TOMB SCULPTURE

Edited by H.W. Janson

SCU

Four Lectures on Its Changin

TOMB
PTURE

spects from Ancient Egypt to Bernini

BY ERWIN PANOFSKY

FOREWORD BY MARTIN WARNKE

HARRY N. ABRAMS, INC., *Publishers*, NEW YORK

Library of Congress Catalog Card Number: 64–15235
ISBN 0–8109–3870–7

Foreword © 1992 Martin Warnke

This 1992 edition is published by Harry N. Abrams, Incorporated, New York
A Times Mirror Company

Printed and bound in Belgium

Contents

Foreword

Tomb Sculpture was the last book Erwin Panofsky published in his lifetime. Friends and students had been enthusiastic about a lecture series on tomb sculpture that Panofsky had given in 1956 at the Institute of Fine Arts at New York University, and they wanted the seventy-two-year-old scholar to publish it in book form. Under the guidance of H. W. Janson they helped him to complete the book, which finally appeared in 1964.

Jan Białostocki pointed out that most of Panofsky's writings published in the United States were revised lectures, complete with footnotes and illustrations.[1] For that reason Panofsky's books have a didactic structure, where great syntheses, uncomplicated conceptual explanations, and vivid depictions with striking metaphors and spirited comparisions are the rule.[2]

The book *Tomb Sculpture* was the first of Erwin Panofsky's books to appear simultaneously in German and English, in Germany and in the United States. In both countries Panofsky had old and new admirers. But holding *Tomb Sculpture* in their hands, Panofsky's German as well as American readers, who had known his publications in their respective mother tongues that he mastered equally well, seemed to find a transformed author. Intellectually and linguistically interspersed with neo-Kantian abstractions, meticulous philological derivations, and scholarly references, the German texts Panofsky had published before his emigration in 1933—among them *Die Perspektive als symbolische Form* or *Hercules am Scheidewege*—had been difficult to read; in short, they had been masterpieces of traditional scholarship and intellect in the best sense. Even when Panofsky had written for a larger German public, as in his 1924 publication *Die deutsche Plastik des elften bis dreizehnten Jahrhunderts*, he analyzed the historical and stylistic connections and interrelations in difficult sentence structures and idiosyncratic expressions. None of his German texts had been probed beforehand for clarity and accessibility through talks and lectures. The universe of the listeners had been very different from the universe of the readers; there, you counted on learners, here on knowledgeable persons. All of that was to change with the first book Panofsky published in Germany after World War II: it had an accessibility and ease that seemed to come more from life experiences than from scholarship.

The American reader had already been familiar with these virtues through Panofsky's English texts. But in the book *Tomb Sculpture,* he encountered traits that had not emerged thus far and were more clearly linked to the experiences of his Hamburg years. He had not only given two lectures open to the public in the winter semesters of 1923/24 and 1930/31 on *Ausgewählte Beispiele der Sepulkralplastik,* but among his later books, this is the only one that reviews and explains thousands of years of cultural history with the help of a single motif or genre. Only the essay on the history of the "idea" concept of 1924 had covered an equally wide field. This approach was possible because it was guided by a philosophical concept, by the "philosophy of symbolic forms" with which Panofsky had familiarized himself in the years from 1920 to 1933, while he was a colleague and a friend of Ernst Cassirer in Hamburg; and once again this concept had an impact on *Tomb Sculpture.* The work of art assumes the status of a "symbolic form," where the essence of an epoch, a

---

[1]   Jan Białostocki, Introduction to E. Panofsky, *Studien zur Ikonologie,* Cologne 1980, page 8.

[2]   Panofsky himself traced this change in style to his "transplantation" from Europe to America. See E. Panofsky, *Epilog. Drei Jahrzehnte* *Kunstgeschichte in den Vereinigten Staaten. Eindrücke eines versprengten Europäers,* in: *Sinn und Deutung in der bildenden Kunst,* German edition, Cologne 1975, page 386f.

developmental stage in human life and striving, objectifies itself. Thus, the tomb sculptures, as interpreted here, are permanent symbols of imagination, wishes, and hopes that the respective cultures and epochs had linked with death: Egyptian tomb art is related to the belief that the deceased continue their earthly affairs in the beyond, whereas Greek tomb sculpture is explained by the idea that death is an uncertain existence in the realm of shades, where life fades to a beautiful memory. Among the many possibilities of Roman sepulchral art, one emerged that promised a beautiful existence in death as a compensation for a virtuous life; whereas in Christianity, all ties to real life have been severed, and only the future prospects of the next world are important. Only in the Renaissance, worldly affairs and needs, and a concern for the glorious continuation of life on earth, emerged again from this exclusive alliance with life after death. The book ends with the discussion of Bernini's tombs in the Baroque age, a time when everything had been said in tomb art. After death had become separated from cult and religion and had become a subjective event, it meant the downfall of an artistic tradition as discussed in this book, because a subjectively limited experience of death that no longer was tied to objective values cannot materialize; it loses its symbolizing capacity.

Among all these general prerequisites, Panofsky sees variations and special solutions throughout the history of sepulchral art, style and iconography. Thus, he observes that in southern Europe the tomb figure is usually portrayed as dead, in northern Europe as a living person; with regard to the portrayal of the deceased as "living" persons lying in state or as "dead" persons standing up, this leads to numerous questions and answers. Among the multilayered historical changes, Panofsky sees again and again phenomena he calls "pseudo-morphoses," i.e., moments separated by time and place in which identical formal solutions can independently take shape. Thus, in the fourteenth century wailing women appear on the tombs of the counts of Hesse in St. Elizabeth's Church in Marburg, which inadvertently remind one of the "wailers sarcophagus" of Gidon from the fourth century before Christ. Virtually the same spontaneous artistic inspirations are emerging over time and space in the same form.

One cannot do this book justice without noting that it was first published almost thirty years ago. Its topic, however, the history of the changes in the perception of death, experienced a boom in recent years. It started with the book of the French historian Philippe Ariès, *L'homme devant la mort*, which was published in 1978 and has been translated into many languages. Today, it is considered a classic because it provided for international cultural and historical knowledge (in the sense of the *Annales*, the school for historians), important ideas for a history of mentality. One can acknowledge that we have learned since then to understand death as more than just a social phenomenon; and examples taken from everyday life, from literature, have shown us how to process and symbolize death in much greater detail, and have helped us to understand better that the survivors are the ones who, with the help of the dead, control and maintain the validity of their norms, interests, and needs. Whoever reads Ariès's work carefully will notice that already in the introduction he gratefully acknowledges what he has gained from Erwin Panofsky. Throughout the text, Panofsky is one of the most quoted authors, and, under the guise of Ariès's strange terminology, the reader of Panofsky's *Tomb Sculpture* will rediscover some of his basic thoughts in this book. This is especially true for the caesura, with which Panofsky's book ends; his justification and definition of this caesura appear almost programmatically in the original title of Ariès's book, *L'homme devant la mort*. And he states along the lines of Panofsky that the actual history of death only begins when death is no longer wrapped in the protective cover of tomb art and those systems of meaning that support and, thus, defy it.

Martin Warnke

Preface

The text of this volume was not intended for publication: it consists of a little series of public lectures delivered at The Institute of Fine Arts of New York University in the fall of 1956. But when some members of the Institute's faculty, particularly its director, Professor Craig H. Smyth, proposed that the material then presented be made accessible in book form, I fell in with this kind and flattering suggestion—with the proviso, however, that my own part in the publication be restricted to a minimum. I would place at the disposal of the Institute a legible but essentially unaltered transcript of the lectures; a list of illustrations; and such scattered bibliographical references and notes as I had happened to jot down. It would be left to the younger members of the Institute to correct palpable errors; to hunt for photographs; to check the citations—in short, to do the work.

Mrs. Mary Lee Thompson, Mr. Joachim Gaehde, and Mr. Howard Saalman were kind enough to share this thankless task, and my old friend, Professor H. W. Janson, who consented to function as an "editor-in-chief," made many valuable suggestions and imparted to the book—if book it can be called—its final shape. He has probably spent more time and labor on this volume than has the author (who, however, remains responsible for all errors of judgment), and I wish to express to him my heartfelt gratitude.

Apart from these editors, my thanks are due to a number of friends and colleagues who assisted me with suggestions, factual information, and, in part, with the gift or loan of photographs: Messrs. Jean Adhémar, Malcolm Campbell, Albert Châtelet, Louis Grodecki, Ragnar Josephson, P. P. Kahane, Ernst H. Kantorowicz, Adolf Katzenellenbogen, Richard Krautheimer, Gerhard B. Ladner, the late Karl Lehmann, Michelangelo Muraro, Carl Nordenfalk, Enoch E. Peterson, Henri Stern, Guy de Tervarent, Richard Turner, Rudolf Wittkower, and Francis Wormald; and Mmes. Anne de Egry, Rosalie Green, Trude Krautheimer, and Marian Wenzel.

In conclusion I wish to acknowledge my long-standing indebtedness to A. della Seta's remarkable book *Religione e arte figurata* (Rome, 1912 [English translation, *Religion and Art*, London, 1914]); and, on the other hand, to express my regrets that Mevrouw Henriette s'Jacob's *Idealism and Realism: A Study of Sepulchral Symbolism*, Leiden, 1954, became available to me only after my text had been completed. This book contains a wealth of useful information and an extensive bibliography; but it would have transcended the modest purpose of these lectures to comment upon or to incorporate its contents.

Erwin Panofsky

8

I. From Egypt to the "Tomb of the Nereids"

An art historian can approach the subject of these lectures only with the greatest trepidation. Trespassing upon the preserves of many adjacent disciplines (classical and oriental archaeology, Egyptology, the history of religion and superstition, philology, and several others), he has to rely largely on secondary sources and often finds himself confronted with a diversity of opinions, at times about crucial points, which he, a rank outsider, cannot presume to evaluate. During my own lifetime the interpretation of the Egyptian Kā has changed several times, finally to revert to more or less what I had learned when I was young. The classicists are still divided as to whether "heroes" are debased gods or immortalized humans (viz., the ancestors of the great families), and whether their cult resulted from the lingering memory of a person or from a lingering feeling of sacredness attached to a place—alternatives which probably cannot be decided on principle at all.

To make things worse, there is hardly any sphere of human experience where rationally incompatible beliefs so easily coexist and where prelogical, one might almost say metalogical, feelings so stubbornly survive in periods of advanced civilization as in our attitude toward the dead.

The aboriginal fears and taboos of primitive man survive all around us (even in ourselves), and primitive rituals continue to be practiced, unbeknownst to those who do so, up to this day. When we close the mouth and eyes of the dead and arrange them in an attitude of peaceful repose, their hands often placed crosswise, we do so in the belief of performing an act of piety; but there is reason to assume that in these very acts of piety *toward* the dead there survive, in a residual or sublimated form, measures taken *against* the dead in order to prevent them from harming us: measures such as putting out their eyes, tying or even mutilating their hands and feet, dismembering them, putting them in tightly closed vessels, often in postures similar to that of the embryo (*pace* the psychoanalysts, these customs prevailed long before the actual position of the embryo was known), or sealing them up in hollow trees.

The Egyptians did just the opposite from what seems natural to us. They opened the eyes and mouths of the dead so that these might be able to see, to speak, and to enjoy whatever life was imputed to them, and we shall see that there was an amazingly widespread and long-lived reluctance, overcome only at certain times and in limited areas, to represent the dead with eyes closed on funerary monuments. This brings us right *in medias res*.

Animals fear death and experience a sense of privation as a result of the death of others, at times to the point of dying or seeking death themselves; most of you have read, I hope, Maupassant's moving short story, *Amour*, where a male teal whose mate has been killed by a bullet keeps circling above the spot with "short, repeated, heart-rending cries" until he is shot down himself. But animals do not know about death. Man, however, has known about it from the remotest times and in the most primitive conditions. He realized that his life was limited—in every sense of the term, that is to say, formed as well as restricted—by death. Yet he could not bring himself to believe that the extinction of life (viz., of the ability to move, to speak, to eat, etc.) meant the end of existence—particularly since dreams, hardly distinguished from "apparitions" at an early stage of human consciousness (see Aeschylus' ἐνυπνίων φαντασμάτων ὄψεις, "the sights of specters appearing in dreams"), seemed to assure the survivors of the continued existence of the dead.

9

This very belief, however, infused into the living a primordial fear of the dead which must have been much stronger than any "sense of bereavement" and, like all primordial fears, was closely akin to religious worship (we still speak of the fear of God as much as of the love or worship of God, and the borderline between the dead and the gods tends to be fluid).[1] The dead, continuing to live without the opportunities—but at the same time without the limitations—of the undead, could do infinite harm. And to prevent this there were two ways, one negative, the other positive. On the one hand (as has already been hinted at), the living might attempt to render the dead powerless; on the other, they might seek to make the dead happy. But we must remember that, in this strange sphere, not even these extreme possibilities were of necessity mutually exclusive. Even where cremation was adopted as apparently the most effective means of reducing the dead to impotence by destroying the matter as well as the shape of their bodies (or where the bodies were allowed to rot away and only the bones were subsequently collected and buried in what are known as "ossuaries"), the relatively small containers of these remains were shaped like figures, like houses, or even, exceptionally, like both[2]—a procedure which, in a sense, reinstated the very situation destroyed by cremation or decomposition. Even the ash urns could be placed on thrones like living rulers; cherished possessions were added; and special drains were provided through which offerings of wine or blood could reach these receptacles.

Some ways of rendering the dead powerless, and their unnoticed survival in modern civilization, have already been mentioned. It is even possible, I believe, that the Roman ritual of *os resectum*—that curious custom of cutting off a finger from the body to be cremated and throwing earth upon this severed member—is not so much a symbolic re-enactment of burial at a period when interment had been superseded by cremation as it is a survival of the quite primitive custom of cutting off one or more fingers of the corpse in order to prevent the dead from using weapons against the living.

The means of making the dead happy were, of course, to provide them with what may be called the necessities of afterlife, that is to say, with everything they used to need or enjoy when alive: food, drink —particularly drink, for the dead were always thought of as extremely thirsty—shelter, tools, weapons, ornaments or toys, animals, and, if they had been prominent enough, servants. The custom of slaughtering not only horses, dogs, and cattle but also slaves (or, in the case of princes, gentlemen and ladies in waiting) at the grave of their masters—or, worse, of burying them alive together with the corpses—is common to all primitive (and so-called primitive) peoples, to the American Indians as well as to the ancient Germans, to the predecessors of the Greeks (when Achilles sacrificed twelve Trojans at the grave of Patroclus, he probably committed an act not so much of vengeance as of propitiation) as well as to the inhabitants of Ur in Chaldea.

I have always spoken of "the dead." But now we must qualify. At a primitive stage of civilization it was indeed the person as a whole that was believed to survive on some unknown and unknowable plane, and to be capable of "coming back" as what the French so eloquently call a *revenant*. It took a great amount of observation and reflection to realize that the body of the dead individual decays and ultimately vanishes of

---

[1] J. G. Frazer, *The Fear of the Dead in Primitive Religion*, London, 1933–36.

[2] Anthropomorphic ash urns, often displaying only the features of the face and then known as *Gesichtsurnen*, have been found in numerous prehistoric sites extending from Troy to Pomerania; for house-shaped urns see F. Behn, *Hausurnen*, Berlin, 1924. Ossuaries combining the features of both types, generally house-shaped but provided with protruding noses or beaks occasionally supplemented by eyes (in at least one case the whole container even bears an intriguing resemblance to an eight-legged ram), have recently come to light in Azor near Tel-Aviv; see J. Perrot, "Little Houses for the Dead of 5000 Years Ago," *Illustrated London News*, CCXXXVII,

itself, while his power—for good or evil—remains unimpaired: that what apparently continues to function and to intrude upon the world of the living is something which persists when the body has perished.

When this difference between "that which perishes" and "that which persists" had been recognized, it was, however, not concluded (by way of mathematical subtraction, as it were) that the surviving entity was, so to speak, the living person minus the body. It was not reasoned: the dead person cannot move, breathe, speak, hear, or feel; consequently, that which survives in death must be identical with that which has enabled his body to move, to breathe, to speak, to hear, or to feel in life but has fled away from it at the moment of death. According to immediate experience (in dreams, etc.), the surviving entity was not an invisible and, so to speak, impersonal "life force"; it was, on the contrary, a mysterious but very concrete and individual being that differed from the dead person only in its lack of materiality: an insubstantial image or shade which, far from being a part of the deceased, was rather a ghostly duplicate thereof.

It took, therefore, a further step to distinguish between this "double" of the dead person—duplicating him in his entirety except for matter—and an invisible and volatile principle that had animated the body when alive: to distinguish, that is, between what I should like to call, purposely using a Germanism, an "image-soul" and a "life-soul," the latter supposed to reside in the blood or (preferably) in the breath and so completely divorced from the individual shape and personality of the former human being that art attempted to symbolize it under the guise of such small, fast-moving creatures as snakes, butterflies, fishes, and, above all, birds.

When this second step was taken, there resulted a tripartition (occasionally further diversified, as in ancient Egypt) which was to survive for millennia and leave its imprint on art as well as language. In Greek we have, in addition to the words for body, σῶμα or μέλη, several words for soul: σκιά, εἴδωλον, and ψυχή. Σκιά and εἴδωλον, needless to say, originally designated the "image-soul" and were, therefore, visually symbolized by human figures, often of small size and dark in color in order to express the lack of life, and winged in order to express incorporeality. Ψυχή (literally: a breeze, a breath) originally designated the "life-soul" and was, therefore, visually symbolized (as has already been mentioned) by butterflies or birds. In Latin a similar contrast is expressed by *manes*, on the one hand, and *anima, animus,* or *spiritus* on the other; and in English by "ghost" (originally only the "image-soul") and "soul" or "spirit." But in all these cases the original distinctions were not consistently respected, so that we can now speak of the Holy Ghost as well as of the Holy Spirit and, if so inclined, may conjure up spirits as well as lay ghosts.

Once the distinction between body and soul (or souls) had been made, it became evident that purely negative measures to render the departed harmless could be of no avail. Neither the "image-soul" nor the "life-soul" could be incapacitated or immobilized by incapacitating or immobilizing the body—with the single exception of souls which for some reason or another had not managed to disengage themselves from their bodies. This was believed to be the case with persons not decently buried, with suicides, and, most important, with maidens who had died between betrothal and marriage *(lamiae)* and sought a belated gratification of their frustrated desires. Persons of this kind were βιοθάνατοι, "living-dead," believed to prey upon the living like—or, rather, as—vampires; for it is in Greece and the Balkan countries that the belief in vampires, to which we owe so many haunting works of literature from Goethe's *Braut von Korinth* and Keats's *Lamia*[1] down to Bram Stoker's *Dracula*, remained endemic at all times and became epidemic as late as the eighteenth century.[2] Vampires had to be killed a second time (preferably by

[1] Through Symmachus the *lamia* found her way into the Vulgate rendering of Isaiah 34:14 ("Ibi cubavit lamia," where the Septuagint has ὀνοκένταυροι; and gave some trouble to the translators, who were reluctant to introduce into the Bible what corresponds to a female vampire. Luther has *Kobold* (demon); the King James Version, "screech owl." A German translation of the Vulgate text, however, has the very graphic expression, *die ungeheure Nacht-Frau* ("the monstrous night-woman"). The Douay Version cautiously retains the term employed by the Vulgate: "there has the lamia lain down."

[2] For a contemporary account of the outbreaks of vampirism in 1725 and 1732, see the remarkable work by M. Ranft, *Traktat von dem Kauen und Schmatzen derer Toten in den Gräbern*, Leipzig, 1734.

driving a stake through their hearts) so that their souls might be freed from their bodies for good and thus come to rest; but the bona fide dead could not be dealt with so harshly. They had to be pacified by providing for the postmortal needs of their surviving souls. Failure to do so was considered the greatest of crimes, while to do it effectively and in perpetuity was the most sacred of duties : a matter of private and public self-preservation.

Under primitive conditions this provision for the needs of the dead was effected, as we have seen, directly and materially: by leaving them in actual possession of what they had owned and cherished in life; according to that "law of inconsistency" which always governs funerary customs, even today children are often buried with their favorite toys, and grownups are provided with some coins, a handkerchief, a hymnal, or a prayer book. On a large scale, however, this direct and material method proved, quite apart from humanitarian considerations, too wasteful as well as too unsafe. It seemed much better to meet the situation by magic imagery, the advantage being that images of men and beasts were cheaper yet less perishable than real men and beasts, and that the persons most interested, if they were circumspect and powerful enough, could provide for their post-terrestrial needs in advance instead of relying on the piety of their survivors. This is why art received as potent a stimulus from the fear of the dead as from the fear of the gods. It had to provide shelter for the dead by the house-shaped sarcophagus, the *mastaba* or pyramid, the mausoleum, the martyrium; it had to duplicate the corpse in a statue; it had to replace the real *Grabbeigaben*—slaves, animals, furnishings, and ornaments—by "counterfeit presentments." And this is why an art historian, all pitfalls notwithstanding, cannot help looking once in a while at the development of funerary art in general and, as it were, in a kind of bird's-eye view.

The transition from real offerings to offerings in effigy—signifying at the same time a transition from human victims to animal substitutes—can best be seen, as you all know, in Ur in Chaldea. At the beginning, the inhabitants slaughtered practically the whole retinue of the sovereign that had died. Later on, however, the departed were satisfied with beautiful things designed for the purpose of giving protection, service, and pleasure forever: weapons, ceremonial standards, precious jewel boxes, harps of gold, silver, or inlaid wood, terminating in superbly chased bulls' heads, and even gaming boards (figs. 1, 2).

In contrast, the famous *Billy Goat* from Ur (fashioned of ivory, gold, and lapis lazuli), which is the "lion" of the University Museum in Philadelphia, is not an implement but a cult object (fig. 3). Sacred to Tammuz and embodying the male principle in nature, the animal served as a stand for bowls with offerings to that god. If it suggests the "ram caught in a thicket" familiar to all of us from the account of the sacrifice of Isaac in Genesis 22:13, this impression is not altogether unfounded. The author of Genesis must have known images similar to the Philadelphia figure, that is to say, herbivores rearing up against a plant on their hind legs. But he accounted for the unusual position of the animal by a miracle: the ram had been "caught in a thicket by his horns" and was revealed to Abraham at the last moment. In this way the Biblical description could act as an intermediary, so to speak, between the Chaldean figure and the innumerable renderings of the sacrifice of Isaac in Judeo-Christian art. If the Bible and all the earlier representations based on it had been lost, many an art historian would assume a direct connection between the *Goat* of Ur and, for example, a panel produced by a German painter, named Bertram, in 1379 A.D. (fig. 4). The case is an amusing illustration of that interplay between texts and images which can be observed so often in the history of art; and in this particular case more than mere coincidence may be involved: Abraham himself—originally called Abram—had emigrated into Canaan, at the behest of the Lord, from "Ur of the Chaldees" (Genesis 11:31 f.).

The fullest documentation of this phase—the phase in which funerary sculpture was intended to provide for the future of the dead on what may be called the "magic" level—is, of course, supplied by the art of the Egyptians. Here infinite precautions were taken to provide the dead with everything they needed to live on and be satisfied forever and ever: "Their will was not to die," says Edna St. Vincent Millay of

12

the Pharaohs, "And so they had their way, or nearly so." If we were, God forbid, sociologists, we might say that the entire Egyptian civilization tended to be "death-oriented" rather than "life-oriented"; Diodorus of Sicily expressed the same contrast much better in the sentence: "The Egyptians say that their houses are only hostelries, and their graves their houses."

In Egypt the now familiar trichotomy of body, "image-soul," and "life-soul," developed in such a way that the resulting doctrine has been called, by analogy to polytheism, "polypsychism";[1] it is a doctrine so variable and complex that I could not think of explaining it here even if I completely understood it—and if the Egyptologists themselves were agreed upon it. A primary and apparently quite old distinction seems to have been made between what corresponds to an incorporeal "image-soul" or "shadow" (Shā), which duplicates the original appearance of the deceased in attenuated form, and a "life-soul" (Bā) which formless and invisible per se, could be represented only in symbolical form. This symbol is a bird with a human face, not unlike the Greek Sirens, who may ultimately derive from it (fig. 5). A beautiful mural in the tomb of Irinufer (or Arinefer) at Thebes (XXth Dynasty) shows Bā and Shā hovering together near that "false door" which will be discussed very shortly (fig. 6).

But this simple division was obscured by a number of other, in part, overlapping distinctions. There was the general "principle of immortality" (Akh); a kind of general world-soul (Chū) of which the individual souls are only particularized manifestations; and, above all, the enigmatical Kā, considered, it seems, to represent the active personality of the deceased, as far as it survives without its body, in its entirety. Supposed to have his being in or near the actual grave, he combined, in a sense, the qualities of "image, soul" and "life-soul" with those of the "principle of immortality." In the end, then, the various forms or modes of postmortal existence tended to merge, though on a higher level, into the primitive notion of "the dead" pure and simple.

Before being assigned his definite place in the universe, the defunct person undergoes a complicated process explicitly described in the Book of the Dead (the data of which are, however, supplemented by numerous other sources). He descends into the nether world, where he is brought before Osiris by dog-headed Anubis, the special god of burial and embalming, or falcon-headed Horus (fig. 7); he is weighed in the presence of forty-two judges and can be condemned to remain in a kind of hell full of malevolent demons (not very well defined) or, conversely, can be admitted to the heavens, the goddess of which, called Nūt, thus came to assume the character of a death goddess.[2] If so admitted, the deceased accompanies the sun god, Rē, on his daily journey around the earth; and it was in anticipation of this journey that a ship (varying in size according to the social status of the deceased) was given the place of honor among the *Grabbeigaben* and was employed in lieu of a hearse for transporting the corpse to its final resting place (fig. 8). The dead person thus became, as it were, a celestial body himself, and this accounts for the fact that tombs and coffins were frequently adorned with images recording the complex system of astronomical reference and time measurement which Egyptian science had evolved.[3] At the same time the soul of the dead person was thought to enjoy the care and custody of Osiris, killed and resurrected like the Greek Dionysus and the Christian Saviour. And its association with this guarantor of immortality became so

[1] F. Cumont, *Lux perpetua*, Paris, 1949, p. 408.

[2] A. Rusch, "Die Entwicklung der Himmelsgöttin Nut zu einer Totengöttin," *Mitteilungen der vorderasiatisch-ägyptischen Gesellschaft*, XXVII, 1922; H. O. Lange and O. Neugebauer, *Papyrus Carlsberg No. 1 (Danske Videnskabernes Selskab Hist.-filol. Skrifter*, I, 2), Copenhagen, 1940. The complexity of Egyptian beliefs can be measured by the fact that the same goddess, because of the alternation of day and night, was also conceived of as a sow devouring her own young (H. Grapow, "Die Himmelsgöttin Nut als Mutterschwein," *Zeitschrift für ägyptische Sprache und Altertumskunde*, LXXI, 1935, pp. 45 ff.). For the Egyptian ideas and

practices concerning the dead, see H. Kees, *Totenglauben und Jenseitsvorstellungen der alten Ägypter*, Berlin, 1956. [For illustrations: M. Fechheimer, *Ägyptische Plastik*, Berlin, 1914; H. Schäfer, *Von ägyptischer Kunst*, Leipzig, 1922.]

[3] See, for example, the Aspalta sarcophagus in the Boston Museum of Fine Arts (D. Dunham, "An Ethiopian Royal Sarcophagus," *Bulletin of the Museum of Fine Arts, Boston*, XLIII, 1945, pp. 53 ff.) and the Cairo coffin brilliantly analyzed by O. Neugebauer, "The Egyptian 'Decans'," *Vistas in Astronomy*, A. Beer, ed., London and New York, 1955, I, pp. 47 ff.

close that the Egyptians could speak of "such and such a person's Osiris" as we may speak of "such and such a person's beatified spirit." Thus apotheosized, the departed "enters the heavens like a falcon / He soars aloft like the crane / He kisses the heavens like a falcon / He springs to the sky like the locust / He flies away from you, mere men / He is no longer of the earth / He is in heaven with his brothers, the gods."

Persons less exalted in life and less effectively deified in death were admitted to the fields of Iaru, a sort of Elysian Fields which, however, had to be cultivated by the inhabitants, and this very materialistic conception, peacefully coexisting with the idea of transfiguration or even apotheosis, was apparently of specific importance to that elusive "double," the Kā.

This Kā, we recall, was thought of as hovering in or near the actual grave; and he always demanded and received concrete service which was supplied by the latter's contents and decoration. His prime need being a material body, the Egyptians developed into a fine art the preservation of corpses. After the entrails were removed—to be preserved in four separate jars often misleadingly referred to as "Canopic vases" or "canopi"[1]—the body was embalmed, sheathed in many layers of linen, equipped with shoes, staff, and breastplate, and placed in an "inner mummy case," carefully painted, which operated both as a container and a duplicate. And this was in turn encased in a sarcophagus, made of materials as time-resistant as possible, which either repeated the form of the "inner mummy case" (anthropomorphic sarcophagi) or imitated a dwelling which in turn represented, on a small scale, the universe, much as the temple did (house-shaped or—to coin a term corresponding to "anthropomorphic"—"domatomorphic" sarcophagi).[2]

Since even the mummy, however well protected, was in danger of decay, the Kā needed a body as imperishable as human artifice could make it: the funerary statue, strongly individualized so that no confusion could occur. Thus monumental Egyptian sculpture begins, so to speak, where the "classic" phase of monumental Greek sculpture ends: with iconic, lifelike portraiture (fig. 9). And cautiousness was carried to such lengths that in certain cases spare heads were provided in case the original head should be lost or become unrecognizable.

Then the Kā, who was always afraid of being "shut in," could enter and leave the grave at will, using a door passable only by him and not by the living (called, not quite correctly, a "false door," whereas it is, as one might say, a "superreal door"; fig. 10). He could take possession of his statue and make use of all the objects either deposited in the tomb or represented on its walls, including all the flowers, food, and drink depicted in the frequent scenes which show the deceased seated at a table and receiving offerings (fig. 11). But in order to make assurance doubly sure, the tombs of the great were usually adorned, in addition, with colored reliefs minutely describing the production of food and artifacts as well as such pleasures as hunting or boating amidst the tall papyrus plants that grow in the marshes of the Nile (fig. 12). Representations of this kind—guaranteeing, as it were, the continuance of the deceased's well-being in perpetuity—must be interpreted as visible and tangible answers to such prayers as:

May I be cool under the sycamores;
May I bathe in my pond;
May my Kā not be shut in;
May I tend my acres in the fields of Iaru.

It is, however, precisely this last requirement, the cultivation of the fields of Iaru, which the deceased does not much like to meet in person (fig. 13). He prefers to leave this part of life in the beyond to menials

---

[1] For the development of these jars and the confusion surrounding their appellation, see E. Panofsky, "*Canopus Deus;* the Iconography of a Non-Existent God," *Gazette des Beaux-Arts*, Series 6, LVII, 1961, pp. 193 ff.

[2] For prehistoric anticipations of both these forms, see above, p. 10.

—to those very slaves who were originally doomed to accompany their masters in the flesh but were later on replaced by little figures known as *ushabtis* (fig. 14). This word means, literally, "they who answer," and we have texts reading as follows: "When I [the master] am called to tend my land, then you, *ushabti*, give ear and answer 'Here I am.'"

Small wonder that these *ushabtis* give the impression of forever waiting—waiting to be called. But the curious and revealing thing is that this applies to the effigies of their masters as well (fig. 15). An Egyptian tomb statue, intended to be occupied by its soul, is not what a Greek or Roman statue is. It is not a representation (μίμησις) of a living being—body plus soul, the former animated by the latter—but a reconstruction of the body alone, waiting for animation.

This, if I am allowed an aside (and a very sweeping generalization), is true, with a few well-motivated exceptions, of all Egyptian art, which, regardless of medium, tends to show movement *in potentia* and not *in actu*. Sculpture in the round avoids all torsions involving foreshortening. In paintings and reliefs—the latter either flat or even *en creux* and thus, in contrast to the high relief developed by the Greeks, tending to confine the forms to one plane instead of permitting free play between two—movement is not directly expressed as a functional transition from one position to another but merely intimated by the graphic junction of opposing aspects (profile and front view). And in architecture the supporting members, particularly papyrus- or lotus-shaped columns, are not conceived as actively carrying a load but as standing freely and quietly in space, their capitals often separated from the ceiling by an abacus invisible from below (fig. 17). Columns and pillars exist rather than act, and where human figures are connected with architecture, they are, unlike the Greek caryatids, loosely attached to the walls instead of playing an active part within the structural system; the very notion of a caryatid—fulfilling the actual function of a column and thereby eloquently illustrating the classical theory according to which different types of columns represent different types of human beings—was thoroughly foreign to Egyptian art (fig. 22). In it, we may say, material space is not as yet activated by time. Greek art (and "classic" art in general) conceives of material space as activated by time in such a manner that the latter is immanent in the former; and Gothic art, to carry the parallel still further, conceives of material space as activated by time in such a manner that the latter transcends the former.

Plato, of course, was not quite right in saying that Egyptian art had never changed for ten thousand years. In spite of its indeed extraordinary conservatism, it could and did not fail to respond to such shifts in the historical situation as the contact with the Aegean sphere in the New Empire (not to mention later developments under Greek and Roman influence) or to such fundamental spiritual events as Amenophis IV's heroic attempt to replace the traditional polytheism—and "polypsychism"—by what may be called an anticipation of modern pantheism and panpsychism. At this period life and death were no longer seen as two absolutes but in relation to each other—with the result that different, even opposite, attitudes became possible toward both.

On the one hand, a dialogue could be written in which the poet convinces his soul that life is not worth living and finally obtains its permission to seek refuge in death:

To whom can I speak today?
Hearts are wicked,
Everyone takes what is his neighbor's.
To whom can I speak today?
The gentle perish,
The forward are welcome everywhere.
To whom can I speak today?
The righteous have gone,
The earth is full of transgressors.

Death stands before me
As though a sick man be healed,
As though he step forth after an illness.
Death stands before me
Like the fragrance of myrrh,
As though one sit beneath the sail on a windy day.
Death stands before me
Like the fragrance of the lotus,
As though one sit on the shores of drunken ecstasy.

On the other hand, there are such glorifications of personal happiness, under the auspices of the all-enlivening sun god, as the famous relief of Amenhotep IV in the circle of his family (fig. 16); and, as the logical counterpart of such happiness, such expressions of sorrow and grief over the end of this life as the relief that shows a group of mourners lamenting the death of a High Priest of Memphis (fig. 18). Ritualized mourning over the deceased had been practiced in Egypt, as almost everywhere else, from time immemorial; but it is only in the period of the New Empire that the manifestation of grief is represented in art and, at the same time, seems to express subjective emotion rather than to conform to a formalized ritual—so much so that the postures and gestures formulated by the artists of this period could re-emerge from what has been called the collective memory of mankind, in the Greek *threnoi* and the Roman *conclamationes*.

Representations of this kind are, so far as I know, the nearest approximation to what may be called a "retrospective" as opposed to a "prospective" point of view in Egyptian funerary sculpture, and even here the "retrospective" attitude is limited to the survivors and not extended to the departed. As far as these are concerned, we are still confronted with a magic provision for the future, and not with an imaginative commemoration of the past. Commemoration of the past was taken care of, with a few late exceptions,[1] by the decoration of temples and palaces, to be seen by everybody; whereas the admirable products of funerary art, revealed to us by archaeological grave robbing, were never destined to be seen by human eyes.

The step from the "prospective" to the "retrospective," from the magic manipulation of the future to the imaginative commemoration of the past, was taken, like so many steps in the development of our civilization, in Greece, where the product of funerary sculpture was called σῆμα (sign or landmark) or μνῆμα (memorial or monument)[2] and was cared for in a spirit of pious remembrance:

’Ανθέμιδος τόδε σῆμα κύκλῳ στεφάνουσιν ἑταῖροι
Μνημείων ἀρετῆς οὕνεκα καὶ φιλίας

("This tomb of Anthemis his friends adorn / With wreaths in memory of love and virtue.")

In fact, this loving care for the funerary monument—in memory of, and not by way of provision for, the deceased—is one of the most frequent subjects in Attic vase painting (fig. 20); and the monuments themselves were intended to commemorate the life that had been lived rather than to meet the needs of a life to come. Even in Homer the shade of Elpenor, Odysseus' faithful companion who had been left unburied

---

[1] One of these is the tomb, at Saqqara, of Horemheb, who was then a general under Amenhotep IV and later became a Pharaoh himself. The reliefs, now scattered in various museums, include camp scenes, groups of shackled captives, and, as chance would have it, what is believed to be the earliest equestrian figure in ancient Egyptian art.

[2] For the original distinction between σῆμα and μνῆμα see F. Eichler, "Σῆμα und μνῆμα in älteren griechischen Grabinschriften," *Mitteilungen des kaiserlich deutschen archäologischen Instituts (Athenische Abteilung)*, XXXIX, 1914, pp. 138ff. (kindly called to my attention by Mr. George Stamires). It should be noted, however, that Homer's Elpenor (*Odyssey*, XI, 75) uses the word σῆμα for a tomb which by his own testimony was destined to recall his memory to posterity.

(ἄθαπτος) on the island of Aeaea, asks not only for decent burial, necessary to himself, but also for a "memorial" impressive to posterity: "Build me a grave [σῆμα] upon the grey sea's shore / So that the future learn of luckless me; / On it there shall be raised the towering oar / I used to ply while I still saw the light" (*Odyssey*, XI, 71 ff.). This oar, then, is no longer a tool to be used by the dead man, but conveys a message to be heard by the living.[1]

Originally, it seems, the Greek ideas of the beyond—ideas which, needless to say, never ceased to coexist with more recent ones—were, as in most civilizations, dichotomous.

On the one hand, there was the notion of a realm of darkness dominated by destructive demons: snakes, dragons or such monstrous beings, dwelling in the bowels of the earth and "eating the flesh" of the buried, as the δαίμων σαρκοφάγος (whose epithet, transferred to a kind of stone quarried near Assos and to the receptacles made thereof, survives in our "sarcophagus"). These monsters were first thought to be more or less localized wherever the tomb was, but later on expanded the radius of their power so as to become the rulers or guardians of a general "realm of the dead," and their memory survives, for example, in the Minotaur, in Cerberus, and in Polygnotus' blue-black demon that gnaws flesh off the bones of the dead.

On the other hand, there was the notion of a realm of light, originally reserved for those select few who are referred to as μάκαρες or "heroes." Their souls were thought to be transported to either the Isles of the Blessed (μακάρων νῆσοι)—accessible only by ship, so that the old symbol could retain its hopeful meaning and some Greek farewell inscriptions could simply read εὐπλῷ, "good sailing"; or to a bright and far-off country generally conceived as the home of the Sun, so that Memnon could be transported to Ethiopia (southwestward from Greece) by Eos, and Sarpedon to Lycia (southeastward from Greece) by Sleep and Death; or to the "pure and radiant ether" (pure and radiant in contrast to the water-diluted and denser air beneath it); or, finally, to the firmament itself, so that the departed could become a star or group of stars (it should be noted that the idea of catasterism must be very old, since Homer already knows the "mighty Orion" as a constellation).

It is, however, characteristic of early Greek thought that these opposites of light and dark tended to merge into the gray of Hades, where feeble, disembodied shades (σκιαί, ψυχαί), squeaking like bats, float about in cheerless, dreamlike fashion; the soul of Achilles, conjured up by Odysseus, says: "Speak not conciliatorily of death, Odysseus. / I'd rather serve on earth the poorest man / Who, owning nothing, leads a meager life / Than lord it over all the wasted dead" (*Odyssey*, XI, 488 ff.). Yet even this comparatively painless existence (the great sinners forever tortured in Hades, Tantalus, Sisyphus, and Tityus, seem to have gotten in by mistake or at least by conflation)[2] was preferable to the fate of those whom Charon refused to ferry over the River Styx: the unburied and, according to a famous interpolation (38–43) in the eleventh book of the *Odyssey*, all those frustrated brides, wicked old men, etc., who were doomed to lead the life of βιοθάνατοι, a life between the nether world and the earth, and were inclined to haunt the living. Thus even under the management of Charon the ship or boat retains its—relatively speaking—felicitous connotations (fig. 21), and there were those who derived the name of the grim ferryman from χαίρειν, "to be of good cheer."

In what we call the classic period of Greek civilization this notion of Hades, and other even more archaic ones, were, however, simultaneously undermined from two opposite directions: if I may express myself somewhat anachronistically, by faith and by reason. On the one hand, there arose those closely inter-connected mystery cults (like those of Demeter, the twice-born Dionysus, etc.) and mystery sects (Pythag-

---

[1] Hazardous though it is for a mere art historian to contradict an eminent archaeologist (G. E. Mylonas, "Homeric and Mycenaean Burial Customs," *American Journal of Archaeology*, LII, 1948, pp. 56 ff., the passage referred to, p. 73), I do not see how the oar erected on top of Elpenor's Tomb as a memorial can be "paralleled" with the carpenter's tools found in a tomb at Mycenae; these would seem to be normal *Grabbeigaben*.

[2] See below, p. 19, Note [1].

oreanism and/or Orphism, their mutual relation still a matter of agitated debate) which insured a more satisfactory form of afterlife—or even rebirth—to all the "initiated." On the other hand, there arose that Greek philosophy which deprived death of its terror by rational analysis, culminating in Epicurus' famous phrase, θάνατος οὐδὲν πρὸς ἡμᾶς, "Death is nothing with reference to us" (for, where we are, death is not, and where death is, we are not).

The mystery religions were "exclusive" much in the sense of a modern country club—a famous inscription in a burial place near Cumae states that "only members (μύσται) may be buried in these precincts"—except for the fact that membership could be acquired regardless of social standing, nationality (at least to some extent), and objective merit. They were, so to speak, mutual afterlife insurance companies guaranteeing heroic immortality at a comparatively low premium. Diogenes, when asked to join the cult of Demeter because he would go to Hades if he did not, is said to have replied: "It is ridiculous to think that Agesilaus and Epaminondas should vegetate in a mud hole while every nonentity goes to the Isles of the Blessed merely because he has been initiated" (Diog. Laert., VI, 2, 6, 39). But just for this reason the mystery religions achieved tremendous popularity. They changed the very concept of Hades in such a manner that it came to have room for bliss and punishment instead of being a place of uniform, anemic drabness (Proserpina herself was, after all, the daughter of Demeter and, according to the believers in twice-born Dionysus, the mother of Dionysus Zagreus); and the Orphics and Pythagoreans have expressed this novel concept in poetry of real beauty.

As early as the fourth and third centuries B.C. we find those beautifully lettered gold plates which may be called passports for the beyond (fig. 19), giving detailed instructions to the soul as to what it must do and even what it must say after having entered the gates of that now bipartite Hades:

> There you will see a fountain on the left,
> And next to it a cypress white of hue.
> This fountain you must shun: it spells disaster.
> But on the other side there is a spring
> Fed by the lake of memory, well-guarded.
> Say to the guards: "I am of earth and heaven,
> Which are my origin, and this you know.
> I die of thirst; oh, let me drink the water
> That issues from the lake of memory."
> Then they will give you water from the fountain
> Divine. And you will live and rule with those
> That live a life of blissful consciousness.[1]

After this—very Greek—prayer for "the blest fact of consciousness," the soul, admitted to the presence of Persephone herself, says:

> I am a child of earth and also of starred heaven.
> I come from what is pure, pure Queen of Death;
> But fate has brought me here, and the immortals.

Upon which Persephone answers with the beautiful χαῖρε παθὼν τὸ πάθημα: "Hail! You have been through the experience./But *this* experience you have not had:/You, once a man, have now become a god./You

18   [1] Kern, *Orphische Fragmente*, 1922, pp. 104ff.

are a kid that has found milk. Hail! You/Have picked the right-hand road that finds the sacred/Meadows and groves of great Persephone.''

It is into a Hades remodeled under the influence of the mystery religions, a Hades which has room for bliss as well as misery, that Virgil's Aeneas descends in the Sixth Book of the *Aeneid*. Homer's Odysseus had not been allowed to penetrate the realm of the dead itself. He had dug a deep trench near its entrance and conjured up the thirsty shades from below (ὑπέξ) by means of a blood offering.[1] Aeneas, on the other hand, actually invades the nether world, and this nether world opens up through a mysterious gate into a kind of Elysian Fields, the inhabitants of which are permitted to pursue their favorite occupations, to feast and to drink, and to look forward to a possible rebirth. The same more hopeful conception of the beyond makes us understand such epitaphs as: ἦλθε πρὸς ἀθανάτους. Θάνατος οὐ κακὸν ἀλλ' ἀγαθόν ("He has gone to join the immortals; death is a good and not an evil"); ψυχὴ ἀθάνατος ("The soul is immortal"); or—an apparent paradox which ceases to be a paradox in the light of what has been said about the reinterpretation of the nether world into a place of promise as well as despair: εἰς ῞Αιδα μακάριστος ("You enter Hades, most blessed of men").

In contrast to sentiments such as these, however, we find reflections not of the hopes aroused and nourished by the mystery religions but also of the agnosticism promoted by philosophy, resulting either in dignified resignation or in frank, at times downright frivolous, hedonism:[2] θάρσει, οὐδεὶς ἀθάνατος ("Take heart, no one is immortal"); or (addressed, of course, to the passer-by rather than to the deceased): παῖσον, τρυφῆσον, ζῆσε, ἀποθανεῖν σὲ δεῖ ("Be cheerful, have fun, live—you must die").

All these new ideas did not, it seems, find direct expression in the funerary art of "classic" Greece. The intellectual detachment of the philosophers was nonvisual by definition; the hopes encouraged by the mystery religions were not only surrounded by secrecy (so that their public exhibition would have been considered sacrilegious) but could be visualized only by way of allegorical or mythological metaphor and allusion—a form as repugnant to the classical phase of Greek art as it was favored at a later date, and quite particularly on non-Hellenic soil, whether in Asia, Africa, or Italy. When we look for Orphic and Pythagorean monuments rather than texts, we have to rely on Hellenistic, Roman, and late antique examples, such as the interesting Pythagorean stele from Philadelphia in Lydia (fig. 23), to which we shall revert in the next chapter.

Indirectly, however, both movements, the mystery religions as well as philosophical rationalism, could not but favor that fundamental change in funerary art so touchingly announced in Elpenor's request: the shift from a "prospective" or anticipatory to a "retrospective" or commemorative attitude.[3] Philosophy was conducive to this shift by de-emphasizing the hereafter in favor of life on earth; the mystery religions, by

[1] *Odyssey*, XI. In verses 568–627, it is true, Odysseus has suddenly left his station outside "Erebos" and penetrates the realm of the dead itself, here to encounter Minos and to perceive, on the one hand, such happily active heroes as Orion and Hercules and, on the other, the "great sinners," Tityus, Tantalus, and Sisyphus. These much debated lines, however, were already athetized in classical antiquity. Probably based on Orphic sources, they must have found their way into the text long after its original composition, though prior to Plato, who (*Gorgias*, 525 E) cites "Homer's" references to Tityus, Tantalus, and Sisyphus. Cf. W. B. Stanford's edition of Homer's *Odyssey*, London, 1955, p. 401.

[2] See, for example, F. Cumont, "Une pierre tombale érotique de Rome," *L'Antiquité Classique*, IX, 1940, pp. 1 ff. In this monument the life on the very Isles of the Blessed is described in terms which Cumont did not dare publish even in the original Greek.

[3] See above, p. 17. Intrinsically, Elpenor's oar is a closer anticipation of the archaic and classical Greek steles than the famous steles surmounting the Mycenaean shaft tombs (G. Karo, *Die Schachtgräber von Mykenai*, Munich, 1930–33, particularly pp. 19, 29 ff., 168 ff.; Mylonas, *op. cit.*), not to mention the crude, imageless markers found on some tombs of the Geometric Period in the Kerameikos. These Mycenaean steles were not as yet personalized: showing only such general subjects as battle scenes or animals in combat and in several cases displaying only abstract linear ornament, they served to identify the site of a specific tomb within a collective burial place rather than to commemorate the life and destiny of an individual: they say, "Here lies a king," and not, "Remember Democleides the sailor who died on the high seas." Yet even these impersonal anticipations of the later, individualized steles seem to occur only on the Greek mainland; nothing of the kind seems to have existed on Crete, and we may well remember that, since the decipherment of the "Linear B" inscriptions, Mycenaean art and civilization, formerly considered a Cretan art and civilization *in partibus*, now tend to be regarded almost as "Greek" as Homer thought them to be.

changing the concept of the hereafter from continued material well-being to a state of bliss which could not be provided for by magic imagery. And it is not by accident that the most vigorous and most beautiful development of a funerary sculpture intended to commemorate the dead rather than to provide for them took place in Attica, particularly in Athens.

A Spartan relief of the sixth century (fig. 24), showing the heroized dead receiving offerings of flowers, fruit, and a cock, is still reminiscent of Egyptian habits not only in style but also in content. And the reliefs from the famous "Tomb of the Harpies" in Xanthos in Lycia, now preserved in the British Museum, while immeasurably more sophisticated in style, proclaim the anticipatory or "prospective" principle as late as the beginning of the fifth century (figs. 25–27). In the two reliefs to which this monument owes its rather misleading name, the souls of the departed, portrayed in the guise of diminutive human figures, are borne heavenward by winged creatures, half bird, half woman, which, though monstrous, are neither ill-intentioned nor terrifying. Resembling, and possibly derived from, the Egyptian soul-bird, Bā (but much enlarged in scale and reinterpreted from an image of the soul flying away into a personification of the power that enables it to fly away, much as a skeleton could be reinterpreted from the portrayal of the body disintegrated after death into a personification of the power that has caused it to disintegrate), they are not so much Harpies (from ἁρπάζω, "to snatch away, to kidnap") as carriers charged with the task of conveying the souls to their destination; and they fulfill this task with touching tenderness, cradling the little figures in their arms as if they were babies (figs. 25, 26). The central sections of the reliefs, however, represent the departed, now restored to their full size and dignity, as hero and heroine, enthroned and receiving gifts appropriate to their sex and status.

In Attica, on the other hand, the idea of commemoration took hold very early and dominated, roughly speaking, the entire "classic" phase of Attic art—so much so that in Athens even the actual *Grabbeigaben* were largely limited to *lekythoi*, small oil vessels intended to insure the continued effectiveness of the funeral rites, in which they played a prominent role, rather than to be used by the deceased (fig. 28). In the end, memory becomes stronger than death itself:

Οὐδε θανὼν ἀρετῆς ὄνομ' ὤλεσας ἀλλὰ σὲ φᾶμα
Κυδαινοῦσ' ἀνάγει δώματος ἐξ 'Αϊδεῶ
("Even in death your virtue's name persists / Fame leads you back from Pluto's gloomy house.")

Thus from the sixth century B.C. down to the beginning of the Christian Era, Attic funerary sculpture —almost exclusively found on steles (fig. 29), "upright slabs or pillars," as the *Oxford Dictionary* defines them—commemorates rather than provides for the dead. These steles—their production only temporarily interrupted by the "Law of Demetrius" (317–316 B.C.), which restricted funerary monuments to *columellae* not exceeding three cubits in height—show the life that had been lived in all its aspects (figs. 30–43). Originally limited to single figures but later, particularly in the "classic" phase of the fifth and fourth centuries, expanding their program to groups of two or three, these admirable works of sculpture commemorate, up to this day, warriors dying in combat or vanquishing the enemy; soldiers going to battle in silent submission to destiny (as in the supremely beautiful Stele of Chairedemos and Lyceas, fig. 32, where the impression of εἱμαρμένη is produced by the simple yet almost unique device of having the two figures move in unison from left to right instead of facing each other); a woman clasped in a last embrace by a young friend or daughter who, in at least one case (fig. 33), has cut off her hair as a sign of mourning;[1] old

---

[1] That women sacrificed their hair to the dead (originally one of the many substitutes for the sacrificial slaughter of the survivors themselves) was so common in Greek and Roman antiquity that the verb κείρεσθαι ("to cut one's hair") could be used almost as a synonym for πενθεῖν ("to mourn over"). When Richard Wagner died, his wife, Cosima, cut off her hair and placed it on his breast to be buried with him!

men leaning on their staffs and accompanied by their faithful dogs (fig. 37); young men exerting themselves in athletic games, playing with their pets, offering libations, or immersed in meditation as if brooding over their own untimely death (an idea also expressed on white-grounded *lekythoi*, fig. 28); beautiful women, often attended by a servant, adorning or unveiling themselves as on the day of their marriage (fig. 43), taking care of their children, or engaging in domestic pursuits; a maiden, Myrrhine, tenderly led to the house of Hades by Hermes Psychopompos, her head bowed in gentle acquiescence (fig. 39); husbands and wives—or a pair of friends—taking leave of each other (fig. 42); sons and daughters taking leave of their parents—so that, a thing impossible before funerary art had turned "retrospective," we are at times unable to distinguish the departed from the survivors. The trade or profession of the deceased is often indicated by such attributes or symbols as the cobbler's last, the actor's mask or ivy wreath, the poet's sweet-singing Siren. And what is perhaps the most touching of all these Attic steles portrays a sailor, Democleides the son of Demetrios, as a small, melancholy figure seated on the prow of the ship with which he went down (or from which he was lost) under foreign skies, an ἄθαπτος mourning over the cruelty of his fate (fig. 38).

In some of these representations—particularly the portrayals of women adorning or unveiling themselves, the scenes of leave-taking (suggestive of a union beyond the limitations of space and time), the gentle "abduction" of Myrrhine (fig. 39), or a particularly beautiful composition where the combination of a heroic youth, an old man, and a mourning boy might convey the ideas of the Three Ages of Man and the "Chain of Being" (fig. 40)—there may perhaps be sensed a hopeful intimation of the future in addition to the mournful evocation of the past, and such an expectation of fulfillment in the hereafter may also be expressed, in more tangible form, in the custom of shaping the steles of unmarried persons into the likeness of a *loutrophoros*, the two-handled jug wherein the water for the nuptial bath was fetched. But even if this interpretation were correct (while there is some literary evidence for the specific significance of the *loutrophoros*, the fact remains that vase-shaped steles were no less often fashioned after the model of a *lekythos*),[1] we should be faced with something fundamentally different from what may be called, for short, the pre-Hellenic point of view: instead of assuring the future of the deceased by way of magic substitution, the funerary imagery would subtly predict it, within the framework of a basically commemorative attitude, by way of symbolic inference.

In the Attic steles, then, the anticipatory element, if present at all, is so delicately and elusively interwoven with the commemorative that it is difficult, if not impossible, to separate the one from the other. Both appear, however, in manifest and explicit juxtaposition in a famous monument nearly contemporary with, say, the beautiful stele of Hegeso (fig. 43) but, significantly, produced on Asian soil: the so-called Tomb of the Nereids in Xanthos, erected in the same place as the so-called Tomb of the Harpies (and, like it, deprived of its decoration for the benefit of the British Museum) but postdating it by almost exactly one hundred years (fig. 45).

The iconography of the earlier, still preclassic, tomb, we recall, had been purely and uniformly "prospective": in its reliefs we saw the souls of the departed carried away to an exalted level of existence where they enjoy the offerings and veneration due to heroes.

The "Tomb of the Nereids," a periptery of fairly orthodox Ionic style (except for the fact that its substructure is unusually high), is iconographically dichotomous. Its reliefs are strictly "retrospective" or commemorative in character, those in the pediments showing the deceased and his family on one side, and an equestrian battle on the other, while the friezes encircling the voluminous base exhibit further

---

[1] It should be interesting to investigate whether or not these giant, vase-shaped steles are in some way connected with the equally colossal "tomb kraters" adorning some graves of the so-called Geometric Period. These giant vessels, their bottoms perforated so as to permit the pouring of libations, were placed in shallow pits more or less directly above the ash urns or corpses; but their upper portion rose well above ground level so that they, like Elpenor's oar mentioned above, may also be reckoned among the forerunners of the later steles.

battle scenes culminating in the conquest of a city (figs. 44, 46, 47), hunting, and other exploits and pastimes befitting an aristocrat; they summarize the life lived by the "hero" without, however, necessarily referring to individual events. The statues in the round (fig. 48), on the other hand, hold out a promise for the hereafter. One of the pediments was crowned with a group which, though too much mutilated to be interpretable without reservations, certainly showed an abduction, and very probably that of the Leucippides by Castor and Pollux, the Celestial Twins, who were to remain, as will be seen, the guides and protectors of apotheosized souls for many centuries. And the intercolumniations of the peristyle were occupied by the eponymous "Nereids" (fig. 49) who are, in reality, no more Nereids than the "Harpies" of the earlier tomb—of whom they are the humanized descendants—are Harpies. Their draperies billowing back like sails, they lightly skim over the water (characterized by little sea animals) rather than live in it. They are, quite obviously, creatures belonging to the air as well as the sea. I am inclined to call them, appropriating the term from Xenophon and Euripides, Αὖραι ποντιάδες, Sea Breezes (Pliny might have described them as *Aurae velificantes sua veste*); and their fleeting movements—far from indicating, as assumed by certain nineteenth-century archaeologists, that they are "frightened by the battles that go on in the reliefs"—would seem to characterize them as spirits of the benevolent elements which, like so many personifications of sea and wind in later funerary art, help the souls of the departed to attain the Isles of the Blessed or the upper reaches of the atmosphere.[1]

[1] The expression αὖραι ποντιάδες occurs in Xenophon, *Hellenica*, VI, 2, and Euripides, *Hecuba*, 448. The Pliny passage alluded to in the text *(Hist. nat.*, XXXVI, 29) refers to two of the many anonymous works that had pleased him in the "schola Octaviae." Professor Karl Lehmann kindly informed me that he preferred to interpret the "Nereids" as clouds—which may improve upon, but would not basically alter, my own suggestion.

For the symbolism of marine personifications and symbols see Cumont, *op. cit.*, pp. 168 ff. and *passim.*, further J. I. Bachofen, *Die Unsterblichkeitslehre der orphischen Theologie (Gesammelte Werke*, VII, Basel, pp. 119 ff). Against the symbolic interpretation of these motifs : A. Rumpf in C. Robert, *Die antiken Sarkophagreliefs*, V, I, Berlin, 1939, pp. 129 ff., and H. Stern, "Les Mosaïques de Sainte-Constance à Rome," *Dumbarton Oaks Papers*, XII, 1958, pp. 159 ff., particularly p. 191.

II. From the Mausoleum to the End of Paganism

The "Tomb of the Nereids" marks not only the beginning of a fusion between the "prospective" and "retrospective" points of view, but also of a tendency toward allegorical indirection. The blissful existence of the deceased in the hereafter is allusively predicted rather than realistically anticipated or magically provided for; and the meritorious conduct of which this "immortality by virtue of Virtue" is the reward is expressed by similes rather than factually recorded.

The aerial or atmospheric deities commonly designated as Nereids no longer physically transport the departed to the beyond, as had been the case with their semihuman forerunners on the so-called Tomb of the Harpies, but merely personify the cosmic forces which, it is hoped, will help them to reach their destination. The abduction enacted by the statues on top of the monument does not actually describe the future state of the soul, but merely compares or equates it with that of mythological characters miraculously carried away and aloft. And the battle and hunting scenes in the reliefs on the base—depicting the conquest of vicious human enemies and wild beasts—are not, or at least not exclusively, representations of real events: they symbolize, as do their parallels in later funerary art down to the sarcophagi of Christian worthies who had never seen a lion or wild boar in their lives, a moral triumph over evil in the struggle of life.

In short, in the "Tomb of the Nereids" direct representation gives way to, or is at least rivaled by, *symbolic parallelization*—symbolic either in the sense of a general moral allegory or in the sense of a specific mythological precedent. And while the mythological element (as represented by the abduction group) is here still limited to the "prospective" part of the program, it can be seen to invade the "retrospective" sphere in a somewhat later and much grander monument—a monument so famous that its name is used as a generic term even now: the colossal tomb erected at Halicarnassus in memory of Mausolus, the ruler of Caria, and his wife Artemisia, that model of marital devotion who is said to have loved her husband so much that she dissolved his ashes in a suitably flavored liquid and drank them.

This "Mausoleum," nearing completion in 362 B.C., probably finished in 351 B.C. (fig. 51), and fairly accurately described by Pliny and Pausanias, may de defined as a Lycian "house tomb" or *heroön* after the fashion of the "Tomb of the Nereids" (it should be noted that Caria is adjacent to Lycia), enlarged, however, to truly heroic proportions and topped by an Egyptian pyramid. From a foundation measuring no less than 35.6 meters square there arose a base 29 meters wide and some 17 meters high. This was surmounted by a periptery about 12.30 meters high; and this again by a truncated pyramid, also about 12.30 meters high, which served as a pedestal for an enormous quadriga. The sculptural decoration (the remains of which are, as usual, preserved in the British Museum) was executed by four of the most famous sculptors of the age, Scopas, Leochares, Bryaxis (famed also for his statue of Serapis in the Serapeion at Alexandria), and Pytheos. It consisted—in addition to the quadriga—of freestanding figures (placed, as in the "Tomb of the Nereids," in the intercolumniations of the periptery) and of three friezes, the original placement of which is still a matter of debate. Two of them, probably encircling the base, showed a battle between Amazons and Greeks (fig. 50) and a battle of Centaurs; the third, probably surmounting the columns of the periptery, a chariot race (fig. 53).

Of the freestanding figures (among them several lions) too little has come down to us to ascertain their iconographical significance (fig. 52); but the meaning of the friezes and the quadriga is not open to doubt.

Both the battle between Amazons and Greeks and the battle of Centaurs evidently express, here in unequivocally mythological form, the conflicts and triumphs of a heroic life, and the chariot race—a prelude, as it were, to the crowning quadriga—would seem to add the idea of a moral victory which, in conjunction with the military and political ones, entitled the dead ruler to a place among the immortal gods. Plato (*Phaedrus*, 248) compares the efforts of the soul to reach a sphere wherein it may participate in the majestic motion of the stars to a race of charioteers (we still speak, without much thinking about it, of the "career" of a man); and Horace (*Carmina*, I, 1) speaks of the godlikeness of those who were victorious in a chariot race:

> . . . metaque fervidis
> Evitata rotis palmaque nobilis
> Terrarum dominos evehit ad deos.[1]

Thus both the racing frieze and the crowning quadriga add up to one impressive symbol of apotheosis.

Like the earlier *heroa*—and, for that matter, the Egyptian *mastabas* and pyramids—the Mausoleum is a gigantic house of the dead. And it is not surprising that similar principles of decoration were applied to the diminutive houses of the dead which we are wont to call sarcophagi, no matter whether these were fashioned in the likeness of actual buildings—"domatomorphic sarcophagi," as I have ventured to term them in contradistinction to the "anthropomorphic" type—or in the likeness of chests, couches, or even, as will be seen, wine vats.

Characteristically, however, the sumptuously sculptured sarcophagus, the dominant manifestation of funerary sculpture throughout the Roman Empire down to the Early Middle Ages, did not originate—and was only reluctantly accepted—in Greece proper, least of all in Attica. Here the dead, if not cremated, were originally buried in comparatively simple receptacles, mostly of terra cotta or wood rather than stone, while the purpose of commemoration was served—and often continued to be served even after the Roman conquest—by the indigenous stele; the Hellenic inclination to perpetuate the memory of life on earth rather than to evoke the vision of a hereafter and the equally Hellenic aversion to the idea of personal apotheosis were unfavorable to the development of an art form which, by virtue of its Oriental antecedents and its analogy to mausoleumlike structures, tended toward anticipatory glorification.

With certain somewhat questionable exceptions, such as the famous "Fugger sarcophagus" showing a battle of Amazons apparently derived from the style of the Mausoleum reliefs, the sarcophagi normally referred to as "Greek"—as a rule "domatomorphic" and carved with equal care on all sides, whereas in "Latin" specimens, normally placed in dimly lit *hypogea* and preferably in *arcosolia* recessed into the wall, the efforts of the artists tended to be concentrated on the front, the ends being treated more summarily and the back often remaining completely blank—are products of semioriental borderline regions such as Cyprus, Asia Minor, and the territories that can be summed up under the general heading of "Syria."

On Cyprus, highly developed and richly decorated sarcophagi were common as early as ca. 500 B.C., and their type may be illustrated by one of the two specimens in the Metropolitan Museum (fig. 54). Shaped like a house, it is adorned with flat reliefs on all sides. Most of these are clearly "prospective" and essentially hedonistic in character. They represent such pleasurable activities as charioteering, hunting, and, most particularly, feasting: reclining on a couch, the deceased enjoys food, drink, and the company of

[1] For these symbolic implications of chariot racing, see F. Cumont, *Recherches sur le symbolisme funéraire des Romains*, Paris, 1942, particularly pp. 460 ff.; cf. also Daremberg-Saglio, *s. v.* "Sarcophagus," "Sepulcrum," "Urna," etc. For a judicious criticism of Cumont's point of view, see A. D. Nock, "Sarcophagi and Symbolism," *American Journal of Archaeology*, L, 1946, pp. 140 ff.

attractive female entertainers. Only on one of the ends do we encounter a mythological subject, the story of Medusa (fig. 55). But since Medusa's head, the so-called *gorgoneion* (employed by her conqueror, Perseus, to petrify his foes if necessary), was always regarded as a most effective *apotropaion*, we may assume that this representation was here intended to serve an apotropaic rather than symbolical purpose. Together with the four lions who, facing outward, guard the corners of the lid, Medusa protects, like the two angels in St. John 20:12, the "head and feet" of the body. In fact, the ends of later sarcophagi frequently show either the gorgoneion itself (which also occurs, at times, on their front walls) or such equally potent deterrents as sphinxes or griffins, the "guardians of treasure" par excellence.

Much more important and instructive than these Cypriote examples are the sarcophagi, no fewer than twenty-two in number, which were discovered in Sidon (Saida), that is to say, on Phoenician soil, by Hamdy Bey in 1887. This impressive series reflects, over a period of several centuries, the far-flung cultural associations and dramatic political vicissitudes of a great colonial empire which, after the decline of its own power, was first conquered by the Persians, then by Alexander the Great, and finally by the Romans, but whose art had submitted to Greek influence long before the advent of Alexander's irresistible armies.

The earliest members of the Sidon series, dating back to the times of Phoenician independence, are anthropomorphic sarcophagi in the Egyptian manner, fashioned of black basalt or diabase and probably imported from Egypt itself (fig. 56). After the Persian conquest (completed by the end of the sixth century B.C.), Greek artists came to be employed by the Phoenician rulers and applied their accustomed style to the unaccustomed task of either producing further anthropomorphic sarcophagi (which continued to be used throughout the fifth and fourth centuries B.C.)[1] or decorating the walls of nonanthropomorphic ones which, at the beginning, tended to be shaped like sturdy chests reinforced at the corners and, later on, turned "domatomorphic," first imitating Asiatic and later purely Greek structures.

As an example of the chest-shaped type we may consider the so-called Sarcophagus of the Satrap (probably late fifth century; fig. 57), whose reliefs, though somewhat archaic in style, conform to classical standards in that their content is of a purely commemorative character: they show the "Satrap" hunting, feasting, attending the "test run" of a chariot, or, as though the Egyptian representations of the field Iaru had taken a "retrospective" turn, supervising agricultural activities.

The earlier "domatomorphic" type (middle of the fourth century B.C.) may be exemplified by the "Lycian" Sarcophagus (fig. 58), so called because it is patterned after the fashion of tombs not infrequently found in that country, its lid being about as high as the body of the sarcophagus and resembling a Gothic barrel vault in shape. The lateral surfaces of this lid are guarded by apotropaic sphinxes while the walls of the sarcophagus itself are adorned with reliefs which, like those on the base of the Mausoleum, exhibit combats of Amazons and Centaurs and are probably invested with similar iconographical connotations.

In the course of the fourth century the "domatomorphic" sarcophagi of Sidon turned to the imitation of purely Greek structures, their lids assuming the shape and proportions of orthodox classical roofs, with low, triangular pediments and acroteria. The walls of these diminutive houses or temples, however, were treated according to two different methods establishing two parallel traditions which can be traced down to the very end of the Early Christian period. They could either be organized, in close analogy to large-scale peripteries, by colonnettes ("columnar sarcophagi") or, when architectural structure was abandoned in favor of continuous narrative, treated as large, unbroken surfaces ("frieze sarcophagi").

On its eastern Mediterranean home ground the columnar sarcophagus—accepted in the Latin West only by appropriation and in somewhat simplified form[2]—was ultimately to develop into the truly

---

[1] E. Kukahn, *Anthropoide Sarkophage in Beyrouth*, Berlin, 1955.
[2] C. R. Morey, *Early Christian Art*, Princeton, 1942, particularly pp. 22 ff.

spectacular scheme known as the "Asiatic" or (after the two splendid specimens preserved, respectively in the town hall of a small South Italian city and the Museum at Constantinople) the "Melfi" (fig. 59) or "Sidamara" (fig. 60) type, where six colonnettes organize the front wall, after the fashion of a *scaenae frons*, into a rhythmical succession of five units: a niche framed by a gabled aedicula in the center, a niche framed by an arched aedicula on either side, and two flat, linteled spaces in between.

At Sidon itself this development began with the austerely simple "Sarcophagus of the Mourning Women," which looks like an architect's model of an Ionic peristyle, except that each of its eighteen intercolumniations shelters a female figure of Praxitelian cast (fig. 61). Expressing grief in various shades from deep dejection to quiet meditation, these beautiful mourners are both the descendants of pre-Hellenic *Klagefrauen* and the precursors (though not the lineal ancestors) of the medieval *pleureurs* and *pleureuses* as well as of the tearful mythological and allegorical figures in which tombs of the seventeenth, eighteenth, and nineteenth centuries abound. The reliefs on the lid represent the funeral cortège of the occupant (Strato I, who reigned from 374 to 362 B.C. [?]) while those on the base show, as usual, a hunt.

The frieze type is represented in the Sidon series by the equally famous "Alexander Sarcophagus" (figs. 62–65) which—probably holding the remains of a Sidonian ruler (Abdalonymus?) who had enjoyed the favor of the great Macedonian conqueror—displays in front and on the ends a victory of Alexander (distinguished by Greek costume and a diadem) over the Persians, quite possibly the battle of Issos in 333 B.C. (figs. 62, 63); the back shows a hunt (figs. 64, 65) appropriately staged in one of those big-game preserves which were a Persian specialty and whose originally Persian name (παράδεισος) survives in our "paradise." The occupant of the sarcophagus can be identified as the prince, appearing in Persian garb but always in close proximity to Alexander, who occurs no fewer than four times—on each of the faces of the sarcophagus —and may be said to have sought, and in a sense attained, immortality not so much by mythological parallelization as by personal association.

In Phoenicia, then, the anthropomorphic sarcophagus type, imported from Egypt, was speedily superseded by the "domatomorphic" one. A curious and lasting synthesis of these two forms took place, however, in the western outpost of the Phoenician empire: in Carthage, which from the fifth century B.C. dominated considerable portions of Sicily (only about 150 miles across the sea) and may thus have extended its influence to the art of the Italian mainland as well. Here the effigy of the deceased is placed—somewhat uncomfortably, it would seem—on the ridge of the roof-shaped lid that covers a "domatomorphic" sarcophagus or ossuary; and since the Carthaginian sculptors, heirs to the Greek as well as to the Egypto-Phoenician tradition, imparted to these images—images as rigidly erect as their Egyptian ancestors— much of the organic vitality characteristic of Hellenic art, we receive the strange impression of human beings seeming to assume a standing posture while actually recumbent on the lids of their sarcophagi, and capable of autonomous action in spite of their apparent immobility.

On the sarcophagus of the priestess of some strange, winged goddess (fig. 66), the deceased—her appearance assimilated, as so often in primitive (and even not so primitive) cults, to that of the goddess herself and thus presenting the aspect of a sirenlike creature, with huge wings folded over her ceremonial garments—offers a dove and a libation. And a libation is also offered by a priest whose sarcophagus is preserved in the Louvre (fig. 67).

In these Carthaginian or "Punic" sarcophagi an intrinsic conflict exists, therefore, between the horizontal placement of the figure and its apparently standing position and apparently conscious activity; and that this conflict was realized is evident from a device which, in attempting to alleviate what was obviously considered a hardship, makes the inconsistency of the scheme doubly noticeable: the head of the figure was often made to rest upon a pillow, or even two pillows, although the eyes are wide open and the hands are busy offering libations and prayers (fig. 69).

We have here a truly remarkable case of what might be called pseudomorphosis: the emergence of a form A, morphologically analogous to, or even identical with, a form B, yet entirely unrelated to it from a genetic point of view. As we shall see in the next chapter, high medieval funerary sculpture, as represented by any number of instances, produced precisely the same situation: a human figure, apparently standing and perfectly alive, is placed horizontally upon what looks like a sarcophagus, a bed, or even a table, its head supported by one or two pillows (fig. 68). But it will be shown that here the contradictory situation resulted not from the fact that an effigy originally three-dimensional and recumbent had come to be precariously placed on the roof of a house-shaped sarcophagus (in the medieval examples the figure rests on a perfectly flat surface) but from the fact that an originally two-dimensional figure, depicted on a slab in the pavement but represented as standing, had subsequently acquired three-dimensional volume, the figure expanding into a statue, the slab raised upon supporting members or growing into what is known as a *tumba*.

After this brief digression into the Middle Ages let us revert to the pre-Christian Era. The ancient Egyptian tomb statue was, we recall, not really a portrayal of that union of body and soul which Erasmus of Rotterdam was to call the *totus homo* but rather, as I phrased it, an imperishable reconstruction of the body alone, a material substratum for subsequent magic animation. The classical Greek stele *was* such a portrayal, and so were, in a sense, those Punic effigies which we have considered: in spite of their inherited immobility they show the deceased as he was and acted while alive, and not in that state of repose which we presuppose and wish for in the hereafter—or, rather, which is part of what we presuppose and wish for in the hereafter. For—and we shall have to come back to this later—it is one of the great paradoxes of human existence that we desire repose after death yet balk somehow at the idea of a repose so complete that it amounts to an extinction of consciousness and thereby to a loss of identity. Epicurus' Θάνατος οὐδὲν πρὸς ἡμᾶς and the Stoics' "Poenam non sentio mortis, poena fuit vita" ("I suffer not from death, my suffering was life") could not satisfy man's ineradicable if illogical wish to (if I may express myself so colloquially) have his cake and eat it too: to be dead enough to have peace and quiet (*securitas, tranquillitas*) but alive enough to enjoy them. "Vorrei morir di morte piccinina," "I'd like to die a quite, quite little death," says a charming Italian folk song, and this is not so very different from what is expressed, in more exalted language, in all those metaphysical or theological doctrines which distinguish between such "lower" forms of psychological activity as can and will be *suspended* by death and a higher, in fact, suprarational principle that can and will be *liberated* by death and ascend to a place beyond all imagination and comprehension—"steaming away," as Henry James said of the Pennsylvania Railroad trains as he knew them more than fifty years ago, "in disinterested, empty form to some terminus too noble to be marked in *our* poor schedules."

It was, it seems, the art of the Roman empire[1] which struggled with, and finally solved, the problem of giving visible expression to the idea of a repose that was perfect but not total. And it would seem that this achievement was predicated, to a considerable extent, upon the intervention of the Etruscan element in the transmission of the Greek style.

It is hazardous to pronounce the name of this weird people, let alone to discuss its religious beliefs and artistic achievements, in the presence of classical archaeologists.[2] Yet the peculiar manifestations of its genius are indispensable for even a superficial understanding of Roman funerary sculpture. The Etruscans, possibly (no one seems to be sure) hailing from the East, were even more death-ridden, if one may say so, than the Egyptians. Wherever they settled, they began by building two separate cities: a city of the living and a city of the dead, the latter subterranean or semisubterranean and closed by a "ghost stone" (*lapis manalis*) which was solemnly removed three times a year, but surrounded with symbolic fortifica-

[1] See Cumont, *op. cit.*, and *After Life in Roman Paganism*, New Haven, 1922.
[2] An instructive survey is found in *Enciclopedia Italiana*, XIV, 1951, pp. 510 ff.; cf. G. Q. Giglioli, *L'Arte Etrusca*, Milan, 1935; P. J. Rijs, *An Introduction to Etruscan Art*, Copenhagen, 1953. In particular, see R. Herbig, *Die jüngeretruskischen Steinsarkophage*, Berlin, 1952.

tions and laid out with elaborate splendor (fig. 70). Its halls and chambers were decorated and furnished with a luxury at times reminiscent of Victorian elegance, no matter whether the dead were entombed or cremated. For it should be noted that in Italy cremation and burial—the latter either in the form of interment or, to borrow Evelyn Waugh's phrase, "ensarcophagusment"—were not considered mutually exclusive but were practiced concurrently. In prehistoric Rome the inhabitants of the Palatine interred their dead while those of the Quirinal cremated them, yet the two groups formed a kind of communal association from the outset; and in historical times cremation and burial coexisted and competed to such an extent that it became fashionable to entomb the body itself while burning an effigy thereof on a pyre. Before the acceptance of Christianity—whose belief in the resurrection of the flesh, anticipated to some extent by certain Jewish sects and by such mystery cults as that of Isis, put an end to cremation for nearly two millennia—the preference for either the one or the other of the two methods seemed to have been, in many cases at least, a matter of family tradition rather than of commonly accepted ritual (the Cornelii, for example, never cremated their dead up to the death of Sulla).

In the Etruscan necropoles, therefore, we find at all periods short, squat ash urns as well as regular-size sarcophagi (though, with the reservations made, cremation seems to have noticeably gained in popularity as time went on). But in addition to entombment and cremation the Etruscans developed—or, rather, elaborated according to their luxurious tastes—a third, essentially even more primitive, practice which strikes the "civilized" mind as stranger than the two others: the bodies were neither cremated nor placed in sarcophagi but preserved, if one may say so, *au naturel*. Beautifully dressed and adorned, they were arranged, in a reclining position, on elaborate couches (some of which have come down to us) as if alive and attending a ghastly banquet. And it is this custom which may have given rise to the Etruscans' most important contribution to funerary sculpture.

No matter which method of dealing with corpses they preferred, the Etruscans believed that not only the bodies but also the souls of the deceased were entombed: "animamque sepulcro condimus," says Virgil's Aeneas in describing the belated funeral of Polydorus (*Aeneid*, III, 67). The dead were thought of as beings no less complete than they had been in life, inhabiting a world of their own in perpetuity and either forever tortured or forever enjoying themselves in a massively materialistic manner. Their fate was believed to be decided—immediately upon arrival, so to speak—by a tug of war between friendly and hostile demons—*lasas* and *charūns*—who in Etruscan monuments (fig. 71) can be seen fighting over the *anima sepulcro condita* much as, in Christian art, devils and angels were to fight over the soul parted from the body in death (fig. 72) or reunited with it on the Day of Judgment (fig. 73).

Etruscan funerary sculpture employed, in addition to marble, all imaginable kinds of material—terra cotta, alabaster, bituminous limestone—and its style reflects all imaginable kinds of influence: Egyptian, Corinthian, Ionic, Attic, Phoenician,[1] all this reinterpreted in the spirit of an "Italic realism" that occasionally verges upon caricature (fig. 74). As a result of this wild mixture, Etruscan funerary art adopted all the types thus far considered: steles, some of the earliest examples reminiscent of archaic Attic prototypes in shape and style (fig. 75) as well as in the purely commemorative nature of their iconography, the later ones often horseshoe-shaped and exhibiting a great variety of scenes (fig. 76) in which Etruscan eschatology and demonology tend to intermingle with Hellenic myth and fable; "domatomorphic" sarcophagi adorned with such familiar combat scenes as Greeks battling with Amazons or heroes fighting monsters and wild beasts (fig. 77); and the so-called Nenfro sarcophagi, resembling the Punic specimens in that the effigies, laid out flat, are placed, if not on the ridge, at least between the triangular pediments of a roof-shaped lid (fig. 78).

---

[1] See J. Carcopino, *Atti della Pontificia Accademia*, 3rd ser., *Memorie*, I, Pt. 2, 1921, pp. 109 ff.; R. P. Lefeyrié, *Revue Tuni-* sienne, new ser., VI, 1935, pp. 1 ff.

In addition, however, we find a number of forms that seem to be original and specific: first, ash urns, some adorned with reliefs of an infinite variety of subjects, among them the feasts and sacrifices offered to the dead (fig. 79) and those ceremonial *conclamationes* (fig. 80) that seem to have made some impression on Duccio and Giotto, others shaped like diminutive buildings (fig. 81) that duplicate Etruscan structures with the same accuracy as the "Sarcophagus of the Mourning Women" does an Ionic periptery; second, sarcophagi, made of terra cotta and painted in natural colors, which imitate beds or couches at times so literally that the body of the sarcophagus is elevated on four legs.

Not only most of the sarcophagi, however, but also most of the ash urns (the chief exceptions being the strictly "domatomorphic" specimens) serve as bases, so to speak, for effigies unheard of before. Like those on the Egyptian and Punic sarcophagi, these effigies are sculpted in the round; but unlike these, they do not seem to transcend the realm of physical, indeed physiological, reality. Even where the figures retained a recumbent position, their attitudes gradually changed from lifeless rigidity to postures of pliant relaxation (fig. 82); two famous sarcophagi from Vulci in South Etruria go so far as to show couples linked in an everlasting embrace so that the roof-shaped lid, characteristic of the Punic type, appears transformed into a *lectus genialis* (fig. 78). The faces acquired an expression varying from rapt attention to brooding despondency; and when—so far as I know, for the first time—the eyes were dimmed or even closed in death (fig. 83), the very possibility of images thus seeming to have "gone to sleep" presupposed their having been emphatically awake before.

More frequent, however, and even more astonishing, is an apparently indigenous type of effigy, developed by Etruscan sculptors as early as ca. 500 B.C. Here the departed are portrayed as though they had never ceased, and would never cease, to possess the advantages of physical existence (fig. 84). They are shown reclining rather than recumbent, the upper part of the body propped up on pillows and supported by the elbow, holding a dish or goblet when represented singly, and heartily enjoying each other's company when represented in pairs (figs. 85, 86).

To represent the dead enjoying food, drink, and love in the beyond was not new. What was new was the idea of concretizing these representations, formerly confined to the narrative or quasi-narrative context of paintings and flat reliefs, into independent and fully three-dimensional effigies which, instead of merely intimating the happiness presumably awaiting the departed in the hereafter, tangibly duplicate their living selves: figures as "real" as the Egyptian tomb statues yet as "alive" as the portrayals on a Greek stele. Instead of either waiting for an animation to come or evoking the memory of an animation that belongs to the past, they represent an attempt to defy the future by perpetuating the appearance of the present, thus serving as artificial substitutes—less perishable and more aseptic—for the corpses gruesomely displayed on couches in the flesh.

Repellent though their probable origin—and, in some cases, their actual aspect—may appear to the modern beholder, these Etruscan effigies constitute an innovation of the greatest importance. Refined and, as we shall see, reinterpreted in various ways, the new type was adopted by the Romans and spread all over their empire as far as Greece and Western Asia, here to become incorporated with the sarcophagi of the Melfi or Sidamara type (figs. 59, 60). And it was not only in this respect that Roman funerary sculpture was indebted to that of the Etruscans.

That the Etruscan artists were exposed to what I have referred to as a wild mixture of influences had one positive aspect: the very variety of these influences was conducive to a certain independence from established traditions with regard to style as well as iconography. Hellenistic relief—even in works so "pictorial" as the friezes of the Mausoleum, the Alexander sarcophagus from Sidon, or, for that matter, the Pergamon altar—remained committed to classical principles in that it was conceived as a composition of figures detaching themselves from a coherent and impenetrable surface ("ground"). In the Etruscan ash urns of the third and second centuries B.C. (mostly modeled of clay or carved out of comparatively soft stone) the "ground" tended to lose the qualities of coherence and impenetrability (fig. 87). The figures are so deeply undercut and form so dense a pattern that the ground is entirely obscured by shadow, thus ceasing to be impenetrable and purely two-dimensional: the figures appear to exist in an illimited or at least not clearly delimited expanse extending in back of an imaginary front plane rather than in front of a material back plane. And it was this style, in a sense more closely conforming to a perspective conception of space than that of contemporary Hellenistic reliefs, which was widely and enthusiastically adopted—and adapted to hard marble—in a majority of Roman sarcophagi and exerted an enormous influence upon the nascent Renaissance from Nicola Pisano to the youthful Michelangelo.

In a similar way the interpenetration of Oriental and Occidental, primitive and advanced ideas in Etruscan art tended to make more fluid the conventions of funerary iconography. In such monuments as the "Tomb of the Nereids" or the Mausoleum the "prospective" point of view intruded upon the "retrospective" owing to a recrudescence of Oriental tendencies within the framework of a Greek memorial. In the Etruscan ash urns the "retrospective" point of view intruded upon the "prospective" owing to the Hellenization of indigenous attitudes; and eschatological or mythological allusions—as in the Actaeon scene adorning the urn of an Etruscan lady perhaps renowned, although she does not look it, for chastity—became so multifarious that the very absence of "system" opened the way to that complexity and universality which is characteristic of Roman funerary art.

In saying that the Romans refined and reinterpreted the reclining effigies introduced by the Etruscans, I was thinking, in particular, of the fact that the idea of material well-being in the hereafter tended to be sublimated into that of spiritual salvation. But this idea itself was subject to a great variety of new interpretations.

To indicate two diametrical opposites, let us compare the stele of an *eques singularis* (in modern terms, an officer of the Horse Guards) named Aurelius Saturninus (fig. 88) with the famous Prometheus sarcophagus (fig. 89) in the Museo Capitolino at Rome.

The stele of Aurelius Saturninus shows in its lower section the late officer's horse brought in by his groom, a purely commemorative evocation of his position and profession in life. In the upper zone, however, we see his reclining figure—here, naturally, reduced to a relief—reposing on a couch and surrounded by symbols of everlasting bliss enjoyed with perfect consciousness: in his left hand he holds the goblet of eternal youth (reminiscent of Hercules) while with his right he grasps the crown of immortality; and the cist of the Dionysiac mysteries is placed behind the headboard of his couch.

In the Capitoline sarcophagus the situation is, in a sense, reversed. Here the image on the lid—the statue of a child which, though borrowed from another sarcophagus, may be accepted as a substitute for the lost original—conveys the impression of life suspended but not extinct. Recumbent instead of reclining, yet relaxed rather than inanimate, his eyes unseeing but, significantly, not closed (only in one or two instances did Roman funerary sculpture follow the Etruscan precedent in this respect), the infant seems to be overcome by sleep rather than to have succumbed to death; in fact, his right hand holds a bunch of poppies, the "gift of Sleep"; other similar effigies hold, instead of poppies, an egg (fig. 90), the symbol of latent life.[1] But it is evident that images of this kind—most nobly represented, perhaps, by the frail figure of the lady portrayed on the Melfi sarcophagus—could tell no more than the story of the body (including, possibly, those lower, "vegetative" components of the soul that were supposed to be inseparable from it and thus to remain in or near the grave).

The story of the immortal soul could be told only in the reliefs; and those on the Prometheus sarcophagus present this story in a language admirable for beauty of diction as well as for the skill with which mythology is placed in the service of philosophy.[2] In the center of the front wall, we see Prometheus fashioning human

[1]   In our fig. 90, this egg is unfortunately invisible as it is held between the thumb and forefinger of the left hand.
[2]   For a recent discussion of the Prometheus subject see A.-J.

Festugière, "La Mosaïque de Philippopolis et les sarcophages au 'Prométhée'," *Revue des Arts*, VII, 1957, pp. 195 ff.

beings of clay but, unlike the Biblical Creator, unable to infuse them with the "breath of life"; his immortal soul—here represented as a butterfly—man receives from Minerva. This central scene is preceded by a prologue and followed by an epilogue. Beginning on the left-hand end wall, there are enumerated, again in mythological guise, the elements and forces necessary for the procreation and preservation of life: Deucalion and Pyrrha; Vulcan at his forge; Cupid and Psyche; Ocean, Sun, and Earth; a wind god; Lachesis and Clotho (viz., the two Fates attending the living). On the other side of the central group, extending to the right-hand end wall, there are arrayed the powers of darkness and death—powers that yet hold out a promise of the future: Night; the Moon; Death himself (portrayed in the very "classical" form of a Cupid placing an inverted torch upon the breast of a dead body); Atropos, the third of the Fates, here writing the record of the life that has come to an end; Earth once more (as if in anticipation of The Preacher's "all are of the dust, and all shall turn to dust again"); and, finally, Prometheus delivered by Hercules with the permission of a reconciled Jupiter.

These two examples indicate the extraordinary amplitude of Roman funerary sculpture in form as well as significance.[1] In addition to steles and sarcophagi, as represented by the instances just seen, we still have ash urns (because, we recall, the custom of cremation survived along with that of burial throughout the pagan era); sepulchral altars often referred to as *cippi* (although this expression should be reserved, strictly speaking, for still another class of monuments, viz., the often richly decorated markers of individual burying lots); and, on the grand scale, funerary chapels, pyramids, *tetrapyla* such as the Tomb of the Julii in St.-Rémy, towerlike structures like the amazing Tomb of a Decurio at Ptuj (fig. 104) or the Tomb of the Secundii in Igel (a village near Trèves which owes its very name not to the German word for "hedgehog" but to a monument popularly referred to as *acicula* [*aiguille*]) as well as mausoleums that could grow to the proportions of the *Moles Hadriani*. And in addition to that frequent combination of the "retrospective" and the "prospective" point of view exemplified by both the stele of Aurelius Saturninus and the Prometheus sarcophagus in the Museo Capitolino, we have great numbers of either purely commemorative or purely anticipatory monuments.

The commemorative principle predominates, of course, in those modest tombstones, descendants of the Greek steles, that show only the portraits of the deceased, whether in full length or, more frequently, in half length or *en buste*, while giving an indication of their status and achievement in life—whether they were cutlers, carpenters, sculptors, cobblers, soldiers (fig. 91), family men portrayed in the company of their wives and children (figs. 92, 93), or decorous ladies, their virtues occasionally emphasized by suitable mythological symbols as when the portraits of Cornelia Tyche and her twelve-year-old daughter Julia Secunda (fig. 94), both of whom perished at sea, were embellished with the attributes of Fortuna (*Τύχη*) and Diana, respectively. But commemoration could also be achieved, in a very modern spirit of industrial self-congratulation, by the frieze on the mausoleum of a successful wholesale baker named Euryaces (the mausoleum itself no less astonishingly modern as a specimen of purely geometrical architecture; figs. 95, 96); or, in an atmosphere of idealizing eulogy, by such "biographical sarcophagi" as that of a Roman general (fig. 97), which selects from the life of the deceased such episodes as could be interpreted as *exempla virtutis*. On the left-hand side wall is the preparation for, and beginning of, a lion hunt; in front, more hunting, a victory over barbarians, the gracious pardon extended to their leaders, the victory sacrifice, and the marriage of the successful commander; and, on the right-hand side wall, his happy family life.

The purely anticipatory principle, on the other hand, is carried to an extreme in a sarcophagus of fairly recent discovery which may be described as a throwback to Egyptian or Etruscan habits, not only in that the life in the beyond is depicted in strictly materialistic terms but also, and more important, in that the

---

[1] For sarcophagi, see C. Robert, *Die antiken Sarkophagreliefs*, Berlin, 1890; W. Altmann, *Architektur und Ornamentik der antiken Sarkophage*, Berlin, 1902. For other forms, *idem, Die römischen Grabaltäre der Kaiserzeit*, Vienna, 1905. See also P. Gusman, *L'Art décoratif de Rome de la fin de la République au IVe siècle*, Paris, 1908–14.

reliefs, all inside, can be seen and enjoyed only by the occupant, whereas an intrusive observer, if any, would see nothing but a plain, prismatic block of stone: the sarcophagus of a lady found in Simpelveld near Maastricht and now preserved in the Archaeological Museum at Leiden (fig. 98). This charming monument of the Antonine period may be described as an Egyptian or Etruscan tomb chamber reduced to the dimensions of a doll's house. The lady herself rests comfortably on a couch placed in the courtyard of her villa; and on the opposite wall of her cozy abode she can behold the interior of this villa with many objects both useful and ornamental—wall cupboards, a chair, a pretty table with lions' feet, a kind of wardrobe, a locked cashbox, and numerous containers for food and drink.

The Simpelveld sarcophagus is an exception. As a rule, Roman funerary sculpture, insofar as it predicts the future happiness of the deceased in the hereafter, either eliminates direct description in favor of metaphorical allusion—mythological or otherwise—or, more often than not, utilizes a combination of both. It was perhaps precisely the much-vaunted matter-of-factness of the Romans which (as in the minds of so many "practical men" of our day) tended to produce that fusion, or confusion, of reality and symbol which is characteristic of their funerary art.

The reliefs from the Tomb of the Haterii (figs. 99–101), found near Centocelle but now preserved in the Lateran, are famed for their "realism." But their content goes far beyond a factual record of what had happened—or, rather, was to be remembered by posterity as having happened—in reality, viz., the *conclamatio* over the most important feminine member of the family, lying in state in the atrium of her house; the road of the funeral cortège along the Via Sacra, passing the Arch of Titus, the Temple of Cybele, and the Colosseum; and, most interesting of all, the construction of what is supposed to be the very tomb for which the reliefs were intended. We find, in addition, such subjects as the eternal repose of the defunct matriarch under the protection of unidentified divinities and the images of the gods especially venerated by the Haterii. But the "architectural portraits" of the buildings on the Via Sacra are provided with imaginary decorations, and the building represented in course of erection is not so much a lifelike portrait of the Tomb of the Haterii (the construction of which hardly required so colossal a machine) as an imaginary structure incompatible with the reliefs that have come down to us but superabundant in such traditional symbols of immortality as bust portraits encircled by medallions (*imagines clipeatae*), funerary garlands, eagles, the Elements, the Seasons, etc.

Similarly, a much-debated sarcophagus in the Vatican (fig. 102) exhibits so bewildering a mixture of personifications, legendary characters (e. g., Odysseus), gods and demigods, and realistic topographical details (among them a recognizable portrayal of the port of Ostia) that its interpretation is still a matter of surmise. The most reasonable assumption is that the two principal figures, their faces merely blocked out and presumably to be carved into the likenesses of the deceased, are Bacchus and Ariadne (Roman portraiture never hesitated to identify its subjects with gods); and that the multiplicity of port installations is meant to convey the idea that the personage portrayed in the guise of Bacchus had, like Odysseus, "seen the cities of many men and come to know their minds." This one sarcophagus, then, attempts both to perpetuate the memory of what the departed had been and done on earth and to safeguard their well-being in the hereafter; it qualifies them, it seems, as votaries of the Dionysian mysteries; and it conveys these ideas in a language as rich in topographical description as in allegorical symbolism.

To give an even moderately adequate idea of the way in which all these elements proliferated and intermingled in Roman funerary sculpture would be futile as well as presumptuous. Nor should we overlook the danger of reading a profound significance into each and every detail. The human race is both playful and forgetful, and many a motif originally fraught with meaning came to be used for "purely decorative" purposes when this meaning had fallen into oblivion or had ceased to be of interest. I am convinced, however, that very few motifs were invented for "purely decorative" purposes from the outset: even so lighthearted an ornament as the garland or festoon (*serta*), ubiquitous in Roman art and enthusiastically revived by the Renaissance, was ritual in origin, and the specific connection of such *longae coronae* with funerary rites is attested by as venerable a source as the *Twelve Tables*.

We shall thus take a middle course, so to speak, and limit our discussion to a small number of monuments, selected more or less at random, of which we can be reasonably sure that they did carry an intelligible and determinable message both for those who made and for those who had commissioned them.

First, let us return for a moment to that modest stele from Philadelphia in Lydia which has been briefly mentioned in the preceding chapter (fig. 23). Poor, late, and ill-preserved as it is, it provides valuable testimony to the fact that the age-old simile of the narrow way that leads to good and the broad way that leads to evil—a simile employed by Hesiod as well as Xenophon, the Psalmist as well as Christ in the Sermon on the Mount, and circumstantially elaborated in such popular tracts as the *Tabula Cebetis*—had been adopted by the so-called Pythagoreans (indeed the graphic symbol of this simile, the letter Y, was known as the *Littera Pythagorae*)[1] and had been invested by them with a significance which made it suitable for a funerary monument.

The Philadelphia stele, its very composition determined by the "Pythagorean Letter," unquestionably alludes to the doctrine according to which the choice between good and evil, made in every life, must be repeated in Hades and determines either perdition or salvation. On top of the composition we dimly recognize a bust portrait, probably that of Pythagoras himself. On the left is seen a personification of ’Ασωτία, Dissipation, surmounted by two scenes depicting the character and fate of her adherents (a couple of lovers disporting themselves on a couch and, farther up, a person falling down head over heels). On the right, we have ’Αρετή, Virtue, surmounted by two representations antithetical to those associated with ’Ασωτία: a laborer in the fields, typifying the strenuous efforts of a life well spent; and farther up, the now familiar symbol of everlasting bliss, the figure reclining on a couch in undisturbed repose. It is this symbol which gives an eschatological touch to a relief which otherwise might serve as a mere illustration of a moralistic parable and firmly connects it with the doctrines of the mystery religions.

From the point of view of these doctrines even the story of Persephone, told on so many sarcophagi (fig. 103), holds out a promise rather than a threat. She was addressed, as we have seen, as the "pure Queen of Death," presiding over the groves of bliss and the fountain of life, and her consent to share the throne of Hades could be interpreted as the self-sacrifice of a goddess for the benefit of her votaries; it is perhaps more than an accident that in at least one instance her story is connected with the myth of Alcestis, who offered to die for her husband but was ultimately restored to life by the intervention of Hercules.

The idea of the god suffering and dying for the salvation of mankind and manifesting this salvation by his own resuscitation or rebirth—the very idea that was to become a reality in the Passion and Resurrection of Christ—pervades, needless to say, the closely interrelated mysteries of Dionysus and Orpheus. But it is significant—and a like aversion to the passional can be observed in Early Christian art—that neither the horrible death of Orpheus at the hands of the maenads nor the equally horrible death of Dionysus-Zagreus at the hands of the Titans seems to occur in funerary sculpture. Orpheus was represented, if at all, not as the victim but as the pacifying savior, charming the animals or casting the magic spell of his music over the nether world as on the monument at Ptuj (fig. 104):

Quin ipsae stupuere domus atque intima Leti
Tartara caeruleosque implexae crinibus anguis
Eumenides, tenuitque inhians tria Cerberus ora,
Atque Ixionii vento rota constitit orbis.

[1] Cf. E. Panofsky, *Hercules am Scheidewege und andere antike Bildstoffe in der neueren Kunst* (Studien der Bibliothek Warburg, XVIII), Leipzig and Berlin, 1930, pp. 37 ff.; A. Friberg, *Den Svenska Herkules* (Kungl. Vitterhets Historie och Antikvitets Akademiens Handlingar, LXV, 1), Stockholm, 1945 (see Index under "Pythagoras" and "Cebes").

("Spellbound remained Death's house and inmost chambers/And, locks entwined with blue-green snakes, the Furies;/Cerberus held his triple mouth agape,/And Ixion's wind-driven wheel stood still" [Virgil, *Georgics*, IV, 481 ff.].)

And the belief in the powers of Dionysus was expressed in reliefs depicting the ecstasy of the Bacchic *thiasos*, the god's triumphal progress through the inhabited world, or his union and reunion with Ariadne—in short, in evocations of an overpowering joy remembered by the votaries of Dionysus as a transitory experience in life and accepted by them as a promise of unending felicity after death (figs. 105–107).

Small wonder that the "Bacchic" sarcophagi surpass all other Roman funerary monuments not only in beauty of form and richness of content[1] but also in numbers. And to these numerous monuments there may be added those in which the Dionysiac element enters the narrative only by implication, so to speak, as in the sarcophagi depicting the myth of Ariadne. An instrument of salvation in that it is she whose help enables Theseus to find his way back from the inferno of the Cretan Labyrinth, she was formally—in fact, doubly—recognized as an object of salvation by her twofold encounter with Dionysus, who rescued her after her desertion by Theseus, abandoned her himself, but finally immortalized her as his celestial bride.

In this sense a particularly charming sarcophagus of the so-called garland type (the central garland consisting partly of ears of grain, sacred to Demeter, and partly of vine leaves and grapes, sacred to Dionysus) may be considered as a "Bacchic" monument even though Dionysus does not appear in person (fig. 108). Its lid shows winged cupids bridling animals that stand for sensual emotion (goats, lions, bulls, and boars) while the ends display foliated masks which may or may not have retained the apotropaic significance of the Medusa's heads referred to in connection with the Cypriote sarcophagi. In front, in the spaces left by the garlands, are seen Ariadne lending a helping hand to Theseus, who is about to enter the Labyrinth; Theseus killing the Minotaur; and, finally, Theseus abandoning Ariadne on Naxos. The happy ending of the story, Ariadne's "sacred marriage" to Dionysus (in commemoration of which her diadem was transformed into the Constellation of the Crown), is not entirely absent from Roman monuments but it is rare and told without enthusiasm (fig. 109); it was left to Titian to write, as it were, the final epilogue to our sarcophagus in his *Apotheosis of Ariadne* in the National Gallery at London.

While, as I said, the passion of Dionysus—originally symbolic of the death and rebirth of nature in general and of the mysterious process by which the juice of the tortured grape is changed to wine in particular—is absent from Roman funerary monuments, it is presupposed and alluded to in a peculiar type of sarcophagus which imitates wine vats and thus suggests, in non-narrative form, both the identity of the god with the plant sacred to him and the identity of the votary with the god. The idea of expressing these two equations by assimilating the shape of the vessel destined to hold a dead body to that of the vessel destined to hold the juice of the grape goes very far back. As early as the fifth century B.C. (Pherecrates the Comedian) the Greek word for wine vat, ληνός, was used as a synonym for sarcophagus, and sarcophagi resembling wine vats in shape (narrower at the bottom than at the top and rounded at the edges) were employed in Greece long before the Roman occupation. But these Greek specimens are cheap, inconspicuous vessels, mostly made of terra cotta. Roman art transformed these modest ληνοί into objects both precious and noble: the strigilated sarcophagi, fashioned of beautiful marble and reminiscent of their humble ancestry only in their tublike form and in the presence of open-mouthed lion heads that took the place of spouts and were originally the only figural element in the decoration (fig. 110).[2]

As time went on, a twofold fusion occurred between the strigilated and what may be called—in analogy to

---

[1] See, in addition to Cumont, *op. cit.*, K. Lehmann and E. C. Olsen, *Dionysiac Sarcophagi in Baltimore*, New York, 1942.
[2] Later on (see, e. g., Reinach, *Répertoire de reliefs*, III, pp. 156, 2; 348, 1) these lion heads developed into complete lions with rams or other harmless animals between their paws. This type survived in Early Christian art (see, e. g., Reinach, II, p. 7, 1), where a figure of the Good Shepherd, placed in the center, tends to make it clear that the rams devoured by lions symbolize the sinners destroyed by the devil.

the term applied by medievalists to capitals adorned with narrative reliefs—the "historiated" sarcophagus. On the one hand, sarcophagi adorned with reliefs *en frise*—particularly with reliefs of a Dionysiac character —could adopt the ovoid shape of the strigilated type (occasionally including even the lion heads, fig. 111). On the other hand, strigilated sarcophagi could be adapted to the square shape of the historiated type and could incorporate figural reliefs narrow enough to leave room for the strigilation: one panel with reliefs could be placed in the center while the corners were reinforced by colonnettes; two panels could be placed on the sides, while the center remained empty; or, most frequently, three panels were distributed symmetrically.

In these panels we find a great variety of subjects from Bacchic scenes and figures to full-length portraits pure and simple: married couples alone or united by Juno Pronuba, portrayed realistically or symbolized by such mythological prototypes as Mars and Venus or Cupid and Psyche (figs. 112, 113, 114), their immortality occasionally insured by the presence of Victories or the Dioscuri; the *imago clipeata* of the deceased, at times between the figures of Sleep and Death (fig. 115); the Door of Hades (fig. 116), its panels adorned with the Four Seasons, now symbols of time which stops, so to speak, once the threshold between this life and the next has been crossed;[1] Ganymede (or a Victory) offering wine to Jupiter's eagle (fig. 117); a seated scholar, physician, or poet holding a scroll (fig. 118) and often accompanied by a veiled woman who may be a Muse or personify some such idea as poetry, wisdom, or invention.

As is evident from a comparison between identical motifs, all the reliefs that can be seen on strigilated sarcophagi are excerpted from historiated specimens, in which the choice and treatment of subject matter were limited only by the structural types which we have had occasion to distinguish. In sarcophagi of the garland type (practically abandoned after the second century A.D.) the narrative, if any, had to be broken up into individual episodes; the frieze type, on the other hand, lent itself to the display of unified compositions of quasi-monumental character, whether epically unfolding in a progression from left to right, dramatically revolving around a center of action, or hieratically crystallized into bilateral symmetry; and the columnar type—the complex rhythmical organization of the Melfi-Sidamara group giving way to a simple division into five intercolumniations of nearly equal width, bridged by either a level entablature, a series of arches, or, at the utmost, a series of arches and gables in alternation—tended to restrict the program to isolated figures or groups (fig. 119) which constitute a coherent narrative only when connected by intellectual effort rather than immediate visual experience (fig. 120).

However, no matter to which of these types a historiated sarcophagus of the Roman period may belong (in Greek territory, where all four sides continued to be decorated, we may even find a relief *en frise* in front and an arrangement of garlands in back, as on the exceptionally fine sarcophagus in St. Irene at Constantinople, fig. 121), the fundamental attitude expressed in its decoration is rarely simple or, to borrow a term from the mathematicians, "uniquely determined."

The "biographical" sarcophagi already mentioned are, of course, essentially commemorative in character (though even here the selection, we remember, of the subjects evokes the idea of such "Roman" virtues as *fortitudo*, *clementia*, *liberalitas*, and *pietas* and thereby implies a suggestion of future reward as well as past merits); and in certain cases—fewer, perhaps, than might be expected—the representation of a myth such as that of Niobe may serve to lend expression to the feeling of bereavement as such.

Conversely, where the deceased is portrayed as the guest of honor at an Elysian banquet graced by the presence of Hercules or Mercury (fig. 123), or where a "heroized child" receives the homage of other children carrying the attributes of the Muses (fig. 124), we are unquestionably confronted with an anticipatory or "prospective" monument. Real apotheosis could be signified by the age-old symbol of victory and

---

[1] E. H. Haight, *The Symbolism of the House Door in Classical Poetry*, New York and Toronto, 1950, p. 151.

ascension, the eagle, which played a prominent role in the funeral rites of Roman emperors and on the Hildesheim bronze doors (fig. 122) could still illustrate the words of the Lord (St. John 20:17): "I ascend unto my Father, and your Father; and to my God and your God." And that the ubiquitous *imago clipeata* also symbolizes an ascent to the heavens is made explicit in innumerable ways. The circular image is borne aloft by such guides to immortality as Victories, Cupids, the Seasons, or—particularly where it is set out against a conch instead of being encircled by a medallion—the Winds, Sea Centaurs, or Nereids (fig. 125). In many instances the terrestrial sphere which the deceased leaves behind him is typified by the figures of Ocean and Earth, and the idea of his rise to higher realms, though clear enough in itself, is often further elucidated by what may be called visual footnotes: his ascent may be compared to the abduction—that is to say, deification—of Ganymede (fig. 126) or, on the contrary, contrasted with the labors, struggles, fleeting ecstasies, and fallacious delights of life on earth (such, it would seem, is the significance of the masks which are occasionally represented beneath the elevated image and bring to mind Seneca's *personata felicitas*). At times the *clipeus* itself assumes the form of the zodiac (fig. 127) so that the mortal being appears, quite literally, transported *ad astra*.

More numerous, however, are representations in which the "prospective" and "retrospective" points of view assert themselves simultaneously, so that the evocation of life on earth merges with the anticipation of a life hereafter into one panoramic vision—the representation of a life well spent in this world prefigures, of itself, unending beatitude in the next.

Where the departed are thought of as being alive, this idea could be expressed, directly, by representing them in the company of such exacting divinities as Juno Pronuba or Diana, the goddess of valor and chastity; by showing them inspired by a personification of creative activity; and, most particularly, by associating them with Minerva, Apollo, and the Muses (fig. 128): the ancients believed that intellectual achievement bestowed immortality in a literal rather than figurative sense (Homer in particular was unanimously held to have been deified), and it is this belief—weakly surviving in our habit of referring to the great philosophers, poets, and artists as "the immortals"—which accounts for the extraordinary frequency of sarcophagi exhibiting Muses, whether alone or gathered around a leader, whether appearing in full force, in smaller groups, or singly (figs. 129–131). Indirectly, or metaphorically, the same idea could be conveyed not only by such familiar symbols as the slaying of wild beasts, the combat with human enemies, or the chariot race (its metaphysical significance frequently stressed by the fact that the horses are controlled by Cupids rather than ordinary charioteers), but also by motifs drawn from the inexhaustible well of mythology, which, in addition to providing such grand eschatological similes as the story of Phaëthon,[1] yielded unforgettable prototypes of the "labor and sorrow" as well as the triumph of human life: Achilles forsaking a long life of idle pleasures for one of heroic action and everlasting glory; Meleager, slayer of the Calydonian boar (but victim of his own mother's vengeance); Theseus triumphant over the Minotaur; Hippolytus, the classical though less fortunate counterpart of the Biblical Joseph; and, above all, the hero of heroes, Hercules (fig. 132), whose labors and ultimate apotheosis were represented over and over again.

Where the departed are thought of as having passed beyond terrestrial existence, it was natural to represent their immortality as a favor bestowed upon them by divine powers rather than as a reward for human virtue; and this idea could again be expressed directly as well as metaphorically: directly, by showing them protected and attended by the benevolent spirits of water and air repeatedly mentioned before, by the Seasons, or, above all, by the Dioscuri, considered as special "patron saints" of the dead because their astral reincarnations, the Twins, are never seen together in the firmament and were thus held to rule the two hemispheres of the heavens where the most privileged souls are permitted to dwell;[2] indirectly, by having recourse to either common symbolism (eagles, garlands, wreaths, etc.) or, again, to

[1] Cumont, *Recherches*, pp. 16 ff.   [2] *Ibid.*, pp. 64 ff.

such mythological parallels (in part already named) as imply immortalization or deification. The future destiny of the deceased could thus be equated, at times to such an extent that the mythological characters bear the individual features of the dead persons, with the fate of the god of whom he had been a votary (most frequently Dionysus), with the abductions of Ganymede, Hylas, or the Leucippides (a theme the more appropriate as the abductors were the Dioscuri), with the death of Adonis (his beauty to be shared between Venus and Persephone), or with the everlasting love of Endymion and Diana, the very goddess whose planet was thought by some, particularly the Stoics, to be the home of the blessed.[1]

All this is complicated enough. But very often the four possibilities which I have treated separately (the presentation, direct or indirect, of immortality as either a matter of merit or a result of divine intervention) were realized in conjunction, and this not only in such exceptionally rich and complex ensembles as the monuments of St.-Rémy, Igel, or Ptuj but also in ordinary sarcophagi, sepulchral altars, steles, etc.

The *cippus* of a high Roman official of the first century called T. Flavius Abascantus (fig. 133), for example, shows, at the bottom, a quadriga driven by "Scorpus," a charioteer so famous in his day that his name was immortalized by Martial, and drawn by his equally famous horses (whose names are also recorded in the relief). On top, Abascantus himself reclines in the familiar attitude of bliss consciously enjoyed (his right hand holding a scroll, his left a cup), and basks in the light of a torch held up by Lucifer or Phosphorus, the Morning Star that signifies the dawn of a new day ("Praevius Aurorae Lucifer"; "Phosphore, redde diem"). Still higher up, finally, we see the now familiar symbol of ultimate triumph, the eagle.

The motif of the quadriga—whether symbolizing, as usual, the struggles and victories of life, or merely alluding to the fact that Abascantus was affluent and generous enough to offer games to the people, or both—is certainly intended to extol the merits of his earthly life. The upper part of the composition, however, describes his blissful state in the hereafter and his ultimate ascension to the realm of the gods. And in its modest way this little monument to a Roman dignitary may be said to embody the same ideas which, as Karl Lehmann has shown, underlie the Arch of Titus.[2]

Even more comprehensive is the program of the sarcophagus from Sidamara (fig. 60), whose columnar organization we have admired before but whose iconography we did not analyze. Intended, as appears from what remains of the reclining effigies, for a married couple, it may be said to epitomize what may be called the double-edged character of funerary symbolism in the Roman era. The front wall shows a poet enthroned between his "Muse" and Diana, each of whom would have been sufficient to characterize him as a person worthy of immortality; but in order to make assurance doubly sure, the Dioscuri are added on either side. The left-hand side wall displays a hunting scene, a motif recurring in the decoration of the lid as well as of the base, one face of which, however, exhibits in addition a chariot race. And on the right-hand side wall we perceive two youthful figures guarding a door which here, since it reveals a table laden with offerings, would seem to represent the Door of Hades—a frequent motif which we remember from one of our strigilated sarcophagi—under the guise of the entrance to the actual tomb.

On two exceptionally beautiful sarcophagi in the Vatican this door, here symbolizing the entrance to afterlife pure and simple, occupies the center of the front wall. On one of these the door is flanked by the portraits of a husband and wife (fig. 134); but each of the spouses is protected by two Muses whose presence at the very door of Death seems to indicate that Hades has lost its terror; and this idea of victory in death is made even more explicit in the other sarcophagus (fig. 135), which is of special interest to art historians because it was to inspire Michelangelo's first plan for the Tomb of Julius II (fig. 417). Here a distinguished family of four, divided according to sex, are portrayed standing in niches on either side of the door, the wings of which—one of them slightly ajar—display the Four Seasons, here as in other cases an obvious reference to Homer's and Ovid's description of the Horae as guardians of the Gates of Heaven (*Iliad*,

[1] *Ibid.*, pp. 246 ff.
[2] K. Lehmann-Hartleben, "L'Arco di Tito," *Bollettino della*   *Commissione Archeologica Communale di Roma*, LXII, 1934, pp. 89 ff.

V, 749, and VIII, 393; *Fasti*, I, 125). The Muses are replaced by two mildly persuasive divinities (Persephone and Hades?), and the door itself is guarded by statues of what would seem to be the personal *genii* of the departed. Represented in the traditional postures of Sleep and Death (legs crossed) but carrying poppy stalks and cornucopias instead of their traditional attribute (the inverted torch), they turn their heads so that their eyes, meeting those of the husband and the wife, seem to invite the couple to enter; and they are crowned by Victories emerging above them *en buste:* "nullique ea tristis imago."

This superficial survey is merely intended to illustrate a complexity and multivalence which had been foreign to classical Greece and was to be reduced to relative simplicity and absolute consistency by the unifying force of Christianity. The funerary sculpture of the Roman period was inspired by an almost boundless variety of beliefs and experiences—the official religion, the literary and representational tradition of mythology, strange mystery cults, and even stranger philosophies—and it was torn between the desire for terrestrial recognition on the one hand and for salvation on the other. The Christian faith gave unity of direction to man's bewildered longing for immortality. It said, in a sense, to Roman art what Christ Himself had said unto Martha: "Thou art careful and troubled about many things; but one thing is needful" (St. Luke 10:41 f.). Even so, Early Christian art, born from an experience spiritually different from, yet psychologically cognate with, that of the mystery religions, could develop a visual mode of expression only by reinterpretative borrowings from paganism.

III. The Early Christian Period and the Middle Ages North of the Alps

What Diogenes is said to have found objectionable in the Eleusinian mysteries—that they promised to the initiated, regardless of merit, a state of bliss from which Agesilaus and Epaminondas were excluded—was, on a higher level of religious experience, the very essence of Pauline Christianity: "A man is justified by faith without the deeds of the law."

In funerary sculpture this essentially Christian conception (in the Old Testament the word *fides* occurs only once, viz., in Habakkuk 2:4, and here, in contrast to St. Paul's interpretation, denotes "faithfulness" rather than "faith") resulted, at the beginning, in a complete elimination of the "retrospective" or commemorative principle—except, of course, for portraits and such references to profession or status in earthly life as may be compared to what is called "distinguishing marks or features" in a modern passport. Apart from these means of identification, especially desirable in view of the Resurrection, Early Christian art emphasized not what the deceased had been or done but what would happen to him on account of his faith.

Where Early Christian sarcophagi—steles seem to have played an important role only in the outlying provinces, particularly in Africa—still exhibit lion or boar hunts, these scenes must be interpreted in the light of such passages in the Vulgate as "Salva me ex ore leonis" (Psalm 21:22) or "Exterminavit eam aper de silva" (Psalm 79:14). And the only important "Early Christian" monument occasionally cited as glorifying the past instead of safeguarding the future, the huge porphyry sarcophagus traditionally connected with St. Helena, the mother of Constantine the Great, is not an Early Christian monument (fig. 136). The very fact that its reliefs show nothing but battles between Romans and barbarians would seem to prove that, even supposing that it ever did contain St. Helena's remains (which is quite doubtful), it cannot have been intended for her from the outset. Originally it must have been destined not for a pious princess but for a military leader proud of his successes in war and not at all concerned with the salvation of his soul. If it is a product of the late third or early fourth century (and not, as has been thought, of the second), it may have been commissioned by Constantine himself before his conversion.

The message of Early Christian funerary sculpture, then, is hardly ever "retrospective,"[1] let alone eulogistic; and the expectations of the faithful which it expressed in visible form—whether their artistic manifestations were as simple and naïve as, say, the *Banquet in Paradise* in the Catacomb of Peter and Marcellinus or as complex and erudite as, say, the sarcophagus in S. Ambrogio at Milan which we shall soon discuss—can nearly always be reduced to Rufus Morey's beautiful formula: "Deliverance from death *(vivas in domino)*, deliverance from sin and the misery thereof *(in pace).*"[2] Where the pagan lady of Simpelveld (fig. 98) craved everlasting comfort in the possession of her villa and its furnishings, a Christian woman of Thabraca in Tunisia longed for everlasting peace under the protection of the "Mater Ecclesia," depicted on her tombstone in the guise of her parish church (fig. 137).

By and large the beginnings of Early Christian sculpture do not antedate the early years of the fourth century,[3] when Christianity ceased to be—literally as well as figuratively—an underground movement

---

[1] For some exceptions in catacomb painting (as opposed to sculpture), see H. Stern, "Les mosaïques de l'eglise de Sainte-Constance à Rome," *Dumbarton Oaks Papers*, XII, 1958, p. 213.
[2] *Early Christian Art*, p. 62.

[3] For earlier (and supposedly earlier) examples, see F. Gerke, *Die christlichen Sarkophage der vorkonstantinischen Zeit*, Berlin, 1940.

and achieved a recognized status among the better and more affluent classes; in a hostile environment it is less difficult to paint catacombs than to keep a sculptor's workshop going, and the numerous Biblical injunctions against "graven images" may have carried greater weight with Christians oppressed by "idol worshipers" than with Christians who had prevailed against them. We can thus easily understand that the makers of Early Christian sarcophagi leaned heavily on painting (first, catacomb painting, later on, book illumination and possibly murals) in subject matter, but equally heavily on the works of their professional predecessors for everything else: artistic syntax, phonetics, and, above all, phraseology.[1]

As regards syntax (or, to abandon the metaphor, over-all organization), the Early Christian sculptors continued to employ the three familiar types of pagan sarcophagi, the strigilated, the columnar, and the frieze type. But they developed, reinterpreted, and, in part, combined them in various ways—and they nearly always omitted the reclining or recumbent effigies in the round which would have been incompatible with both their feeling for style and their religious convictions.

The strigilated type remained essentially unaltered. Except for the peculiar "chest-shaped sarcophagi" of Aquitania, where strigilation is replaced by vegetal ornament (fig. 138), the Christian specimens differ from the pagan ones only in the subject matter of their relief panels; and since this subject matter was frequently adapted from pagan art, it is not always possible to determine whether or not the occupant of a given sarcophagus was a Christian. Orpheus Taming the Animals or the Good Shepherd, for example, were long employed by votaries of the pagan mystery religions as well as by Christians, and it is only by the character of the accompanying scenes (absent from strigilated sarcophagi) that a definite decision can be made.[2] The "Orant" (viz., a rigidly frontalized figure, raising both hands, which may be taken to personify either the ideas of prayer and beatitude in the abstract or to portray an individual *anima beata*), the Fisher of Men, Christ the Teacher, and portrait medallions surmounting a personification of heaven rather than a group of masks or such subjects as the Abduction of Ganymede, may be taken as indications of Christian beliefs; and any doubt is removed where such portraits are replaced by the monogram of Christ (figs. 139–42).

The development of the columnar and frieze types, on the other hand, was subject to dramatic vicissitudes.[3] On Greco-Asian soil, the Sidamara scheme sporadically survived intact (except, of course, for changes in proportions and technique) up to the beginning of the fifth century (fig. 143). In the Latin West, however, the quinquepartition typical of pre-Christian specimens evolved—largely owing to a strengthening of Eastern influences which was the inevitable concomitant of Christianization—in several directions. The five intercolumniations could be elaborated into regular niches, the flutings of the conchs radiating either upward or downward, the former scheme originating in (but not limited to) the Greek-speaking East, the latter in the Latin West (fig. 144). They could be bridged by a level entablature, by arches only, by alternating arches and gables, and also, Sidamara fashion, by alternating arches and lintels (fig. 145). Their number could be increased from five to seven (fig. 146), the treatment of the

[1] As I learn from Dr. Kahane, this even applies, *mutatis mutandis*, to what may be called the Jewish counterpart of Early Christian art and civilization. In Beth She'arim in Galilee, where Greek inscriptions are intermingled with Hebrew ones (one of the latter significantly alluding to the idea of "resurrection"), there have been found numerous sarcophagi, dating from the second to the fourth centuries A.D., which show a decoration of distinctly Greco-Roman character, including all kinds of "graven images" and in part carved by pagan hands; one of them even displays the very un-Jewish story of Leda and the Swan. See N. Avigad, "Sarcophagi at Beth She'arim," *Archaeology*, X, 1957, pp. 266 ff.; *idem*, "Excavations at Beth She'arim, 1955," *Israel Exploration Journal*, VII, 1957 ff., pp. 73 ff., 239 ff.; and "Excavations at Beth She'arim,

1959," *ibid.*, IX, pp. 205 ff.

[2] For the Good Shepherd, see T. Klauser, "Studien zur Entstehungsgeschichte der Christlichen Kunst, I," *Jahrbuch für Antike und Christentum*, I, 1958, pp. 20 ff., a most interesting article which, however, goes perhaps a little too far in eliminating representations of the Good Shepherd from Christian art and apparently ignores the most important previous treatment of the subject: F. Saxl, "Frühes Christentum und spätes Heidentum in ihren künstlerischen Ausdrucksformen," *Wiener Jahrbuch für Kunstgeschichte*, II, 1923, pp. 63 ff., especially pp. 90 ff.

[3] M. Lawrence, "Columnar Sarcophagi in the Latin West," *Art Bulletin*, XIV, 1932, pp. 103 ff.; *eadem*, "City-Gate Sarcophagi," *Art Bulletin*, X, 1927, pp. 1 ff.

individual units varying, again, between uniformity and alternation (figs. 147, 148). The dividing colonnettes or pilasters could be replaced by Paradisial laurel or olive trees such as traditionally flank the Good Shepherd (fig. 149). And, above all, the columnar type as such could interpenetrate with the frieze type: either by way of infiltration, so to speak (in that the intercolumniations were widened or even organized into a kind of triptych, so as to accommodate scenes involving from four to eight figures), or, more important, by way of genuine fusion (fig. 150). Instead of being placed *between* the figures, thus forming five or seven separate aediculae, some or all of the dividing members were placed *behind* the figures, thus forming a backdrop for either several distinct crowds of people or one continuous composition *en frise* (figs. 151, 152). In a further development this backdrop was concretized into a series of crenellated "city gates," perhaps symbolic of the Heavenly Jerusalem and, by implication, of the Church itself (fig. 153); while, on the other hand, the figures themselves, especially the Apostles, disposed on either side of the Lord or of the *crux triumphans* (fig. 154), could be arranged and shaped in what may be called columnar fashion. And friezes as well as a series of scenes divided by colonnettes could be superimposed upon each other so as to form a two-register composition—a concept unprecedented, so far as I know, in pagan antiquity. Two friezes superimposed tend to appear in combination with an *imago clipeata* representing a married couple or a pair of brothers (figs. 155, 156); whereas the superimposition of two "colonnades"—the lower one organized by alternating arches and gables, the upper one exhibiting a level entablature—is exemplified by what is perhaps the best known of all Early Christian sarcophagi, that of Junius Bassus, Prefect of Rome, who died in 359 A. D. (fig. 157).

In addition to illustrating several different possibilities of structural organization, this famous monument displays—and arranges with an almost scholastic passion for system—much of the iconographical subject matter that was at the disposal of Early Christian funerary sculpture by the middle of the fourth century.

The program of the front wall (the ends, carved by a somewhat inferior hand, display the familiar symbols of time, the Seasons) is centered around what may be called the eternal and the temporal triumph of Christ. The central relief of the upper tier shows the so-called *traditio legis*, viz., the Saviour enthroned (His feet here resting not upon the earth, according to Isaiah 66:1, but upon Heaven in the guise of Coelus), entrusting Saints Peter and Paul with their respective missions; the central relief of the lower tier shows His entry into Jerusalem. The *traditio legis* is flanked by the Arrest of St. Paul on the left, which corresponds to the Arrest of Christ on the right; and, farther out, by the Sacrifice of Isaac (viz., Isaac's "deliverance from the hands of his father, Abraham," as it says in the prayers *in extremis)*, which—antithetically—corresponds to Christ before Pilate (viz., Christ's deliverance into the hands of the Jews).

The parallelism between Christ and St. Paul, conferring upon the latter a distinction which many other sarcophagi reserve for St. Peter, can also be observed in the lower zone, where St. Paul's Martyrdom, represented at the extreme right, corresponds to the Afflictions of Job—*exemplar patientiae* and, more specifically, *typus Christi patientis*—which we perceive on the extreme left; whereas that best-beloved example of salvation, Daniel in the Lions' Den, corresponds to the event which made salvation necessary: the Fall of Man.

In the spandrels of the lower colonnade, finally, the theme of salvation is further elaborated in six scenes, all of them enacted by lambs instead of human figures (a substitution based, of course, upon the frequent Biblical references to Christ as the Lamb and to the faithful, particularly the Apostles, as lambs): the Three Hebrews in the Fiery Furnace, Moses Striking the Rock, the Baptism of Christ, the Multiplication of Loaves and Fishes, Moses Receiving the Tablets of the Law, and, at the end, the Raising of Lazarus.

The elements of this highly developed program exemplify at least four different classes of imagery: first, "historical" representations, viz., the scenes from the life of St. Paul; second, "doctrinal" representations, viz., the *traditio legis*; third, "typological" representations, viz., renderings of such events as can be interpreted, either by virtue of analogy or contrast, as "prefigurations" of others, particularly scenes from the Old Testament foreshadowing the New; fourth, "symbolical" representations, viz., renderings of objects or figures to which a certain significance is attached by way of metaphor, as when an anchor is understood as a symbol of hope, a shepherd carrying a sheep on his shoulders as a symbol of the Saviour, or, in our case, lambs as symbols of Biblical characters, including Christ Himself.

This classification is neither exhaustive nor, since the four classes differ in method as well as in subject, exclusive: evidently, a prefigurative or symbolical interpretation, and frequently both, could be imposed on scenes which in themselves fall under the heading of historical events. Thus, the Wedding of Cana was held to foreshadow the Last Supper, and the Raising of Lazarus to announce the resurrection of the flesh; the Washing of the Feet was understood—in certain quarters at least—as a substitute for the Apostles' Baptism;[1] the Three Angels Entertained by Abraham could be interpreted as both a prefiguration of the Last Supper and a symbol of the Trinity, the manger in the Nativity as both a prefiguration of the grave in the Entombment and a symbol of the altar in the celebration of Mass. As we have just seen, the sarcophagus of Junius Bassus exhibits three "historical" scenes from the Old Testament and three from the New, all enacted by symbols (viz., the lambs), which in addition carry a prefigurative significance. And in the magnificent sarcophagus in S. Ambrogio in Milan (figs. 158–60), postdating that of Junius Bassus by about thirty years, a colossal doctrinal superstructure—a kind of visual summary of the teachings of St. Ambrose, beautifully analyzed by Katzenellenbogen—was imposed upon a program which in itself comprises, in addition to historical, prefigurative, and symbolical scenes, a very sophisticated version of the *traditio legis* (both Christ and the Apostles represented in human form as well as in the now familiar guise of lambs) and a no less sophisticated version of Christ the Teacher (Christ represented *in cathedra*, with the Lamb that "stood on the Mount Sion" at His feet).[2]

In spite of all these elaborations, however, the dominating principle of Early Christian funerary art remained, as has been said before, the preoccupation with deliverance from death and sin; and even the highly complex iconography of the sarcophagus of Junius Bassus includes a number of themes—notably the Fall of Man, Daniel in the Lions' Den, the Afflictions of Job, the Sacrifice of Isaac, and all the lamb-enacted scenes in the spandrels—which can be traced back to the very beginning of Christian art and which continued to be invested, quite apart from their intelligible significance (whether historical, prefigurative, or symbolical), with what may be called a charismatic or "salvational," not to say magical, power—a power which in the liturgy of the Church (and, on a level comparable to that of the Early Christians, in Negro spirituals) asserts itself up to our day. The beautiful "Didn't My Lord Deliver Daniel?"— citing, along with Daniel, "Jonah delivered from the belly of the whale," and "the Hebrew children delivered from the fiery furnace"—still selects its examples from those invoked in the *Oratio Severi*, the *commendatio animae*, and the prayers *in extremis*. And it is of these and other Old Testament prototypes of deliverance from evil—augmented by such congeneric scenes from the New Testament as the miracles of Christ and by such manifestations and promises of salvation as the Orant, the Good Shepherd, Christ teaching, the Adoration of the Magi, and the Baptism—that the repertory not only of catacomb paintings but also of sarcophagi was originally composed.

What is perhaps the oldest Early Christian sarcophagus in existence (fig. 161) shows only an Orant— here probably to be interpreted as a personification—and the Good Shepherd in Paradise, the latter indicated by trees, between the portraits of the departed. On another sarcophagus (fig. 162), which has the distinction of having furnished the subject of the first article ever published by Charles Rufus Morey, we see Jonah "vomited out of the fish" (always as popular a theme as Daniel in the Lions' Den); a group resembling the familiar Poet-and-Muse combination except for the fact that the poet has become a Chris-

---

[1] E. H. Kantorowicz, "The Baptism of the Apostles," *Dumbarton Oaks Papers*, IX–X, 1956, pp. 203 ff.

[2] The scene on one of the pediments (the infant Jesus between the ox and the ass) would seem to be based on Habakkuk 3:2 according to the Itala version, which reads: "Domine, opus tuum ... in medio *animalium* [instead of *annorum*] notum facies."

tian absorbed in a pious text and that the Muse has been transformed into an Orant; the Good Shepherd; and the Baptism of Christ. And a third specimen, from Le Mas d'Aire (fig. 163), neatly epitomizes what may be called an "invocational" program. On the lid (its corners formed by huge heads of Winds, here substituted for the traditional masks and, later on, to be replaced by heads of Christ or *akroteria* displaying His monogram) are seen, reading from left to right, the Sacrifice of Isaac, the Healing of the Paralytic, Jonah Disgorged by the Whale, and Tobit with the Fish; and on the sarcophagus itself, the Raising of Lazarus, Daniel in the Lions' Den, the Fall of Man, the Baptism, and in the center the Good Shepherd between the portraits of the dead persons (husband, wife, and son) who have drawn close to Him like sheep craving protection. A special group of sarcophagi (fig. 164) shows, in fact, nothing but sheep, shepherds, and trees—representations which in pre-Christian art would be described as pastoral genre scenes; we may recall on this occasion that the very word *pastor* means "shepherd," so that we use the word "pastoral" as a synonym for "bucolic" and yet speak of "pastoral dignity."

It was apparently fairly late in the development of the Early Christian sarcophagus that Christ appeared as the victim of the Passion rather than the divine Infant, the Teacher, or the Thaumaturge; but even then the narrative stops short of actual martyrdom and is limited to scenes which represent, as it were, a triumph in disguise: the Crowning with Thorns (where the instrument of torture resembles and suggests the symbol of victory) or Christ before Pilate—an event often depicted opposite the Washing of the Feet so that the administration of a sacrament in the guise of self-humiliation[1] is balanced by an affirmation of kingship ("Art thou the King of the Jews? . . . Thou sayest it") in the guise of a humiliation inflicted by others. Even in cycles devoted exclusively to the Passion, the Flagellation, the Derision, the Bearing of the Cross (in a scene occasionally so interpreted the cross is in fact carried by poor little Simon of Cyrene rather than Christ; fig. 145), and the Crucifixion are absent. And where the cross appears on a sarcophagus at all, it is a symbol not of the Saviour's death but of His resurrection, triumphantly rising above the figures of the huddled guardians, or, even more eloquently, those of the Marys who have come to see the sepulcher and meet the Risen Christ.

As I said before, the funerary sculpture of early Christianity depends on pagan motifs not only for artistic syntax but also for artistic phraseology.

Many elements of this phraseology could be incorporated into the system of Christian eloquence without change in either form or significance: such personifications of natural phenomena as Coelus, the Seasons, or the Elements (particularly the Winds); the hunting scenes as symbols of the struggle between good and evil; the *imago clipeata* as an indication of immortality. Others were either reinterpreted, that is to say, invested with a new meaning while their external appearance remained unaltered, or remodeled, that is to say, subjected to a change not drastic enough to obscure their original aspect.[2] Bacchic motifs such as putti engaged in making wine (fig. 165) could be accepted as symbolizing the joys of paradise because the mysterious "transubstantiation" of wine into the blood of the redeeming god, like the complementary symbolism of the "fountain of living waters," had its place in the cult of Christ as well as in the cult of Dionysus; the formula πίε ξήσαις (drink and live) was used, and the rites connected with the interpretation of the hereafter as a *locus refrigerii* ("place of refreshment," often taken most literally) were performed by Christians and pagans alike.[3] Representations of Orpheus as well as shepherds and fishermen were reinterpreted, we recall, as images of Christ Himself. Victories could become angels without changing in appearance (God "sends not Victory, who is without substance, but His angel," says

[1] Kantorowicz, "The Baptism of the Apostles."
[2] For the Christianization of several mythological themes (reinterpretation of Endymion into Jonah, the Childhood of Bacchus into the Childhood of Christ, the Ascent of Helios into the Ascent of Elijah), see the recent, illuminating article by Marion Lawrence, "Three Pagan Themes in Christian Art," *De Artibus Opuscula*

XL; Essays in Honor of Erwin Panofsky, New York, 1961, pp. 323 ff.
[3] See Alfred Stuiber, *Refrigerium interim. Die Vorstellungen vom Zwischenzustand und die frühchristliche Grabeskunst (Theophaneia, XI)*, Bonn, 1957.

St. Augustine in *De civitate Dei*, IV, 17); and these "angels" continued to bear aloft a *clipeus* which, in turn, could be transformed into a laurel wreath and made to encircle the monogram of Christ rather than the portrait of the deceased (fig. 166). The group of poet and Muse could be transformed not only, as we have seen, into a group of reader and Orant but also into a group of teacher and pupil and—though in painting rather than sculpture—into an Evangelist inspired by a personification of "faith as wisdom" (πίστις σοφία). The Door of Hades could be reinterpreted as the Gates of Paradise.

In one form or another the soul of Christian content slipped, so to speak, into the skin of pagan form. And I shall conclude this brief and rather haphazard discussion of Early Christian sarcophagi with an exceptionally beautiful specimen of the two-register type which comes from San Paolo fuori le mura (fig. 167) and is now preserved in the Lateran. Here a Christian sculptor, probably active in the fourth century[1] and obviously familiar with a Prometheus sarcophagus (fig. 168) such as the one in the Louvre, has produced what seems to be the earliest known representation of the Trinity. The seated figure of Prometheus, who puts the finishing touches to a tiny human figure standing before him on a pedestal, is replaced by what I take to represent the Second Person of the Trinity: the enthroned figure of Christ Who, being the Word, blesses a proudly erect little Eve disengaged from the prostrate form of Adam; and as Prometheus is assisted by Helios and Minerva, prepared to instill animal life and an immortal soul into the body of the new creature, so is the Second Person in the Lateran sarcophagus assisted by the First, viz., God the Father, portrayed as an impassive older man standing behind the enthroned Christ, and the Third, viz., the Holy Spirit, portrayed as a man of Christ's age who stands before Him and gently touches the head of Eve. The sculptor thus proclaims the fundamental dogma (established for all time by St. Augustine but not explicitly spelled out in most artistic representations and therefore often forgotten by art historians) according to which the world and man were created not by "God the Father" but by the Trinity in Its entirety; but, in addition, he may have made a touching effort to find a visual expression for St. Augustine's famous parallel between the Three Persons of the Trinity and the three basic faculties of the human soul: the Father corresponds to memory, the Son to intelligence, and the Holy Spirit to love (*De Trinitate*, XV, 41 f.).

Compared with works like this, most Early Christian steles—largely confined, as has been mentioned, to the outlying provinces and particularly plentiful in Christianized Egypt, where they belong to the most frequent specimens of Coptic art—give an impression of rusticity and stagnation. Yet I should like to show three of the hundreds of specimens which came to light some twenty-five years ago in Terenouthis (now Kom Abou Billou) in Lower Egypt and are now divided between the Kelsey Museum of Archaeology at Ann Arbor, Michigan, and the Museum of Cairo: they are of interest not so much despite, as because of their archaic tendencies. Most (about 90 per cent) of these steles, datable between ca. 275 and ca. 350 A.D., retain the ancient Egyptian technique of the *relief en creux*, and in many of them the deceased is represented in what I have called the attitude of blissful repose (fig. 169): reclining on a couch, goblet in hand, and with plenty of flowers, food, and drink at his disposal, a man called Ptolas enjoys a banquet which, if we did not know that he was a Christian, would hardly suggest the Banquet in Paradise. In other instances, however, a theme as old and pagan as that of the banquet appears combined with the specifically Christian motif of the Orant: the theme of the ship. In one case an Orant named Apion is shown in the ship itself (fig. 170); in another the Orant, here feminine, is shown on the shore (fig. 171), hopefully waiting for a boat steered by a youthful figure which would seem to represent her predeceased husband rather than Christ in person.[2] Whichever interpretation may be correct, the ship is

[1] The dating varies between the Constantinian period and the end of the fourth century.

[2] The interpretation as Christ was proposed by C. Bonner, "The Ship of the Soul in a Group of Grave-Stelae from Terenuthis," *Proceedings of the American Philosophical Society*, LXXXV, 1942, p. 84; but the reposeful attitude with legs crossed, recurring in other steles from Terenouthis, would rather seem to indicate a deceased person.

no longer a means of postmortal transportation, as is the case in ancient Egyptian imagery, much less the real vessel which had carried the departed to their death, as is the case with Attic steles even in Roman times: it has become a symbol of salvation (fig. 172).

The Terenouthis steles thus represent, at the same time and in the same place, two opposite concepts of everlasting beatitude. Where the reclining figure admitted to the Banquet in Paradise typifies self-sufficient repose, the Orant carried off by, or waiting for, the ship of salvation typifies self-abandoning surrender to a transcendent power. And it is perhaps more than an accident that in another African cemetery, Aïn Zara near Tripoli (and we should not forget how important Africa was for the formation of Early Christian doctrine and expression), no fewer than twenty-six funerary inscriptions contain, several centuries before its official incorporation in the Mass of the Dead of the Gallican liturgy, that magic formula from Esdras[1] which, once heard, can never be forgotten: "Requiem aeternam dona eis, Domine, et lux perpetua luceat eis" ("Grant them, O Lord, eternal rest, and may the perpetual light shine upon them").

There is a significant contrast between the adjectives *aeternus* and *perpetuus*. *Aeternus* (from αἰών, timeless duration) excludes, while *perpetuus* (from *petere*, to strive, to travel) implies, the idea of movement. We speak of a *perpetuum mobile* but could not speak of an *aeternum mobile*. The Christian Requiem formula managed to reconcile the irreconcilable opposites of absolute rest and never-ending but ever-vibrating illumination. Mozart, I believe, sensed and expressed this antinomy in that miraculous passage where the word *perpetua* is twice echoed in such a manner that the intervals change from a minor second to a fourth, then back to a minor second, and then to a fifth—so that we receive an impression comparable to the strange experience of infinite reverberation that we have when looking in a mirror directly facing another.

In touching upon the Requiem we have stepped into the Middle Ages proper. And this is, all historical continuity notwithstanding, quite a considerable step to take.

To us it seems self-evident that the history of funerary sculpture can be studied in churches. We expect to find, and do find, the tombs of popes in St. Peter's, the tombs of bishops and archbishops in their cathedrals, the tombs of the kings of France in St.-Denis, the tombs of the great men of England in Westminster Abbey, and the tombs of local worthies, from dukes and country squires to mayors, doctors, lawyers, and businessmen, in their parish churches. Few of us stop to think how utterly impossible it would have been for the remains of even Pericles to be buried in the Parthenon or for those of Julius Caesar to be buried in the temple of Jupiter Capitolinus.

From the pagan point of view a dead body was an abomination abhorred by the very gods—in fact, abhorred by gods even more thoroughly than by mortals. Artemis has to bid farewell to her favorite, Hippolytus, when his death is approaching because "it is not right for me to see the dead / Or to be present when they breathe their last" (Euripides, *Hippolytus*, 1437 f.); Apollo has to leave the house of Admetus before the passing of Alcestis (Euripides, *Alcestis*, 22 f.); and when the whole island of Delos was dedicated to him, all the graves were emptied and the dead henceforth had to buried on the neightboring island of Rheneia. It was, therefore, a rule hardly ever violated in classical antiquity that the dead were not only kept out of the sanctuaries but even buried *extra muros*. In Rome only the *triumphales* ("those who had had the honor of a triumph") were entitled to be buried within the city walls, though not, of course, in sacred precincts; but if we can trust Eutropius *(Breviarium historiae Romanae, VIII, 5, 2)*, this happened so rarely that the deified Trajan, whose ashes were placed in a golden urn and laid to rest in the column named after him, was "the only man ever buried within the city" ("inter divos relatus est solusque omnium intra urbem sepultus est"). That founding "heroes," such as Theseus in Athens, Battus in Cyrene, Adrastus in Sicyon, could be buried in the market place and that their tombs—"invested with a dim and

---

[1] Cumont, *Lux perpetua*, pp. 458 ff.

dusky grandeur," as Nathaniel Hawthorne would say—could become sanctuaries in their own right is, of course, an entirely different matter; and so is the fact that a kind of cemetery chapel, dedicated to—and occasionally containing the cult image of—a deity connected with afterlife could be erected on the extra-mural burial grounds themselves. In the first case, the dead had become gods; in the second, the goddess of the dead extended, as it were, her protection to the resting place—considered sacred ground, ἱερὰ χώρα—of her subjects.

The rise and final acceptance of Christianity produced a revolution almost Copernican in scope. From very early times the Christian churches contained the tomb of a martyr in direct conjunction with the altar table, and there was an ever-increasing tendency among the faithful to be buried near this martyr, that is to say, if at all possible, within the church itself. The graves huddled, as it were, around the sacred relics so that their occupants might benefit by direct contact with what a French scholar calls *un protecteur ultraterrestre*:[1] "where the bones of martyrs are buried devils flee as from fire and unbearable torture," says St. John Chrysostom. As recent excavations have shown, this tendency asserted itself—apparently first in Rome, where tombs in great numbers have been found in the subsoil of St. Peter's, in SS. Pietro e Marcellino and in the old Basilica of San Lorenzo lately discovered by Richard Krautheimer—from as early as the end of the third century. The custom then spread all over the Christian world, and the little basilica of Thabraca in Tunisia, already mentioned, is literally crowded with graves arranged in almost hierarchical order, the tombs of children, who were apparently considered to be less important (and, perhaps, less in need of "ultraterrestrial" intercession) being placed at the greatest distance from the altar-tomb of the unknown martyr.

This development can be explained in various ways. In a temporal way, the churches themselves greatly benefited from the cult of martyrs and the admission of graves. In a spiritual way, the belief in the resurrection of the flesh—not entirely without precedent in pagan mystery religions and certain Jewish sects yet, by and large, so new that the Greeks found it more difficult to swallow than any other axiom of the Christian faith (Acts 17:32)—intensified the wish of the faithful to be as close as possible to the focus of salvation on the last day. And even more important was the fact that the Christian system of thought as such not only minimized the fear of death but also the fear of the dead.

The "dead which die in the Lord" were no longer considered "impure." Every one of them was an Anointed and, in a sense, a *triumphalis*; in fact, we find on many Early Christian tombs inscriptions such as "*N. N. triumpha.*" Their souls were received at the gates of the Heavenly Jerusalem as gloriously as were kings and emperors at the gates of a city on earth;[2] and their very bodies were taken, as it were, to the bosom of the Church.

Whether enclosed in a coffin or "lying in state," the departed spend, if possible, the interval between death and burial within the church. During the night before the interment the Office of the Dead is said, and the impression which these "Vigils" in the dark-enshrouded church made upon the medieval mind is attested by the fact that the beginning of the beautiful antiphone which, like a muted drum roll, opens the first Nocturn of Matins ("Dirige, domine Deus meus, in conspectu tuo vitam meam") survives in our word "dirge" up to this day. The Mass of the Dead also was, and often still is, said in the presence of the body, so that pictorial representations of this Mass are indistinguishable from those of the Vigils without an inscription (figs. 173, 174).

As time went on, problems of overcrowding and, possibly, hygiene made it necessary to restrict burial within the church to such an extent that it became a privilege of the few rather than a right of the many;

[1] P. Gauckler, "Mosaïques tombales d'une chapelle de martyrs à Thabraca," *Monuments Piot*, XIII, 1906; for the problem in general, see E. Dyggve, "The Origin of the Urban Churchyard," *Classica et Mediaevalia*, XIII, 1952, pp. 147ff.; R. Krautheimer, "Mensa-Coemeterium-Martyrium," *Cahiers Archéologiques*, XI,

1960, pp. 15ff.
[2] E. H. Kantorowicz, "The 'King's Advent' and the Enigmatic Panels in the Doors of Santa Sabina," *Art Bulletin*, XXVI, 1944, pp. 207ff.

but "ordinary" graves were placed, at least, in the immediate proximity of a church. Monks and nuns were laid to rest in the cloisters of their monasteries and convents, and laymen in "churchyards" (in German, *Kirchhof*), until in the eighteenth and nineteenth centuries not only burials within the church but even *intra muros* began to be prohibited, wherewith the development may be said to have come full circle.

This wholesale invasion of graves—which in such extreme cases as the basilica at Thabraca could transform an entire church, continuing to serve its regular purpose, into a huge collective burial chamber—produced a new, specifically medieval, type of funerary monument: the tomb *slab* as opposed to the tomb *stone* ("*dalle* tombale" as opposed to "*pierre* tombale," "*lastra* tombale" as opposed to "*pietra* tombale," "Grab*platte*" as opposed to "Grab*stein*"). Defining and, as it were, staking out the particular area beneath which a body was buried in the ground, flat slabs of stone—each not much larger than the coffin, of which they are, so to speak, a surface projection, and occasionally reflecting its trapezoidal shape—were set flush into the pavement so as to form an integral part thereof; and where the classical (and very practical) custom of covering floors with mosaics survived as vigorously as in North Africa, it was only natural that the decoration of these slabs should be executed in this very technique.[1]

This decoration varied from the half-realistic, half-imaginary rendering of an ecclesiastical structure such as we saw on the tomb slab of Valentia (fig. 137) to the almost hieroglyphic symbolism of crosses, vases flanked by animals, triumphal wreaths, and the like. But many of the specimens found in Thabraca, Sfax, and other North African centers show full-length portraits of the departed as Orants (fig. 175), their beatified status indicated by the familiar references to paradise: flowers, trees, and, most particularly, birds symmetrically placed on either side of the figure.

Conceivably there survived in these images a dim recollection of those "mummy portraits" from the Fayyum, painted on wood or canvas and mostly dating from the second and third centuries of our era, which were affixed to the mummy itself so as to give it a "face" and thus to transform it into a kind of effigy (fig. 176); and if this possibility—which I suggest with all imaginable reservations—were admitted, we should see one more reason why funerary portraits in mosaic (that is to say, in a technique akin to painting) apparently originated in, and long remained peculiar to, North Africa.

Less hypothetical and more important, however, is the connection which exists between these mosaic slabs and sculpture, steles as well as sarcophagi. And while many of them are even cruder than those Coptic steles, where the Orant motif was fairly ubiquitous, a relatively accomplished work such as the funerary portrait of a lady from Thabraca named Cresconia (fig. 177) may be described as a pictorial translation of the central figure on one of the strigilated sarcophagi just shown (fig. 141), and thus reminds us of the fact that, in spite of the difference in medium, the ancestry of the iconographical type exemplified by this portrait, including the bird motif, must be looked for in the metropolitan—and cosmopolitan—tradition.

On a stele or a sarcophagus, portrayals of this kind were "standing" figures not only in artistic conception but also in that they were placed vertically. The North African tomb slabs, however, were placed horizontally; and yet the men and women portrayed thereon continued to be conceived as "standing" figures, just as the church depicted on the slab of Valentia (fig. 137) continued to be conceived as a "standing" structure. Once more—and on the same Punic soil where it had happened for the first time—a potential conflict arose between artistic conception and physical placement. But it was not until many centuries had passed that this potential conflict, indiscernible as long as art was so little concerned with plastic verisimilitude as was that of the fifth and sixth centuries, became acute and demanded a solution.

---

[1] My remarks about African mosaic slabs were formulated before I received an interesting letter from Mrs. Margaret A. Alexander, who is preparing a study of the subject. I am glad to note that Mrs. Alexander's conclusions do not seem to be at variance with my own views, except that the possible connection with the "mummy portraits" was not mentioned in our correspondence.

In the medieval world—or, to be more precise, in the medieval West, for Byzantine civilization had no room for funerary sculpture at all—the general acceptance of interment (or, in privileged cases, what Evelyn Waugh would call "envaultment"), the almost universal decay of sculpture in stone and, possibly, the aversion to "graven images" diminished the importance, and ultimately caused the virtual disappearance, of the two principal forms of funerary sculpture thus far in use: the historiated sarcophagus and the stele. And in the Northern countries—where major sculpture was ultimately to recapture its place in medieval life—both these principal forms lost, quite literally, their *locus standi:* the historiated sarcophagus—as opposed to the silver-gilt, jeweled and enameled "shrine" which sheltered sacred relics rather than the body of a contemporary and, though probably deriving from the sarcophagus in structure and in turn occasionally reinfluencing the monuments of unsainted personages, does not concern us here—came to be obsolete because the bodies, entombed inside the church and normally buried deep in the ground or shut away in sealed vaults, were placed in comparatively simple receptacles which, even if fashioned of stone (like those quite recently discovered in St.-Denis), cannot be classified as sculpture; the stele came to be obsolete because the individual graves in cemeteries were marked, as if in protest against pagan custom, by nothing but modest crosses or tablets (headstones), with only the consecrated area as a whole placed under the protection of a huge cross or crucifix. It was not until after the end of the Middle Ages, particularly in the seventeenth and eighteenth centuries, when burial within the church had come to be a rare privilege, that funerary sculpture re-erupted into the open air.

After the collapse of the Roman Empire, historiated sarcophagi became so scarce that the remains of exceptionally prominent personages, including Christian saints, were occasionally laid to rest in pagan specimens: those of St. Lusorius in a hunting sarcophagus at Déols, those of Charlemagne in a Persephone sarcophagus at Aix-la-Chapelle. The sarcophagus of St. Agilbert at Jouarre (d. 672; fig. 178) is an exception which still awaits investigation, and later examples seem to be limited (apart from Italy and Spain, where sculptured sarcophagi (fig. 179) are found as late as the middle of the thirteenth century) to periods animated by a conscious desire to bring about a revival of classical antiquity—periods which I once proposed to call "medieval renascences" in contradistinction to the real Renaissance with a capital R.

The first of these renascence movements, the Carolingian *renovatio* of the ninth century, has been credited with the sarcophagus of Hincmar, archbishop of Reims (d 882)—a monument transmitted only through an engraving in Montfaucon's *Monuments de la monarchie française* (fig. 180), so that its period as well as the iconography of its relief (which, according to Montfaucon, represents the archbishop doing homage to the king but more probably shows him in prayer for the intercession of Christ) remains rather doubtful. The second renascence movement, the "proto-Renaissance" of the eleventh, twelfth, and thirteenth centuries, produced—in addition to the nonfigural porphyry sarcophagi of the Normanno-Sicilian dynasty, including Frederick II, in Palermo—such specimens as a sarcophagus believed to have been commissioned by Bishop Arnulf of Lisieux (d. 1181; fig. 181) and adorned with five medallions which, though in my opinion intended to represent a Biblical subject (viz., the Four Monarchies and the Ancient of Days according to Daniel 7:9), are for the most part inspired by Roman coins and cameos; the sarcophagus of the first Abbot of Airvauld, Petrus a Fonte Salubri (d. 1110; fig. 182), which looks as if a Roman or Early Christian columnar sarcophagus were seen in a mirror placed at an angle; or the "faux sarcophage" (not actually containing a body) from Javarzay, which goes so far in what I am inclined to call a revival rather than a survival of classical traditions as to exhibit a pagan hunting scene (though only on the lid).

In what may be called the nuclear territory of medieval Christianity, then, sculptured sarcophagi continued to occur throughout the Middle Ages, but only sporadically and intermittently. Steles adorned with figural representations, on the other hand, persisted fairly continuously for several centuries, but only in such marginal areas as the British Isles, the Netherlands, and Germany, and hardly ever after the Carolingian *renovatio* movement had done its work: they belong to a pre-Carolingian *imagerie populaire*—

pre-Carolingian in a stylistic though not always in a chronological sense—still dominated by Celtic and/or Germanic traditions.

The famous "Reiterstein" from Hornhausen in Saxony (fig. 183), for example, shows a horseman proudly proceeding above a "lacertine" (viz., an ornament composed of animals fantastically shaped and interlaced), which is here probably intended to represent the conquered monsters of the nether world; the monument translates the tombstone of a Roman horseman into a purely Germanic idiom and may, for all we know, commemorate a believer in Wotan as well as a Christian. But even where a stele of this kind unquestionably marked the grave of a Christian, its decoration reveals in form and content a strange interfusion of Early Christian, Roman, and Celtic or Germanic elements; the figures of Christ and the devil were seen through a Nordic mist which made them look like Baldur or Sigurd, on the one hand, and like the dragon Fafnir or the "Fenris-wolf," on the other.

Thus the fragment of a tombstone from the Isle of Man (fig. 184) exhibits on the obverse Christ armed with book and cross-staff, carrying the captured Leviathan and "trampling the dragon underfoot" (according to Psalm 91:13)—all Early Christian motifs except for the fact that the book, and not the cross-staff, is here employed as a weapon: insular Christian art always revealed an acute perception for the uniqueness of a religion built, as it were, on the foundation of a book and, in sharp contrast to Greco-Roman as well as Nordic paganism, conceiving of this book as the chief attribute of the Deity. On the reverse, however, the fragment shows Christ forcing open the jaws of a wolf while holding in readiness a staff which will be inserted into the wolf's mouth in order to keep it open forever after. The same procedure is also applied to the big dragons in the reliefs of the Cross of Gosforth in Cumberland (about forty miles across the sea from the Isle of Man); representations like these help us to understand why it was English art that first replaced the Gates of Hell by the mouth of a gigantic monster.

Similarly, the front of a remarkable stele from Niederdollendorf in the Rhineland (fig. 185) represents a fierce warrior—characterized, however, as a Christian by the presence of a pilgrim's flask—in valiant combat with a three-headed monster, whereas the back of the monument shows Christ Himself triumphant over death and hell. But here again the forces of evil are symbolized by a huge lacertine, and the Saviour is portrayed in a guise halfway between a Teutonic chieftain and a Roman emperor: His right hand carries a big spear, while His breast is adorned with a disk that seems to represent the sun but may have been suggested by the gorgoneion so often seen on a Roman ruler's breastplate.

A tombstone from nearby Gondorf (fig. 186), finally, looks so "Germanic" that it has been thought to represent Odin with his ravens. Yet the very fact that the man here portrayed clasps a book to his bosom suffices to prove that we are confronted not so much with the image of a Nordic god (the Nordic gods did not excel in scholarship) as with the portrait of a Christian protected from the evil spirits lurking in the spandrels by the magic ring of an *imago clipeata* and by the two paradisiacal birds familiar to us from Roman sarcophagi as well as from the mosaic slabs of North Africa (fig. 175).

In view of that law of affinity according to which any given style tends to react positively only to one with which it has, as it were, a common denominator, as well as for purely historical reasons, an artist as primitive as the author of the Gondorf stone is more likely to have been influenced by the flat schematism of the North African mosaics than by the still relatively plastic and naturalistic style of a Roman sarcophagus. And this brings us to what happened to funerary sculpture in Romanesque and Gothic art.

From what has been said it is evident that a new efflorescence of funerary sculpture could result only from an elaboration of the tomb slab as opposed to the tombstone (stele) and the sarcophagus. And in this process the influence of the mosaic slabs of Thabraca, Sfax, etc., seems to have played a more important part than one would be inclined to suppose.

In the semibarbaric Northern stone carvings thus far considered, this influence had led, as it were, into a blind alley. Portraits—if portraits they can be called—were restricted to vertical tombstones; the decoration of horizontal tomb slabs was, so far as we know, limited to abstract symbols such as crosses, vases between symmetrically "affronted" animals, etc.; and no attempt was made at the mosaic technique (figs. 187, 188).

At the same time, however, the North African predilection for full-length portraits executed in mosaic was transmitted to northwest Europe by what may be called the southern route, that is to say, via Spain—a process of transmission which has its parallel in many other spheres of cultural life, in scholarship and liturgy as well as in the arts, including architecture.[1]

Mosaic tomb slabs closely reminiscent of, and only slightly later than, those of Thabraca and Sfax—one of them showing the Good Shepherd surmounted by the familiar pair of doves, the other the portrait of one Optimus (fig. 189)—have been discovered, amidst sculptured sarcophagi, in an Early Christian necropolis at Tarragona, and it is, I believe, by intermediaries of this kind that we can account for a whole series of analogous monuments on the other side of the Pyrenees. The tomb slab of Queen Fredegund (d. 597) in St.-Germain-des-Prés has come down to us only in a later replica executed in a kind of inlay technique rather than genuine mosaic, and such twelfth-century plaques as that of Geoffroi Plantagenet (fig. 190) in the museum at Le Mans or that of Bishop Eulgerius (or Ulger) formerly seen in the Cathedral at Angers (transmitted through a trustworthy drawing in the Gaignières Collection)[2] belong in an entirely different class of monuments: much too small to serve as tomb slabs (the Plantagenet plaque measures only 63 cm by 33 cm, and that of Bishop Eulgerius was of similar size), they occupied the central position in the colonnaded front wall of shrinelike cenotaphs (that of Geoffroi Plantagenet is referred to as a "mausoleum" in a contemporary source). Plaques of this kind must be considered as memorial portraits rather than funerary effigies; in fact, Geoffroi Plantagenet is represented, like one of the donors (Sizzo) in the choir of Naumburg Cathedral, in the very act of administering justice, threatening the lawbreakers with his sword while protecting the Church with his shield:

ENSE TVO PRINCEPS PREDONVM TVRBA FVGATUR

ECCLE[S]IISQVE QVIES PACE VIGENTE DATVR

("The host of robbers flees, O Prince, thy sword; the churches, peace restored, are undisturbed.")

The "real thing," however, is represented by the mosaic slab of William, Count of Flanders (d. 1109; fig. 191), its surviving portion transferred from St.-Bertin in St.-Omer to the local museum; that of Gilbert, the first abbot of St. Maria Laach (d. 1152; fig. 192), his half-length portrait emerging from behind a tablet that bears a long encomium; that of St. Arnulf of Metz, formerly in St. Maria im Kapitol in Cologne (fig. 193), destroyed in the Rhenish campaign after the French Revolution but known to us from a drawing which seems to indicate that the original plaque was executed some five or six hundred years after the death of the saint in 640 but seems to have retained, perhaps from an earlier archetype, the then obsolete Orant gesture; that of Bishop Frumald of Arras (d. 1184; fig. 194);[3] and, as late as about 1300, that of the Dominican General Muñoz de Zamora (d. 1300; fig. 195) in S. Sabina in Rome.

[1] For scholarship, suffice it to mention the names of Isidore of Seville and Martin of Bracara; for the liturgy, see E. Bishop, *Liturgica historica*, Oxford, 1918, pp. 161 ff.; E. H. Kantorowicz, "Ivories and Liturgies," *Journal of the Warburg Institute*, V, 1942, pp. 79 ff.; and, most recently, L. Eizenhöfer, "Nochmals 'Spanish Symptoms,'" *Sacris Erudiri*, IV, 1952, pp. 27 ff.
[2] E. Rupin, *L'Oeuvre de Limoges*, Paris, 1890, pp. 92 ff., figs. 157, 159.
[3] According to Henri Stern, *Recueil général des mosaïques de la Gaule (Gallia, suppl. x)*, Paris, 1957, p. 96, the mosaic slab of Bishop Frumald was placed in the middle of the choir; whereas the tomb proper, unmarked, is separated from it by an interval of about ten feet. The reasons for this arrangement are a matter of surmise; but it may be that there was involved a feeling of formalized humility of which many other instances are recorded. Pepin the Short was buried, "face downward," at the entrance of St.-Denis; Emperor Maximilian wished (although this wish was ultimately not respected) to be buried in similar fashion at the entrance of the Church of Ingolstadt; and Sir Lewis Clifford forbade his tomb to be marked by "ne stone ne other thing" whereby anybody might know where his "stinking careyne" reposed (R. Gough, *Sepulchral Monuments in Great Britain*, London, 1786–96, I, p. lxi).

It is interesting to note that the earliest and the latest members of this series—the tomb of William of Flanders and that of the Dominican general—have one feature in common: in both cases the deceased is represented not, as in the intervening monuments, as the *totus homo* enjoying everlasting beatitude in the possession of his pastoral dignity (though no longer as an Orant) but as a dead body, its eyes closed in eternal slumber. As will be seen, this interpretation was, for many centuries, the rule in Italy and was not infrequent in Spain. In the North, however, it was and remained an exception[1] even as late as the fourteenth and fifteenth centuries. I have, therefore, no doubt that the nonconformist representation of William of Flanders as a "dead" person—accentuated by the fact that he is enveloped in a shroud rather than clad in courtly dress or armor as well as by the precocious appearance of a pillow which, as a rule, was not used until the following century—can be explained only by assuming that the Northern tradition of the isolated effigy, portraying the deceased erect and forever alive, was here deflected by the intrusion of a narrative representation dramatizing the contrast between the dead body, recumbent on its bier or in its grave, and that of the immortal soul, carried aloft by angels. And it is, I think, more than an accident that the earliest and most notable representation of this kind which has come down to us is dedicated to the memory of the very prelate in whose church and under whose reign William of Flanders was laid to rest: the "Death and Transfiguration" of Abbot Lambert of St.-Bertin (d. 1125) to which we shall shortly revert (fig. 240).

Mosaic tomb slabs—executed in a technique which, as we know from Suger of St.-Denis, struck the Northern taste as somewhat out-of-date as early as the middle of the twelfth century—were rare at all times outside North Africa and Spain and disappeared, even in Italy, after 1300. They were displaced, as happens so often in history, by the very thing which they had helped to bring into being: the *sculptured tomb slab*, which made its first appearance in the eleventh century and achieved a dominant status during the High Romanesque and Gothic periods.

That a demand for funerary portraits in three rather than two dimensions should have arisen about eight hundred years after the disappearance of the recumbent or reclining effigy in the round is understandable in view of the general resurgence of major sculpture, integrated with architecture, in the eleventh and twelfth centuries. But it is equally understandable that, in the absence of both a continuous tradition and appropriate models, this demand could be met only by borrowing from another medium. Setting aside so isolated a case, possible only in Provence, as the tomb slab of St. Isarn, abbot of St.-Victor (d. 1048; fig. 196), which can be derived from a Gallo-Roman sarcophagus (itself of a very unusual pattern), it was by translating such portraits as those on the Afro-Iberian mosaic slabs (supplemented, perhaps, by such portraits as were occasionally painted on the wall above a grave)[2] into the language of sculpture—a sculpture gradually adapting itself to a symbiosis with architecture—that funerary imagery could be revived within the framework of high medieval civilization.

The first step in this direction was taken in the bronze-cast tomb slab of Rudolf of Swabia (d. 1080) in Merseburg Cathedral (fig. 197). Rudolf was probably the first layman ever to be honored by a sculptured effigy in a medieval church, and not without reason. Elected and crowned as "anti-king" in 1077, he had been killed in a victorious battle against Henry IV, the archfoe of Pope Gregory VII; and it is precisely on this account that the cathedral nearest to the battlefield opened its doors to his remains and that everlasting bliss was promised to him in the inscription of his tomb: *Qua vicere sui, ruit hic sacra victima belli;/ Mors sibi vita fuit; Ecclesiae cecidit* ("Where his men won, he, war's pure victim, fell;/His death meant

---

[1] For some of these exceptional cases, see figs. 221, 224–226. Several others are illustrated in the Gaignières Collection, and one is preserved in Notre-Dame in Paris: the tomb slab of Bishop Guillaume de Chanac (d. 1348). Closed—or nearly closed—eyes were the rule, however, in the papal tombs at Avignon (see below, p. 57).

[2] See A. Fink, *Die figürliche Grabplastik in Sachsen von den Anfängen bis zur zweiten Hälfte des XIII. Jahrhunderts*, Diss., Berlin, 1915, with reference to the portrait of Gebhard, Bishop of Konstanz (d. 995).

life; he perished for the Church"). From a stylistic point of view, his portrait—executed in a relief so flat and delicate that the forms appear suggested by the interplay of fluctuating lights and shades rather than defined in terms of measurable volume—may be described as a Late Ottonian painting or book illumination converted (including the frame) into a life-sized bronze plaque; though technically a work of sculpture, this plaque strikes us as more "pictorial" than a miniature exhibiting a somewhat similar figure (that of St. Pantaleon; fig. 198) but executed some fifty years later.

The transition from the "pictorial" to the "statuesque" can be observed in the twelfth and thirteenth centuries, when the style of European art developed from Early to High Romanesque and from High Romanesque to Gothic. About 1130 the Saxon Duke Widukind, a favorite son of the Church (in fact, a *beatus*) because he had accepted the Christian faith after his defeat at the hands of Charlemagne, received a monument (fig. 199), executed in stucco applied to a slab of sandstone, in which the effigy has gained a substance and stability absent from the frail and floating figure of Rudolf of Swabia. The relief is much higher, and its mass is organized by means of almost stereographical surfaces and firm, incisive outlines; the feet are made to stand upon a kind of plinth which, later on, was to develop into an elaborate console; and the head is surmounted by a canopy as if the classical niche, reduced to an ornamental band in the mosaic slab of Optimus at Tarragona (fig. 189), had been transformed from a receding into a projecting form.

When the Romanesque style had reached maturity, Frederick of Wettin (d. 1152), bishop of Magdeburg, and one of his successors (probably Wichmann, d. 1192) were commemorated in bronze plaques (figs. 200, 201) the relief of which is so high that their portraits might be described as figures in the round were it not for the fact that they still retain a kind of consubstantiality with the flat background. And the High Gothic effigies of the thirteenth century would be indistinguishable from the architecture-integrated statues adorning the portals, piers, and buttresses of the contemporaneous cathedrals—statues whose style the "tomb-makers" deliberately strove to imitate—were it not for the more and more frequent addition of a pillow, which had made a precocious and, in this exceptional case, quite logical appearance in the mosaic slab of William of Flanders in St.-Bertin (fig. 191). In the tomb of Bishop Evrard de Fouilloi of Amiens (d. 1220; fig. 202) the portrait of the deceased prelate, shown within a rich architectural framework to whose iconographical significance we shall shortly revert, resembles, in spite of the pillow, the saints and prophets which adorn the façade of his cathedral; and some twenty or thirty years later, in conformity with the general development of High Gothic sculpture, the funerary effigy had reached such a degree of plastic independence and, as it were, detachability that it almost demands to be "read" vertically rather than horizontally and could even be fashioned from a material other than that of its support. The limestone image of Pope Clement II in Bamberg Cathedral (fig. 203), for example, executed ca. 1235–40 and now attached to a pier in the east choir, originally reposed upon a marble tomb. The image of Henry III (fig. 204), the last Count of Sayn (d. 1247), and his little daughter (which combination gave rise to the legend that the Count, a kindly giant, had inadvertently killed a child by a friendly tap on the head) is carved, together with its canopy, of a huge piece of oak.

In short, in the century and a half between the bronze plaque of Rudolf of Swabia and the effigies of Evrard de Fouilloi, Clement II, and Henry of Sayn, the funerary portrait had attained the dignity of a "statue," that is to say, an image in the round (or nearly in the round) able to "stand on its feet" and often so lifelike that an Austrian chronicler, Ottocar of Steier (d. about 1320) could make fun of a sculptor who, entrusted with the effigy of Emperor Rudolf during the latter's lifetime, allegedly attempted to keep it up to date by periodic check-ups, carefully adding the wrinkles developing on the Emperor's face as time went on.

Here, then, medieval funerary sculpture has reached a point at which its productions resemble—by way of what I have called a pseudomorphosis—those Punic sarcophagi where a figure in the round, or nearly in the round, conceived as maintaining a standing position, was placed horizontally upon the ridge of a "domatomorphic" sarcophagus—a conflict occasionally "mitigated," even then, by the addition of a pillow; but in the Punic specimens this "contradiction between artistic conception and physical placement" had resulted from the ex post facto combination of an image, three-dimensional from the very beginning, with a house-shaped sarcophagus; in the Middle Ages it resulted from the spontaneous expansion of a figure originally flat and flush with the pavement, and its subsequent elevation.

This progress from mosaic portrait to flat relief, from flat relief to high relief, and from high relief to "statue" created two problems, one, so to speak, technical, the other aesthetic.

To take up the technical problem first: as long as the tomb slabs were executed in mosaic or a comparable technique, even in a relief as flat as in the case of Rudolf of Swabia, there existed, so to speak, no traffic problem; you could walk over them (and that this was unhesitatingly done is all too evident in many cases) without stubbing your toe or breaking your neck. Once, however, the effigy had developed into a very high relief approaching the volume of a real statue, one of two measures proved necessary.

On the one hand, the trend of development could be reversed, that is to say, the three-dimensionalized effigy, while retaining its style and often even its architectural framework, could be reduced to relative or absolute two-dimensionality again, so that it appeared, if one may say so, in planimetrical projection. This in turn could be effected either by diminishing the height of the relief or, more radically, by projecting its design onto a perfectly flat surface. Such is the case with those "brasses" which came into fashion by the middle of the thirteenth century (particularly in the Netherlands, the Rhineland, and the British Isles) and thus do not anticipate, but evolve from, the "monumental effigies" of which they are, if one may say so, linear or graphic abstractions;[1] the same is true of the fairly ubiquitous niello plaques, stone slabs exhibiting incised contours which were filled in with a black paste. One of the best-known and most beautiful examples of this kind is the famous tomb slab of Hugues Libergier (d. 1263; fig. 205), the admirable architect of St.-Nicaise at Reims, which might be described as a diagram of such episcopal tombs as that of Evrard de Fouilloi (fig. 202) just mentioned.

On the other hand, the trend of development could be brought to its logical conclusion, that is to say, the three-dimensional effigy, while retaining its volume, could be raised above ground level. And this, again, could be done in one of two ways: by incorporating the image with either a *tumba* or a "table tomb."

The *tumba*—from τύμβος, the mound of earth "poured over" a grave—is a solid parallelepiped, originally fairly low but later developing to the height (though not assuming the practical function) of a full-fledged sarcophagus; its walls were either organized and ornamented after the fashion of columnar sarcophagi (which was the most usual practice) or displayed coats of arms; but only under very exceptional circumstances were they adorned with figures freely distributed over an undivided surface (figs. 253, 254). Occasionally protected and glorified by a canopy, this *tumba* could either be treated as a freestanding object placed in the center of a choir or chapel, which was the rule in Germany; or it could be attached to, or recessed into, a segment of the wall suitably decorated and normally enframed by a more or less elaborate archivolt. And such ensembles—resembling an altar plus retable and therefore often referred to as "altar tombs" by English writers, whereas the French call them *enfeus*—were very popular in all the other European countries, especially in France (where they apparently originated) and, even more so, in Italy.

Whatever its emplacement and accessories, the *tumba* was the most representative form of funerary monument in the Middle Ages—so much so that this late-classical term (first occurring in Prudentius) became the most widely used designation for any sepulchral monument in French, English, Italian, and

In this respect I beg to differ, e. g., from K. A. Esdaile, *English Church Monuments 1510 to 1840*, London, 1946, p. 5: "It [this early but unconscious experiment in the art of engraving] was in its inception an art of Flemish origin, but the best metal, as proved by the contract for the brasses at the Beauchamp chapel in St. Mary's, Warwick, was 'Cullen plate,' which means, in fact, the latten of Cologne. By the middle or end of the thirteenth century the portrait brasses were in the full vigour of their expression, anticipating, that is to say, the monumental effigies, which were a little later in reaching to perfection."

Spanish *(tombe,* "tomb," *tomba, tumba)*; when a German woodcut designer of 1502 was called upon to represent the tomb of Daphnis (fig. 206) in Virgil's *Fifth Eclogue*—the first "Tomb in Arcady," so to speak—he conceived of it as a genuine medieval *tumba,* inscribed "Daphnis ego in sylvis" but exhibiting, in lieu of the effigy, a huge cross on its upper surface.

In the "table tomb" the image of the deceased is placed, by definition, not upon a solid base but upon freestanding supports: lions (or other animals) or just a suitable number of feet. This form, announcing itself as early as the twelfth century, also remained in fashion throughout the Middle Ages (fig. 207). A late-thirteenth-century specimen, the tomb of St. Erminold (fig. 68), was mentioned in the preceding chapter, and an instance in which it was employed to accommodate two effigies, one on top of the other, may be adduced for curiosity's sake (fig. 208). In the course of the Gothic revival the table tomb even invaded, minus the effigy, the cemeteries of New England and other parts of the United States.

The aesthetic problem created by the resurgence of funerary sculpture in the High Middle Ages follows from the situation already encountered, under entirely different circumstances, in the Punic sarcophagi: from the fact that a figure conceived as standing, and increasingly growing in substantiality and lifelikeness, is placed in a horizontal position, its head more often than not supported by a pillow. In the case of the Punic sarcophagi the overt appearance of this contradiction had been the end of the story. In the case of medieval art it was the beginning. A period which—as will be seen—expected the funerary monument to establish the status of the departed as terrestrial members of the City of God, enthusiastically welcomed the possibility of representing them in such a way that their existence on earth appeared, to speak with St. Augustine, "inextricably intermingled" *(invicem permixta)* with their existence in heaven and tended to exploit this possibility to the limit. But with the increase of naturalistic tendencies the results of this procedure began to verge upon the paradoxical.

When the Bishops Frederick of Wettin and Wichmann (figs. 200, 201), eyes wide open, raise their hands in benediction, and when the former, in addition, transfixes a little replica of the *spinario* (fig. 209)—the pagan "idol par excellence" (fig. 210)—with the ferrule of his crozier, the conflict between the apparent aliveness of the effigies and their actual position may pass unnoticed, not only because no pillow is in evidence but also because the style of these High Romanesque monuments does not encourage the beholder to interpret them from a naturalistic point of view. In the High Gothic effigy of Pope Clement II (fig. 203), however, all the details are rendered with such verisimilitude, the expression of the face is so intense, and the gesture of the hand—completely disengaged from the body—is so vivid that it becomes difficult to conceive of so vigorously active a personage as recumbent; and, more specifically, to reconcile the arrangement of the drapery (the alb, the dalmatic, the chasuble, and the stole behaving as is possible only in a standing figure) with the presence of a pillow. In spite of this pillow the image of Clement II looks more "natural" in its present vertical position than it could ever have looked *in situ,* and it is interesting to note that it seems to have invited a curious and, so far as I know, unique experiment in the very workshop in which it was produced: a fellow sculptor, entrusted with the task of commemorating the long-deceased Bishop Gunther (d. 1066), converted—with suitable changes, among them, naturally, the omission of the pillow—the statue showing the Pope in front view into a flat relief showing the Bishop in full profile (fig. 211), thereby producing—again by way of "pseudomorphosis"—what would constitute a fairly close medieval approximation to a Greek stele of the fifth century B.C. were it not for the fact that the relief remained a tomb slab intended to be placed horizontally.[1]

---

[1] In a most interesting article, "Historismus in der Sepulkralplastik um 1600; Bemerkungen zu einigen Grabmalen des Bamberger Domes," *Anzeiger des Germanischen Nationalmuseums 1940 bis 1953,* pp. 61 ff., W. Lotz has convincingly shown that the two other Bamberg tomb slabs showing portraits in profile, those of Ekbert of Andechs and Berthold von Leiningen, are postmedie- val imitations of the tomb of Bishop Gunther. I doubt, however, that the latter is based upon an eleventh-century model because there does not seem to be any evidence of Early Romanesque funerary effigies in profile and because the form of the miter seems later than would be expected about 1065.

The contradictions confronting us in the effigy of Clement II and countless similar monuments are, however, negligible as compared to those with which we are faced in other cases. English and English-influenced tomb slabs and brasses, for example (fig. 212), show a married couple, both recumbent, in the process of taking the matrimonial oath, occasionally in such a manner that the head of the lady reposes on a pillow while that of her husband does not; and a climax of absurdity is reached in those curious monuments in which the archbishops of Mainz proclaimed their often-flouted right to crown the German kings. In the earliest of these (fig. 213), Archbishop Siegfried III of Eppstein (d. 1249), his head peacefully resting on a pillow, appears trampling the basilisk and the dragon according to Psalm 91:13, while simultaneously placing crowns on the heads of not one but two kings, Heinrich Raspe of Thuringia and William of Holland; and the same scheme was followed in the tombs of two of his successors, one of them possibly but not demonstrably identical with Gerhart II of Eppstein (d. 1305), the other known to be Peter of Aspelt or Aichspalt (d. 1320). While still ostensibly reposing on a cushion, the latter even crowns three kings (Louis of Bavaria, Henry of Luxembourg, and John of Bohemia) at the same time (fig. 214).

A conclusive solution of this antinomy—which in less blatant form was allowed to persist in North European art throughout the fifteenth and sixteenth centuries and at times even longer—was possible in three ways and in three ways only. First, the physical placement of the figure could be adapted to its artistic conception. Second, the artistic conception of the figure could be adapted to its physical placement. Third, the whole problem could be evaded by substituting for the tomb slab what may be referred to as an epitaph, that is to say, a memorial "Andachtsbild," not even necessarily connected with the actual tomb, which could represent a great variety of religious subjects and within which the funerary effigy normally plays the part of an ordinary donor's portrait.[1]

The first of these possibilities—that of abandoning the horizontal placement of the effigy in deference to its artistic character—was often realized ex post facto whenever a tomb slab, originally set into the pavement of a church, was subsequently lifted and raised to a vertical position in order to make room for a newcomer or in the course of architectural remodeling. From the fifteenth century on, however (though, so far as I know, only in the monuments of German prelates), the vertical position was not infrequently planned in advance: with the pillow omitted and the architectural framework developing into an elaborate structure which, like a church portal, could accommodate "jamb statues" of saints, the tomb slab was converted into a monument designed for a wall or pier from the outset and often growing to the impressive height of from twelve to sixteen feet. Suffice it to refer to the tombs of such archbishops of Mainz (it is perhaps more than an accident that the Gordian knot was cut where it had become, if one may say so, more Gordian than anywhere else) as John of Nassau (d. 1419; fig. 215), Konrad von Daun (d. 1434; fig. 216), or Adalbert of Saxony (d. 1484; fig. 217), and to the series of episcopal tombs in nearby Würzburg magnificently exemplified by Tilman Riemenschneider's famous monument of Rudolf von Scherenberg (d. 1495; fig. 218).

The second possibility—that of revising the artistic character of the effigy so as to harmonize it with its horizontal placement and thus transforming it into what the French call a *gisant*—required, in theory, three basic changes: first, the rearrangement of the drapery in such a way that it seems to be spread over an inert body instead of being worn by a living person (it will, for example, form a depression between the legs and tend to display a pattern of curves and diagonals which would not be possible if the figure were standing) and the representation of the attributes, if any, in such a manner that they seem to be held in place by sheer gravity rather than by a muscular effort on the part of the bearer; second, the omission of such obviously "supporting" motifs as consoles, the lion-and-dragon combination of Psalm 91:13 or other animals; third, the suppression of all active gesticulation and the closing or, at least, dimming of the eyes.

---

[1] See now A. Weckwerth, "Der Ursprung des Bildepitaphs," *Zeitschrift für Kunstgeschichte*, XX, 1957, pp. 147 ff. I am glad to see that the definition arrived at in this instructive article substantially agrees with mine.

In practice, however, it took a long time until all these requirements were consistently met; and in this respect, too, considerable importance attaches to the difference, already touched upon, between the Southern and the Northern tradition. As we remember from the mosaic plaque of Muñoz de Zamora (fig. 195) and will see confirmed by the examples to be considered in the following chapter, the Italian and—though less regularly—Spanish artists conceived of the recumbent image as a body immobilized and rendered insensible by death: the hands are invariably crossed before the breast or abdomen in a gesture of perfect repose, and the eyes are nearly always closed or dimmed. The "Gothick North," however, was reluctant to deprive the departed of their ability to face with open eyes that perpetual light which was to shine upon them and to deny them the use of their hands for prayer or other ceremonial gestures.

When—significantly, chiefly after the Black Death—Northern art attempted to represent the actual condition of "being dead," it solved the problem, not by replacing the effigy apparently endowed with everlasting life by that of a corpse, but by dramatically contrasting it with that of a corpse: the *representacion au vif*, viz., the image of the complete person (Erasmus' *totus homo*), arrayed as befits his state and dignity and unaffected by decay,[1] was contrasted with the *representacion de la mort* (normally referred to as *transi*), viz., the image of the dead body covered—if at all—only with a shroud and either reduced to a skeleton or exhibiting the horrid traces of decomposition.

In the *representacion au vif*—that is to say, the *gisant* as more or less standardized from the eleventh and twelfth centuries—the effort to make the recumbent position of the effigy visually explicit instead of merely symbolizing it was, as a rule, confined to an appropriate rearrangement of the drapery and, though less consistently, the attributes—apart from such exceptional monuments (exceptional even in a country famed for iconographical nonconformity) as those astonishing tombs of English thirteenth- and fourteenth-century knights who have been nicknamed "dying Gauls" because these valiant warriors are shown prostrate and *in extremis* yet, pillow or no pillow, attempt to draw their swords or even struggle with Death on a stony battlefield.

The series of these "dying Gauls" begins with an effigy preserved in the church at Dorchester in Oxfordshire (fig. 219)—an effigy which for stylistic reasons cannot postdate the second quarter of the thirteenth century. And it is here, so far as I know, that we find for the first time the specifically English custom[2] of representing knights—and only knights—with their legs crossed. The inference is that this position, though later transferred to effigies stiffly recumbent, was originally intended to distinguish a warrior dying in battle—and still alive—from a man who had breathed his last under less dramatic circumstances and is expecting the resurrection in the tranquil attitude of the ordinary *gisant*. There may then be, after all, some truth in the traditional assumption that the motif of the crossed legs initially designated a Crusader. Since this position resulted from an attempt to represent the act of dying rather than the state of death (thus introducing a parachronistically "retrospective" or commemorative element), it is permissible to consider it a special distinction bestowed upon those who had died for the faith and thereby achieved a sanctity comparable to that of the Holy Martyrs. Nothing militates against the assumption that the knight so honored in the Dorchester monument had met his death in the Fourth Crusade (1218–21) in which more English knights participated than in any other; and Sir Roger Kirdeston (fig. 220), of whom we know that he died in 1337, may easily have been killed in the first engagement of the Hundred Years' War, the invasion of Catzand, an island strategically important in that it blocked the mouth of the Oosterschelde and was situated almost directly across from Sir Roger's native Reepham.[3]

---

[1] Only very exceptionally do the two motifs merge in that a *transi* is shown with hands joined in prayer. The only example I can remember is the tomb of Geoffroi Suet, the last Abbot of Beaulieu near Le Mans (Cabinet des Estampes, Rés. Pe 1, Tome 7,2, fol. 216).

[2] For a few isolated Spanish examples, all produced in the same workshop and obviously evincing English influence, see H. s'Jacob, *Idealism and Realism: A Study of Sepulchral Symbolism*, Leiden, 1954, pp. 20f., 230.

[3] If, as has been proposed, the motif of the crossed legs merely

The earliest attempt at making recumbency "visually explicit" in the normal *gisant* appears, it would seem, in the series of Plantagenet tombs (four of six preserved) at Fontevrault Abbey (fig. 221), which begins with that of Henry II (d. 1189) and his wife, Eleanor of Aquitaine, and continues far into the thirteenth century. Here the effigies repose not on a flat slab of stone but on a draped *lit de parade*, and their garments are carefully arranged so as to conform to the idea of bodies lying in state. It is, in fact, easy to understand why such an innovation should have been made in France and at a period dominated by what Vöge has called the *Bahnbrecher des Naturstudiums*. And since a Plantagenet princess—Mathilda, a sister of Richard the Lion-Hearted—had become the second wife of Duke Henry the Lion of Saxony, the cousin and rival of Frederick Barbarossa, it seems to have been from Fontevrault that the new idea of "explicit recumbency" spread to Germany and was spectacularly employed in the powerful double tomb, datable about 1240, of Henry the Lion and his duchess in Brunswick Cathedral (fig. 222). This is all the more probable for two other reasons. First, the very idea of displaying the recumbent images of a married couple side by side on the same base seems to have been an innovation which first appeared at Fontevrault and cannot be presumed to have been invented twice; second, and more important, the statue of Mathilda of Saxony is, as far as is known, the earliest effigy to show the deceased with hands joined in prayer, the feminine piety of the duchess impressively contrasting with the masculine dignity of the duke. This contrast, as well as the new praying gesture itself, is also anticipated at Fontevrault, where Henry II of England holds his scepter with the same quiet authority as Henry the Lion does his sword, and where the hands of Eleanor of Aquitaine, while not as yet joined in prayer, are already brought close together in holding a small, open prayer book.

In the Brunswick tomb, however, novelty is contrasted rather than reconciled with tradition, and harmony is sacrificed to expressiveness. In comparison with the Fontevrault tombs, the arrangement of the garments leaves even less doubt of the fact that they are, as I phrased it, spread over, rather than worn by, the figures, and the model of the cathedral rebuilt by the duke is placed in such a way that it seems to repose on his breast rather than to be held in place by his arm; yet the *lit de parade* has been abandoned in favor of the more traditional block-shaped *tumba*; and, in spite of the horizontalized drapery (and, of course, the pillows), both effigies are supported by consoles.

More than two and a half centuries later the tomb of Bernhard von Breydenbach (d. 1497; fig. 223), dean of Mainz Cathedral and still remembered as the author of a famous, beautifully illustrated book, the *Peregrinationes in terram sanctam*, sharpens rather than eliminates these contradictions: the forms of the body delineate themselves beneath the clerical vestments as in a transparency; the hands of the deceased are crossed, and the symbol of his dignity, the chalice, lies flat on his chest; his eyes, however, are still wide open.

To represent a recumbent effigy not characterized as a *transi* with eyes closed and thus to erase, as it were, the borderline between the *representacion au vif* and the *representacion de la mort* was, as I have said,[1] fairly unusual even in late medieval Northern art and presupposes, as a rule, either an uncommon degree of self-willed originality on the part of the author or an uncommon art historical situation (as, for example, in the papal tombs at Avignon which, though mostly produced by indigenous artists, understandably conformed to the Italian custom).

---

expressed "status," it would be difficult to understand why it should not have been used much more widely than it was, apart from the fact that nonfunereal figures in which the crossing of the legs does reflect high rank (as in representations of princes), dignified equanimity (as in representations of judges, who were occasionally required by statute to assume this position), or quiet meditation (as in representations of poets), are always seated in medieval art. That, on the other hand, funerary sculpture extended the motif to knights who had perished in other, from their point of view, equally just wars, and ultimately transferred it to persons who may have died in their beds may be explained as one of those imitative or residual survivals in which the history of art and customs abounds, particularly in England. Even now extremely peaceful men wear, on certain occasions, a "dress sword" neither used for nor capable of inflicting lethal wounds.

[1] See above, p. 51.

An example of the first kind is the beautiful tomb of Bishop Wolfhart von Roth (d. 1302) in Augsburg Cathedral, the exceptional nature of which is documented by the very fact that both the sculptor and the bronze caster were permitted to immortalize their names in a (somewhat halting) leonine hexameter: "Otto me cera fecit Cunratque per era" ("Otto made me of wax and Conrad of bronze"). Here not only the fall of the drapery and the position of the attributes conform to the recumbent position of the effigy but the eyes of the fine ascetic face—apparently modeled with the aid of a death mask—are firmly closed (fig. 224); moreover, the face and neck are intentionally lengthened in such a manner that the prelate's countenance discloses its serene beauty only to a beholder standing at the foot of the tomb (fig. 225) and thus observing it in perspective foreshortening—a device anticipating the methods of such Quattrocento sculptors as "Simone Ghini," Donatello, and Pollaiuolo but apparently unique in Northern medieval art. The latter was, as a rule, so little concerned about perspective effects that the author of the impressive double tomb of Louis II of Bourbon (d. 1410) and Anne d'Auvergne (d. 1416) in Souvigny (fig. 226), while—*more solito*—treating the recumbent statues as though they were jamb figures and even placing them under the protection of semidecagonal canopies, had no hesitation to adorn the "upper" surface of these canopies with elaborate reliefs (a Crucifixion for the duke, a Coronation of the Virgin for the duchess) which, all but negating the existence of the effigies, are visible to the beholder only when he creeps up, as it were, on the tomb from behind.

As an example of the second kind, I should like to adduce—in addition to the papal tombs at Avignon just mentioned—such fifteenth-century monuments as the red marble tomb of Ulrich Kastenmayer (d. 1432), apothecary and mayor of Straubing in Lower Bavaria (fig. 227). Here the influence of Eyckian naturalism, combined perhaps with that of not too distant Italy, resulted in an image which may be described in the sibylline phrase "vivit et non vivit." The late mayor is represented at the moment of transition from life to death, his head resting on a pillow and drooping to one side, his eyes not entirely closed but dimmed by death. As a whole, however, the figure, arrayed in a fashionable surcoat and a huge clochelike hat, cannot conceal its derivation from a standing portrait in full length and gives the impression of a Giovanni Arnolfini *in extremis*.

There remains the third and most conclusive solution to the problem posed by the emergence of the sculptured tomb slab: the epitaph in which, we recall, the effigy is, as a rule, reduced to the role of an ordinary donor's portrait (fig. 228).[1] Varying in size as well as content, such epitaphs—making their appearance in the fourteenth century—may show a bust portrait reminiscent of Roman and Gallo-Roman steles except for the fact that the bust, in anticipation of the deceased's admission to heaven, emerges from a band of clouds; or they may even represent the dead man's own funeral rites, as in the epitaph of Jean Fiévez (d. 1425) in the Brussels Museum (fig. 229), which looks like the Vigils of the Dead from a contemporary manuscript translated into stone. More often than not, however, funerary monuments of this kind are hardly distinguishable from nonfunerary ones: an epitaph such as that of Jean du Bos (d. 1438) and Catherine Bernard in Tournai Cathedral (fig. 230) has rightly been compared with both Claus Sluter's portal of the Chartreuse de Champmol and Jan van Eyck's *Van der Paele Madonna* (fig. 232). Sponsored by patron saints or alone, the departed are represented kneeling before the Man of Sorrows, the Trinity, the crucified Christ or the Cross alone (fig. 233). They may witness a scene from the Passion (preferably the Crucifixion but also other events such as the Agony in the Garden) or the Last Judgment; but most frequently they are shown venerating the Madonna. This iconography, already known to us from the epitaph of Jean du Bos and Catherine Bernard, may be illustrated once more by an earlier and exceptionally charming specimen distinguished by the fact that its fine, almost Eyckian donors' portraits have escaped the iconoclastic mutilation which has defaced so many others: the monument of the Tournai goldsmith Jacques Isack (fig. 234), who died on October 24, 1401.

[1] E. Redslob, *Die fränkischen Epitaphien des 14. und 15. Jahrhunderts*, Nuremberg, 1907; Weckwerth, *op. cit.*

In the further course of the fifteenth century—first, as Vöge has shown, in Holland[1]—epitaphs of this kind assumed an even less funerary and almost intimate character by being reduced to compositions in half length. And it is this tradition which culminates in the charming monument (dated 1464) of a Strasbourg canon, Conrad von Busang, one of the most enchanting works of Nicolaus Gerhaert von Leyden (fig. 231). Here the only Northern peer of the great Quattrocento masters succeeded in translating, almost without loss, the language of Early Netherlandish painting into that of sculpture. Like them, he miraculously defied the distinction between heavenly and earthly things and transformed the vision of a distant beatitude into the experience of a world which mortals are permitted to share with the Deity.

The inscription on the scroll that issues from the praying hands of Nicolaus Gerhaert's canon, again a somewhat questionable leonine hexameter, reads as follows: "Ora prece pia pro nobis, virgo Maria," "Pray for us with pious invocation, O Virgin Mary." And this brings us to the iconographical as opposed to the formal problems with which the funerary sculpture of the Northern Middle Ages had to cope.

Its primary purpose, needless to say, was still, as in the Early Christian period, to insure salvation; and its point of view was and remained, therefore, "prospective." In fact, the simple standing portrait, as exemplified by the tomb slab of Rudolf of Swabia, originally anticipated, like the Orants on the African mosaics from which it is derived, the future status of the departed among the Blessed in Paradise. Medieval art, however, always inclined to be literal, attempted to express the idea of a posthumous ascent to heaven more concretely and thereby to place the deceased in the center of a more or less complex narrative.

In the famous sarcophagus of Doña Sancha (daughter of Ramiro I of Aragon) and her two sisters, executed around 1100, this is achieved by a characteristic combination of "Spanish realism" and Early Christian reminiscences. The back of the monument—one of its ends still exhibiting the familiar apotropaic griffins, the other the monogram of Christ—shows a battle of horsemen and Samson Rending the Lion (fig. 235); its front displays, between a group of three priests (a bishop and two deacons) about to celebrate the Mass of the Dead and the seated portraits of the three ladies, what may be called a medievalized *imago clipeata:* the soul of Doña Sancha, represented as a sturdy nude infant and enframed by a mandorla instead of a circular medallion, is carried aloft by two angels while eagles, perched in the spandrels, complete the apparatus of apotheosis (fig. 236).

Some thirty or thirty-five years later, however, in the tomb slab of St. Reinheldis (fig. 237) in the little church of Riesenbeck in Westphalia, the effigy itself appears incorporated into a scene reminiscent of such late antique "assumptions" as the so-called Apotheosis of Romulus in the British Museum (fig. 239). The slender figure of the legendary saint (supposedly killed for excessive piety by her mother at the instigation of her stepfather) is still represented frontally and in a general way retains the Early Christian Orant position; but by an ingenious shift in the position of her hands and face she is brought into gesticulative and emotional contact with an angel who, descending headlong from the heavens, receives her soul—portrayed in the guise of a second, smaller Orant, fully clothed—so as to convey it to the *sidereas sedes* of Christ.

In the tomb of Reinheldis, then, a dramatic assumption scene has been constructed, as it were, by combining two Orants, different only in size, the large one representing the deceased as a *tota mulier*, the other only her soul. But since the Orant figure carries, per se, an implication of ultraterrestrial beatitude, we are confronted with a kind of duplication.

This duplication could be avoided in one of two ways: either by representing the soul not in the act of ascent but as enjoying a secure existence in heaven; or by representing the soul in the act of ascent but

[1] Wilhelm Vöge, "Nicolaus von Leyens Strassburger Epitaph und die holländische Steinplastik," *Oberrheinische Kunst*, IV, 1929–30, pp. 35 ff.

contrasting its upward movement with the inertia of the dead body. The first of these possibilities is exemplified by the tomb slab of Sulpicius Cultor (fig. 238), canon and priest at St.-Martin in Plaimpied (Cher), where the soul of the good canon (still alive in 1136) is shown, quite literally, "in Abraham's bosom"; the second by a work, already mentioned, which, though a narrative miniature rather than a funerary monument, is of the greatest importance in our context: the "Death and Transfiguration" (fig. 240) of Lambert, fortieth abbot of St.-Bertin in St.-Omer (reigned from 1093 up to his death in 1125). Here the deceased, though appearing *in pontificalibus*, is quite dead, reposing on his bier, his hands inertly resting on his thighs and his eyes closed. The Orant figure representing his soul, however—as small as that seen on the Reinheldis tomb but as nude as the one on the sarcophagus of Doña Sancha—is intensely alive. Rushed to heaven by two angels, it ecstatically raises its arms and lifts its head; and Christ in Majesty, attended by Maria-Ecclesia carrying a model of the church completed under Lambert's administration, by one of the latter's predecessors (Martin), and by two Virtues (Patience and Charity toward the Poor, the latter inscribed *Elemosina*), is ready to receive it.

The iconography of this miniature not only accounts, we recall, for the unusual features that can be observed in the mosaic slab (fig. 191) of William of Flanders (executed during Lambert's reign!) but also contains—except for the absence of clerics performing the funeral rites, who, however, occur in an iconographically related miniature from St.-Sauveur d'Anchin executed ca. 1150–60[1]—all those elements which, transferred from the illuminated page to stone or bronze, were to constitute what may be called the "liturgical" type of funerary monument, perhaps the most important innovation of the High as opposed to the Early Middle Ages.

An early example of this "liturgical" type is the remarkable tomb slab of Bruno, priest and cellarer of Hildesheim Cathedral (d. 1194; fig. 241). The lower zone shows Bruno's effigy, here interpreted as an enshrouded corpse ready for burial, his head reverently supported by two tonsured priests: the artist has represented, in fact, a part of the funeral rites, known as the "Elevatio corporis," which is performed immediately before Matins, when the body is placed in the center of the choir, feet toward the altar if the deceased has been a layman, head toward the altar if he has been a cleric. In the second zone Bruno's soul, portrayed in the guise of a small nude Orant, is carried heavenward by two angels; and in the third there appears the figure of Christ in half length, His right hand raised in blessing and His left extending a book inscribed "Venite benedicti patris mei." The whole is surrounded by an inscription reading: "Brunoni cuius speciem monstrat lapis iste/Qui sua pauperibus tribuit, da gaudia, Christe" ("To Bruno, whose likeness this stone displays and who gave what he had to the poor, grant everlasting joy, O Lord"); and this claim to the virtue of charity in the sense of *elemosina*—particularly stressed in the Office of the Dead by the inclusion of Psalm 41:1 ("Beatus qui intelligit super egenum et pauperem," "Blessed is he that considereth the poor") and represented in person, we recall, in the "Death and Transfiguration" of Lambert of St.-Bertin—is visually supported by the presence of four beggars and cripples, placed at the feet of the body, who seem to mourn the death of their benefactor.

The five components of this iconographical scheme, viz., the effigy of the deceased, the elevation of his soul, the image of Christ, the priests performing the funeral rites, and the secular mourners (the latter also appearing, though not as paupers, in such French tombs as that of Bernard de Mèze in St.-Guilhem-le-Désert [fig. 242] and that of St. Hilary in St.-Hilaire-de-Poitiers [fig. 243]) entered into the program of what may be called the *tombeaux de grande cérémonie* which were apparently developed in France from

---

[1] The frontispiece of a *De Trinitate* by St. Augustine, formerly Douai, Bibliothèque Municipale, MS. 257, destroyed in the war but illustrated in Michel, *Histoire de l'art*, II, 1, p. 306, fig. 233. The manuscript was written and illuminated by two scribes named Baldwin and John. Since Baldwin died before the manuscript was completed, he is shown on his bier and attended by monks while an enormous angel carries his soul to heaven; above this elevation scene the surviving John, flanked by the patron saints of the Abbey, Gotwin and Augustine, is shown kneeling and receiving a crown, while the figure of Christ, here represented in half length, appears on top. For the mosaic slab of William of Flanders, see above, p. 51.

the end of the twelfth century. These may be divided, very roughly, into two classes different in form as well as content: the freestanding *tumba* (or table tomb), occasionally surmounted by a canopy; and the tomb attached to—or, even more often, recessed into—the wall, a form which I shall designate by the French term *enfeu* in preference to the not always accurate English term "altar tomb."

As typical examples of the complete *enfeu* there may be adduced the tomb of Abbot Arnoult(?), formerly in St.-Père at Chartres (ca. 1220–25; fig. 244), or that of Bishop Simon de Bucy (d. 1304) in Notre-Dame at Paris (their composition unfortunately transmitted only through seventeenth-century drawings).[1]

These monuments contain all the elements seen in the tomb of Bruno except that the dead body is replaced by the traditional effigy *au vif* (its support frequently inclined toward the beholder so as to improve visibility from below)[2] and that the secular mourners are often omitted. Two features, on the other hand, tend to be added. First, the officiating priests are joined by angels manipulating candles, censers, and incense boats: we witness, in addition to the funeral service performed on earth, a Mass of the Dead performed in heaven as if to celebrate, in anticipation, the *adventus animae*.[3] Second, an image of the Madonna enthroned is placed above the effigy of the deceased. The worship of Our Lady had grown to such a fervor during the twelfth century (the century which invented the Coronation of the Virgin) that it seemed fitting to invoke the intercession of *Maria mediatrix*.

Of what would have been, perhaps, the most beautiful *enfeu* ever produced by Early Gothic sculpture in France, presumably intended to commemorate one of two archbishops of Reims (either William I of Champagne, who reigned from 1176 up to his death in 1202, or his successor Guido Paré, who died as early as 1206) nothing remains but the Madonna and the figures originally surrounding it (fig. 245): the censing and soul-carrying angels in the archivolts, and the officiating priests—one of them, characteristically, exhibiting sorrow rather than attending to his functions—in the embrasures. Appropriated by the energetic Aubry de Humbert (who was suspected of having set fire to his own cathedral in order to be able to begin a new one on May 6, 1211), these *disiecta membra* now decorate the right-hand portal of the northern transept, the so-called Porte Romane.[4]

In a freestanding *tumba* (not to mention a table tomb), where neither wall space nor archivolts were available, the images of Christ, the Madonna, and the soul-carrying angels had to be eliminated. What could be retained, however, was the officiating clerics and, most important, the angels equipped with the implements of Holy Mass. Both features appear in conjunction in the now familiar tomb of Evrard de Fouilloi, bishop of Amiens (fig. 202); and censing angels alone occur, down to the fifteenth century, in countless tombs of ecclesiastical dignitaries in England and Germany (fig. 216) as well as in France, even on the comparatively modest plaque of Hugues Libergier, the architect of St.-Nicaise in Reims (fig. 205). And what could and did attain even greater prominence than in the normal *enfeu* was, in addition

---

[1] Cabinet des Estampes, Rés. Pe 9, unfoliated page inserted between fol. 22 and fol. 23.

[2] This inclination of the effigy can best be observed if the *gisant* is preserved out of context, as is the case with that of a king (ca. 1300) preserved in the depot of St.-Denis. In the Museum at Lyons there is even a niello slab the cross section of which is not a square but a trapezoid so that the incised surface is similarly inclined. It may be conjectured that it was originally placed on supports and accessible only from one side so that the design faced the beholder like a book or drawing placed on a writing desk.

[3] The censing angels also occur in the much cruder but nearly contemporary tomb slab of Bishop del Soler at Elne. This monument (illustrated, e. g., in A. Kingsley Porter, *The Romanesque Sculpture of the Pilgrimage Roads*, Cambridge [Mass.], 1923, fig. 623) represents a specifically Iberian mixture of motifs. The censing angels have been merged with the angels bearing the soul aloft in a cloth; while the deceased is represented as a dead body with arms crossed and while his reclining position is emphasized, as in the

Plantagenet tombs at Fontevrault, by the arrangement of the drapery, his eyes are wide open; and above his head there appears, as in other Spanish examples, the very archaic motif of the Hand of God.

[4] As to the date of its execution, I—as an "elder statesman"—am still in favor of the first decade of the thirteenth century; whereas the younger generation prefers a considerably earlier date. For arguments in favor of this revision, see W. Sauerländer, "Beiträge zur Geschichte der 'frühgotischen' Skulptur," *Zeitschrift für Kunstgeschichte*, XIX, 1956, pp. 1 ff., who dates the monument ca. 1180 and thus attributes it to the reign of William of Champagne—without, however, stating his opinion as to whether the latter belatedly ordered (or permitted) its execution in honor of his predecessor, Henri de France (1162–75), or cautiously commissioned it, more than twenty years ahead of time, for himself. The possibility that so sumptuous a tomb should have been devoted to the memory of a person other than an archbishop can safely be excluded.

to the heraldic and sacramental elements, the figures of mourners *(pleureurs, plorants)*. Placed on the walls of the *tumba*, they grew, as time went on, not only in physical volume (as was only natural in view of the general evolution of Gothic sculpture) but also in significance and, if one may say so, in social status.

In the thirteenth and fourteenth centuries the nondescript grief-stricken characters (on the tomb slab of Bruno, even beggars), rendered in comparatively flat relief, developed into such dignified, semidetached figures as can be seen on the tomb of Louis de France (d. 1260) in St.-Denis (fig. 246) or on the well-known tombs of the Landgraves of Hesse in the church of St. Elizabeth in Marburg (fig. 247); and here we have, for the third time, a case of pseudomorphosis. *Tumbae* of this description inevitably bring to mind the "Sarcophagus of the Mourning Women" from Sidon (fig. 61); but while the classical monument came about by filling the interstices of a columnar structure with mourners, the medieval ones resulted from making room for mourners in the body of a massive block.

At the end of the fourteenth century these semidetached figurines developed into independent statu-ettes—removable and often actually removed in the course of the centuries—in the world-renowned tombs of the Burgundian dynasty in the Chartreuse de Champmol (figs. 248, 249), designed and partly executed by Claus Sluter; and in the second half of the fifteenth century these independent statuettes, now often cast in bronze rather than carved in stone, abandoned their grief-stricken attitudes as well as their anonymity. In the nearly identical tombs of Louis de Mâle in Lille, Joan of Brabant in Brussels, and Isabella of Bourbon in Antwerp (fig. 250), modeled by Jean Delemer and cast by Jacques de Gérines, the assembly of mourners turned into a collection of family portraits, ten of which have been preserved. The whole development ended, within the framework of an altogether different style, in the spectacular if not very tasteful tomb of Maximilian I in the Hofkirche at Innsbruck (fig. 251), where the statues of the Emperor's ancestors and relatives, now grown to "overpowering life size" *(gewaltige Lebensgröße)*, surround the *tumba* of the Emperor in such a manner that Heinrich Heine, characteristically mistaking the time-darkened bronze for cast iron, could compare them to "black wax figures in a booth at a fair."

From the monuments thus far discussed it is evident that the funerary sculpture of the Northern Middle Ages, while still essentially "prospective" or anticipatory in purpose, differed from that of the Early Christian Era in that terrestrial values were no longer ignored. Quite apart from such laudatory inscriptions as those on the bronze plaque of Rudolf of Swabia—or, for that matter, on the mosaic slab of Abbot Gilbert of St. Maria Laach, who is called "praeclarus genere, praeclarior meritis"—we have seen several purely visual references to the deceased's position and accomplishments in life: the little pagan *spinario* transfixed by the crozier of Bishop Frederick von Wettin of Magdeburg; the beggars testifying to the charity of Bruno of Hildesheim; the German kings crowned by the archbishops of Mainz; the model of Bruns-wick Cathedral rebuilt by Henry the Lion. Scholars could be shown teaching (though this apparently Italian motif[1] does not seem to occur in Northern funerary art until the fourteenth century and seems to have been limited to niello plaques which hold, as it were, an intermediary position between sculpture and painting or book illumination). And in one memorable monument, that of Hugues Libergier just mentioned (fig. 205), the honor of carrying a church model, normally reserved to princely or ecclesiastical donors, was even granted to a great architect. An archbishop of Cologne, Philip von Heinsberg (d. 1191), who had provided his metropolis with fortifications, was posthumously honored by a tomb (fig. 252) erected after the rebuilding of the Cathedral in the fourteenth century, which shows his effigy enframed by turrets and crenelations. And in the case of a very few saints or near saints, who, to quote Thiofrid of Echternach, had "entered their graves in an abundance of virtues" ("qui in abundantia virtutum ingrediuntur sepulchrum"), we even find these virtues represented on their monuments—or, rather, shrines: on the almost identical sarcophagi of St. Giles in St.-Gilles and of St. Junian in St.-Junien and on that most intriguing marble tomb of Pope Clement II (figs. 253, 254) in Bamberg Cathedral

[1]   See below, p. 70f.

(executed toward 1240), where the elements of a much earlier composition, perhaps not unlike the miniatures from St.-Bertin and St.-Sauveur d'Anchin, appear to have been flung, as it were, onto the walls of a *tumba* without regard for either symmetry or decorum.[1]

Most of these references to the qualities and achievements of the departed are, however, of a "gentilitial" and, above all, institutional rather than personal character. The status of the family was, in a sense, deemed more important than the accomplishments of its individual members (hence the great emphasis on heraldry, which from the fifteenth century on occasionally displaced, and replaced, the portrait altogether; fig. 255);[2] the office was deemed more important than its incumbent; and the latter's merits were extolled not so much in order to glorify his life on earth as in order to insure his admission to heaven. It was for the good of their office that the archbishops of Mainz insisted on their right to crown the German kings. It was possible for Hugues Libergier to be represented with the model of St.-Nicaise and for Henry the Lion to be accompanied by that of Brunswick Cathedral; it would not have been possible to add to Hugues' effigy a personification of architecture lamenting over his death or to show Henry the Lion in battle. If I may be permitted a self-quotation, I should like to repeat what I once said of Abbot Suger's tendency toward self-glorification: "Yet there is a fundamental difference between the Renaissance man's thirst for fame and Suger's colossal but, in a sense, profoundly humble vanity. The great man of the Renaissance asserted his personality centripetally, so to speak: he swallowed up the world that surrounded him until his whole environment had been absorbed by his own self. Suger asserted his personality centrifugally: he projected his ego into the world that surrounded him until his whole self had been absorbed by his environment."

Perhaps it is also by this feeling for the collective, as opposed to the individual, relevance of the life lived on earth, and not only by the general preoccupation with the macabre that can be observed all over Europe after the Black Death, that we can explain the strange and fascinating phenomenon to which I have repeatedly alluded in employing the terms—documented in a contract of 1526—*representacion au vif* and *representacion de la mort:* the placing of a "lifelike" effigy, arrayed in a costume befitting the dignity

---

[1] After the excellent study by A. von Reitzenstein, "Das Clemensgrab im Dom zu Bamberg," *Münchner Jahrbuch der bildenden Kunst*, new ser. VI, 1929, pp. 216 ff. (see also a recent pamphlet by J. J. Morper, *Der Sinngehalt des Bamberger Papstgrabes*, Bamberg, 1956), scholars seem to agree that the tomb of Pope Clement II, originally surmounted by a canopy adorned with censing angels, is not a postmedieval imitation but an authentic product of the same local workshop that was responsible for the Portal of the Last Judgment. It would seem to reflect, however, a prototype presumably dating back to the time when the remains of Clement II, originally Bishop Suidgar of Bamberg, were secretly transferred to his home town after his death in 1047, and I incline to believe that this prototype was not so much a tomb as a memorial tablet iconographically similar to the two miniatures referred to in the text and possibly resembling, from a technical point of view, the triptych reliquary in the church of Ste.-Croix at Liége (H. Swarzenski, *Monuments of Romanesque Art*, London, 1954, pl. 170, fig. 375). On such a memorial tablet the river-god (probably framed by a semicircle as in the silver niello from the head reliquary of St. Oswald illustrated in Swarzenski, *ibid.*, pl. 209, fig. 485) would have been placed at the bottom; the deathbed scene in the center; the four Virtues on the sides; and the figure of Christ (probably in half length) on top (His present rather undignified posture can best be accounted for by the sculptor's attempt to convert a bust portrait into a complete figure which would, nevertheless, fit into an oblong space). The iconographical program has been traced back to St. Ambrose's *Liber de paradiso*, III

(*Patrologia latina*, XIV, cols. 296 ff.), where the four rivers of Paradise are likened to the four cardinal virtues which issue from a common source; but since St. Ambrose correctly refers to this source as *fons*, and not as *fluvius* or *flumen*, the appearance of only one river-god may be connected with the fact that the funeral office includes, at Lauds, Psalm 64, the tenth versicle of which reads: "*Flumen* dei repletum est aquis." That Pope Clement II should have been honored by the presence of Virtues and thus have been treated as a peer of Sts. Giles and Junian (for their shrines, see R. Hamann, *Die Abteikirche von St.-Gilles und ihre künstlerische Nachfolge*, Berlin, 1955, pp. 300 ff., figs. 381–85) has been convincingly explained by the fact that local tradition did consider the excellent but short-lived Clement II, the only pope buried in German soil, as one of the saints although at the time of his death and "translation" the procedure of canonization was not as yet formalized. The phrase "in abundantia virtutum ingrediuntur sepulchrum" is a quotation from Thiofrid of Echternach's interesting *Flores epitaphii sanctorum*, II, 1 (*Patrologia latina*, CLVII, col. 339, kindly brought to my attention by Professor Adolf Katzenellenbogen), where the all-important word *virtutum* is boldly inserted into Job 5:26.

[2] An ecclesiastical parallel to such purely heraldic monuments are the tombs of abbots and abbesses, particularly in France, which show noting but an habbatial crozier either quite isolated or clasped by a schematized hand; in the Gaignières Collection this type is represented, for example, by the drawings (copies), Cabinet des Estampes, Rés. Pe 1, Tome 5, fols. 9, 53.

of a prince or princess, a prelate or at least a knight, on top of a "deathly" figure showing the deceased as a mere corpse, wrapped only in a shroud which may conceal his form almost entirely, as in the effigy of Jacques Germain (d. 1424), formerly in the Carmelite Church at Dijon (fig. 256), or, conversely, may reveal as much of his nude form as was compatible with modesty, but nearly always divested of all signs of worldly power and wealth and often represented in a state of more or less advanced decomposition.

The moral significance of these grisly *transis*—often expressed by such inscriptions as "I was what you are; you will be what I am" or "Wretch, why are you proud? You are nothing but ashes and will, like me, be the food of worms"—is, of course, that of a *memento mori*[1] (a notion eloquently expressed by the term *"representacion de la mort"*), and some of them occur singly rather than in contrastive juxtaposition with a *representacion au vif*. Apart from the tombstone of Jacques Germain just mentioned, this is also true of one of the earliest recorded instances, the monument of a nobleman named Francis de La Sarra (d. 1362) which can still be seen in the church of La Sarraz some ten miles north of Lausanne (figs. 257, 258).[2] Watched over by members of his family in full dress, he is represented as he was supposed to look after several years in the grave: long worms slither in and out of the body, and the face is covered by toads in such a manner that two of their heads replace the eyes in a macabre anticipation of the effects achieved, more than two hundred years later, by Giuseppe Arcimboldo when he constructed human heads out of sea creatures or vegetables.

As a late-fifteenth-century instance of an isolated *transi* we may adduce another mayor of Straubing in Lower Bavaria, Johannes Gmainer (d. 1482; fig. 259), whose red marble tomb shows him as an almost skeletonized cadaver, as violently attacked by vermin as is the body of Francis of La Sarra and addressing the beholder as follows: "Sum speculum vitae, Johannes Gmainer, et rite / Tales vos eritis, fueram quandoque quod estis" ("In me behold the looking glass of life: / Such you will be, for I was what you are"). Yet—such is human nature—the mayor's armorial bearings are proudly displayed at the skeleton's feet; and a gentleman named Felix Ueblher, whose image *en transi*, dated 1509, can be admired in St. Nicholas at Merano (fig. 260), was even careful to inform posterity that he had been ennobled and allowed a coat of arms by Emperor Frederick III.

More often than not, however, and quite particularly in the tombs of persons of much higher standing in life than the four worthies just mentioned, the *representacion de la mort* is combined with the *representacion au vif* into what may be described as a "double-decker tomb," wherein the disintegrating body of the deceased, divested of all that which distinguishes the high from the low and the rich from the poor, occupies, as it were, the lower berth while his stately effigy, proudly proclaiming his station in life, reposes above. This was the arrangement favored by the great in France for about two centuries, from the end of the fourteenth century to that of the sixteenth; and how eagerly it was accepted in England is shown, for example, by the tomb of Bishop Richard Fleming (d. 1431) in Lincoln Cathedral (fig. 261), by that of John Fitzalan (d. 1435; fig. 262), seventeenth Earl of Arundel, in Arundel (Sussex), by that of Archbishop Henry Chicheley (d. 1443) in Canterbury Cathedral, and by that of Bishop Thomas Bekington (d. 1451) in Wells Cathedral.

In all these cases, it would seem, the idea that the individual is subject to death and decay is contrasted with the idea that his "dignity," be it that of a nobleman, a prince of the church, or a secular ruler,

---

[1] The thirteenth century had suggested this idea not by parading the gruesome effects of decomposition but only by reminding the spectator of such moralistic allegories as the well-known tale of the thoughtless mortal who has climbed a tree and enjoys its fruits without thinking of the fact that this tree is constantly gnawed at by two mice, standing for "Day" and "Night," and that he is bound to fall prey to Death and the Devil, symbolized by a unicorn and dragon; see the Tomb at Joigny, published by L. Pillion, "Un Tombeau français du 13ᵉ siècle et l'apologue de Barlaam sur la vie humaine," *Revue de l'art ancien et moderne*, XXVIII, 1910, II, pp. 321 ff., and kindly called to my attention by Professor W. Sauerländer.

[2] The *transi* does not seem to have become popular until near the end of the fourteenth century; the second earliest specimen is the tomb slab of Thomas de Saulx (d. 1391), formerly in the Sainte Chapelle at Dijon and known to us only from an engraving in Dom Plancher, *Histoire générale et particulière de Bourgogne*, II, Dijon, 1741, p. 31. After that, the examples multiply.

enjoys a permanence which has nothing to do with the immortality of his soul but attaches to his social or institutional status per se: "Dignitas numquam perit, individua vero quotidie pereunt," says a great jurist of the thirteenth century.[1] The famous "double-decker tomb" of Jean Cardinal de Lagrange (d. 1402) in Avignon further accentuated this difference between celestial immortality and terrestrial permanence in the row of statues and in a series of reliefs—all now lost—which surmounted the Cardinal's two effigies and which, if they had come down to us singly, would have been interpreted as independent epitaphs.

What has been preserved of the Cardinal's monument is only his image *en transi* (fig. 263). Originally, however, this image was placed at the bottom of a many-storied structure—justifiably referred to as a *mausolée* in French writing—which with its crowning pinnacle touched the very ceiling of the church (figs. 264, 265). Above the *transi*, expressing the corruptibility of the individual body, there could be seen, as usual, the *representacion au vif* symbolic of what may be called the terrestrial permanence of preter-individual dignity. On top of this, however, provision was made for the Cardinal's immortal soul. The *representacion au vif* is surmounted by the statues of Christ and the Apostles, and these again by no fewer than five narrative reliefs in each of which the prelate is represented, like a donor's figure, on his knees:[2] being presented to the Virgin Mary; witnessing the Annunciation, the Nativity, and the Visitation; and, finally, praying in the company of three crowned figures who may or may not represent the Three Kings from the East.

Be that as it may, for nearly two hundred years French, Franco-German, and English art abounded in funerary monuments dramatically contrasting an image of the body rotting in its grave with an image of what may be called the total personality lying in state. And when an indifferent Northern English illuminator of ca. 1450, perhaps a Carthusian monk, had to illustrate such well-worn phrases as "What thou art, and here aftyr sal be" or "Thy fayr flesche falles and fadys away," he automatically produced what optically, though not technically, corresponds to two "double-decker tombs" (fig. 266). He showed the effigies of a king and a queen, each lying in state on a *tumba*, the walls of which proudly display a multitude of coats of arms; and, beneath them, their nearly nude cadavers, almost reduced to skeletons by the destructive action of corruption and vermin.

It is only in one entirely isolated monument—unfortunately destroyed in the French Revolution—that Northern fifteenth-century art reversed the relation between *transi* and *gisant* (so that the former was placed above rather than below the latter), and left the *representacion de la mort* in possession of all the attributes of worldly power and glory; but this unique monument, provided that we can trust the seventeenth-century drawing through which it has come down to us, was not only distinctly Italianate in style but must be understood, I believe, as an intentional and tragically ironic parody of a famous Italian model about one hundred years earlier in date but demonstrably known and dear to the occupant (and probable designer) of the later tomb. I am referring, of course, to the tomb (formerly in Angers Cathedral) of the good but unlucky René of Anjou, titular king of Naples and Sicily, and his first wife, Isabeau of Lorraine (fig. 267), in relation to the tomb of his mighty ancestor and predecessor, Robert the Wise of Anjou, in S. Chiara at Naples (fig. 398).

Both these tombs show *gisants* contrasted with figures enthroned—an arrangement exceptional, as we shall see, even in Italy and, so far as I know, unique in the North. But where the effigy of the enthroned Robert is a paradigm of active strength and unshakable majesty, the enthroned figure on the tomb of

[1] Damasus, quoted in E. H. Kantorowicz, "Zu den Rechtsgrundlagen der Kaisersage," *Deutsches Archiv für Erforschung des Mittelalters*, XIII, 1957, pp. 115 ff., particularly p. 142. For the whole problem of the "double-decker tomb," see now the same author's remarkable book, *The King's Two Bodies; A Study in Mediaeval Political Theology*, Princeton, 1957, particularly pp. 431–37, figs. 28, 30, 31.

[2] For the Italian antecedents of this arrangement, see below, p. 77.

René, begun about eight years after the dismal failure of his expedition to Naples in 1438–42, is a nearly skeletonized corpse, crowned and arrayed in regal robes but collapsing, as it were, on the very seat of power, and with its foot thrusting aside the scepter and the orb that have slipped from its impotent hands.

In Italy itself representations of the dead as decaying skeletons or corpses—not, of course, to be confused with personifications of death—are of the greatest rarity in funerary sculpture, and this is all the more significant as the motif of the *transi* as such was by no means unknown. A *tumba* supporting a stupendously naturalistic skeleton, possibly meant to be that of Adam, serves as a predella for Masaccio's *Trinity* in S. Maria Novella in Florence (fig. 269),[1] and in Jacopo Bellini's *Sketchbook* we find the tomb of a scholar (fig. 268) where an entirely nude and particularly gruesome corpse is placed upon a sarcophagus the front wall of which shows the deceased delivering an exceptionally well-attended lecture (there are about a hundred and fifteen students, twenty-one of them standees). But in both cases the motif of the *transi* was used by painters as a symbol of mortality instead of being carved by sculptors on the real grave of a dead person; for there can be no doubt that Bellini's bold combination of a Northern *transi* with an elaboration on the North Italian "lecture scene"—a theme which had made its first appearance in the tombs of Bolognese professors about 1300 and to which we shall revert in the following chapter—is pure fantasy, an *invenzione* bearing witness to the imaginative powers of a great artist who lived, as it were, on the borderline between the cisalpine and the transalpine world.

As far as actual monuments are concerned, the only Italian example that has come to my knowledge is the tomb slab of a jurisconsult named Antonio Amati in S. Trinita in Florence (probably executed in the third quarter of the fifteenth century; fig. 270), where the figure of the deceased wears a death's-head on its shoulders. But just this apparent exception serves to throw light upon the basic difference between the cisalpine and the transalpine point of view. It evinces Northern influence not only in the death's-head motif, but also in the epigraphy of the long metrical inscription whose rather ungainly Gothic lettering forms a startling contrast with the pure Renaissance style of the architectural framework. Yet this figure is very different from a Northern *representacion de la mort*, that is to say, from the image of an individual not only reduced to a state of physical decomposition but also divested of his terrestrial dignity (the symbols of which were shown, if at all, with purely negative intent, as is the case with the unique portrayal of René of Anjou as a "dead king" and in such tomb slabs as show the skeletons of a bishop or abbot retaining the miter and/or the crozier; fig. 271).[2] In the Amati tomb we have before us an image which tends to defy the antithesis between *transi* and *gisant* as such.

The Italian *gisant*, we recall, was nearly always conceived as the portrait of a "dead" person—a person incapable of action and sensation but otherwise remaining what he had been in life. This also applies, appearances notwithstanding, to Antonio Amati. Although his face is transformed into a death's-head, his body does not exhibit any signs of decay or even excessive emaciation; and he still wears his academic gown and hood. He is, if one may say so, somewhat more dead than the normal Italian *gisant*; but he is emphatically not a *transi* in the hyperborean sense of the term: death's-head or no death's-head, he remains Antonio Amati, LL.D., "toto clarissimus orbe." Here, as in a flash, we see the difference between the Northern Middle Ages and the Italian Renaissance.

---

[1] The skeleton is obviously not that of a donor. It either represents Adam (according to Charles de Tolnay, *L'Oeil*, January, 1958, pp. 37ff.) or, more plausibly, "Everyman," since the inscription (in Italian) says: "I was what you are, and you will be what I am"; see Ursula Schlegel, *Art Bulletin*, XLV, 1963, p. 25.
[2] In addition to the tomb of Jean de Beauvau illustrated in fig. 271, there may be mentioned, for example, the tomb of an abbot in St.-Maurice at Angers (Cabinet des Estampes, Rés. Pe 1, Tome 7, 2, fol. 169). As a secular parallel, though of much later date, we may refer to the tomb of the Comtesse Françoise de Cossé (d. 1535), formerly in the Jacobins at Angers, where she is shown as an enshrouded *transie* but with her countess' crown on her head (*ibid.*, fol. 10).

IV. The Renaissance, Its Antecedents and Its Sequel

As biologists have had to recognize the fact that the principles of heredity and mutation are complementary rather than mutually exclusive, so must historians accept the complementary relationship between continuity and innovation. It is impossible to deny that the Renaissance, which took its inception in Italy at the beginning of the fourteenth century, proclaimed itself as something "modern" in the course of the fifteenth, and began to spread all over the transalpine countries from about 1500, was and remained inextricably linked to what we call the Middle Ages. But it is equally impossible to conclude from this continuity that there was no such thing as the Renaissance at all (a conclusion, incidentally, which would imply that there was no such thing as the Middle Ages either). And it is precisely in its attitude toward the dead that the new epoch most vigorously asserted its "modernity."

In funerary sculpture there can be observed in many cases a basic change in outlook:[1] a rejection of Christian concern for the future in favor of pagan glorification of the past. But we must not expect this change to be universal and unequivocal. Revealing though the picture of Renaissance funerary sculpture is, it is also very confusing—not only because the intrusion of the new upon the old took place in innumerable different ways and with extremely varying intensity, from almost imperceptible changes of detail to a complete reversal of attitude, but also because one of the basic characteristics of the Renaissance period as such is what I once proposed to call, for want of a more euphonious word, its tendency toward decompartmentalization: a tendency to abolish all those barriers which had kept things apart (but also in order) during the Middle Ages and thus to produce an apparently—and often really—chaotic fusion of art, religion, scholarship, science, and technology which, just by virtue of being chaotic, prepared the ground for the emergence of a Galileo, a Descartes, a Harvey, and a Grotius at the beginning of the seventeenth century, and of a Newton, a Leibnitz, a Bentley, and a Mabillon near its end.

It is not surprising, therefore, that in the domain of funerary sculpture the hitherto distinct types began to interpenetrate in various ways and that the most fundamental quality of the medieval tomb, its religious character and purpose tended not so much to be supplanted by as to commingle with more secular intentions.

Since our survey of the medieval development was largely limited—and for good reasons—to the Northern countries, I propose to begin the last chapter of our discussion where the penultimate chapter stopped. We shall try, as Kepler would say, to catch the Renaissance "by the tail which we hold in our hands": instead of turning at once to what happened in Italy in the fourteenth and fifteenth centuries, we shall begin by looking at what happened in the North at the beginning of the sixteenth and then attempt to find our way back.

Throughout the transalpine world the familiar medieval types—the tomb slab, the *tumba* and table tomb, and the epitaph everywhere, the wall tomb in France and Spain, and that particularly impressive

[1] Of the extensive literature on the funerary sculpture of the Renaissance, the following contributions may be mentioned: F. Burger, *Geschichte des florentinischen Grabmals*, Strasbourg, 1904; G. Davies, *Renascence: The Sculptured Tombs of the Fifteenth Century in Rome*, London, 1910; G. Ferrari, *La tomba nell'arte italiana*, Milan, n. d.; R. Orneta, *La escultura funeraria de España*, Madrid, 1919; K. A. Esdaile and S. Sitwell, *English Church Monuments 1510 to 1840*, London, 1946.

structure, the tomb slab enlarged to monumental proportions and raised to a vertical position in the German Rhineland—survived and coexisted during the sixteenth century. The adaptation of these traditional types to the *maniera moderna* was originally confined to form, particularly to the architectural setting and decorative accessories; and while such a partial or limited modernization could not fail to have its effect upon the spirit or content of the monuments ("All art is one, remember that, Biddie dear"), it should be distinguished from a total modernization which extends to iconography as well. To give some random examples, beginning with France: the tomb of Raoul de Lannoy and his wife (completed in 1507 by Antonio della Porta and Pace Gaggini in collaboration with indigenous artists) in the church of Folleville (fig. 272) remains, as far as the program is concerned, an ordinary *enfeu* even though the couple's coats of arms are supported by Italianate putti and the decoration of the wall on either side of the Madonna includes such motifs as centaurs, sirens, and profile heads reflecting the influence of Roman coins. The tomb of the two dukes of Orléans in St.-Denis (fig. 273), produced by another Italian, Girolamo Viscardi, in 1502, remains a *tumba*, guarded by saints, even though the style of the architectural features and the shape of the "sarcophagus" are pure Renaissance.

In Germany, the famous Nuremberg workshop founded by Peter Vischer the Elder and continued by his sons produced—and distributed as far west as Lower Saxony and as far east as Poland—not only *tumbae* (I limit myself to showing that of the Count and Countess of Henneberg in the little church of Römhild in Saxe-Meiningen [fig. 274] because the effigies can be traced back to a design by Dürer) but also table tombs (fig. 275), epitaphs, and tomb slabs figural as well as heraldic (fig. 276). And all of these reveal a change in style but not in subject matter.

This also applies to the only type of monument that the Vischers, *Rotgiesser* (bronze casters) by profession, left to the stone sculptors: the monumentalized and verticalized tombstones of the archbishops and bishops in Mainz, Würzburg, etc. Riemenschneider's monument of Bishop Lorenz von Bibra of Würzburg (d. 1519; fig. 277) differs from his tombstone of Rudolf von Scherenberg (fig. 218), executed a quarter century before, only in the presence of Renaissance colonnettes, Renaissance putti, and Renaissance garlands as well as in the fact that the figure has, if I may say so, more "presence" (even though Lorenz von Bibra, in contrast to his predecessor, thought it advisable to invoke the intercession of his personal saint, St. Lawrence, and the titular saint of his cathedral, St. Kilian). And while the masterpiece of Riemenschneider's younger (and, in my estimation, more gifted) contemporary, Hans Backofen, the tombstone of Archbishop Uriel von Gemmingen of Mainz (d. 1514; fig. 278), represents a bold iconographical innovation in that he dared to demote the ceremonial archiepiscopal effigy, traditional for many centuries, to the status of the donor's portrait in an epitaph, this very innovation (subsequently emulated, e. g., in the beautiful tombstone of Archbishop Johann von Greiffenklau of Trèves) served to make the spiritual climate of the composition less anthropocentric and more fervently religious than ever before. Instead of facing the beholder as a commanding figure portrayed in full length and pure front view, the Archbishop, all but dwarfed by the two diocesan saints, Martin and Boniface, has fallen on his knees before the crucified Christ, and at his feet there can be seen a magnificent "vanity still-life": the book and crozier that have fallen from his hands, his liturgical gloves and rings, and, lurking behind the hem of his pluvial, the truly terrifying skull of Adam (fig. 279).

In all these monuments, then, the intent of the iconographical program remains unequivocally "prospective." And the same is true even of the remarkable Fugger tombs in Augsburg, designed by Dürer in 1510 and completed, with considerable variations, by local sculptors in 1515 (fig. 280). Possible only in what may be called the most Renaissance-minded city of Germany, they differ from the Italian wall tombs which they attempt to emulate, first, in representing the departed as enshrouded *transis*; and, second, in placing them under the protection of two time-honored symbols of deliverance, the Resurrection of Christ and Samson Carrying Away the City Gates of Gaza (the latter replaced at the last moment, and apparently for purely aesthetic reasons, by Samson Fighting the Philistines).

In one specific group of German and Austrian monuments, however, the change from a medieval to a modern point of view extends to program as well as style, and it is a radical change indeed. I am referring to the epitaphs of poets, scholars, men of letters, and erudite naturalists, in short, of those whom we are wont to call humanists.[1]

The pattern for these inconspicuous but truly revolutionary monuments—revolutionary in that they reveal an attitude not only purely commemorative but even boastful and almost entirely devoid of religious sentiment—was set, as early as 1507, in a remarkable woodcut by means of which Conrad Celtes, the favorite humanist of Frederick the Wise and Maximilian I, informed his friends of his impending death much as a modern couple announces its forthcoming marriage (fig. 281). This "Sterbebild" is, to be sure, an epitaph on paper only and a slightly proleptic one at that; but it is doubly interesting because it was devised by Conrad Celtes himself and was executed according to his instructions by no less illustrious a master than Hans Burgkmair. It shows the bust portrait of the first German poet laureate emerging from behind a memorial tablet, lids lowered as if grieving over his own demise, lamented not only by cupids but also by the classical gods to whom he had devoted his life, viz., Apollo and Mercury, and resting his arms on four of his books (two of them still in print at the time). The picture proper is interspersed with inscriptions—ranging from the Biblical "and their works do follow them" (Revelation 14:13) to Ovid's "Exitus acta probat" (*Heroides* II, 85)—which laud Celtes' merits and complain about the interference of death with friendship; and the two couplets on the memorial tablet exhort his fellow humanists to mourn for him with tears and breast-beating yet to take comfort in the thought that he would always converse with them through his writings.

In more tangible form, but with the classical divinities only invoked rather than actually depicted, this new spirit is represented, for example, by the epitaph of one of Celtes' friends and colleagues, Dr. Johannes Cuspinianus (*recte* Spiessheimer, d. 1527) in St. Stephen's at Vienna (fig. 283). It shows the bust portrait of the deceased, who was a medical man as well as a poet, flanked by those of his two wives and separated from his eight children by an enormous memorial tablet the metrical inscription of which proclaims him a votary of Apollo and the Muses but does not fail to mention that the Emperor had appointed him Rector of Vienna University; it ends as follows: "Historiae immensae monimenta eterna reliqui;/Vivus in his semper Cuspinianus erit" ("To endless history I left eternal works; / In these Cuspinian will live forever").

Here we have indeed a complete reversal of the medieval attitude. Glorification of intellectual achievements and academic honors has taken the place of pious expectations for the future of the soul, and such "immortality" as the deceased hopes for is limited to the continued reputation and popularity of his books. Apollo and the Muses are invoked instead of Christ and the saints. And the desire to revive the *sacrosancta vetustas* ("hallowed antiquity") not only in style but also in iconography is evident from the fact that epitaphs of this kind are patterned upon a classical type of funerary monument extremely popular throughout the Roman Empire but absent from the medieval scene (fig. 91).

In Italy this type had been revived from about the middle of the fifteenth century,[2] so that the closed-eyed *gisants* were supplemented by bust portraits so intensely alive that the deceased could be shown praying (fig. 284). Suffice it to adduce two specimens particularly close to classical prototypes but exploiting them in different ways: the epitaph of Stefano Satri and his family in S. Omobono at Rome (fig. 288), which is literally copied from an Augustan original in the Vatican (fig. 93); and the epitaph of the able sculptor Andrea Bregno (fig. 285) in S. Maria sopra Minerva (dated 1506), which freely combines the *imago*

[1] Cf. A. Chastel, "La Glorification humaniste dans les monuments funéraires de la Renaissance," *Atti Congresso Studi Umanistici 1950*, Milan, 1951, pp. 477 ff.

[2] For a collection of early instances, see U. Middeldorf's review of A. Grisebach, *Römische Porträtbüsten der Gegenreformation*, Leipzig, 1936, in *Art Bulletin*, XX, 1938, pp. 111 ff. Cf. L. Bruhns, "Das Motiv der ewigen Anbetung in der römischen Grabplastik des 16., 17. und 18. Jahrhunderts," *Römisches Jahrbuch für Kunstgeschichte*, IV, 1940, pp. 253 ff.

clipeata with a memorial tablet and professional attributes. In Germany this revival started two generations later; but while Celtes and his humanist friends were thoroughly familiar with the developments on the other side of the Alps, there is no reason to doubt that, as enthusiastic archaeologists and epigraphers, they also drew direct inspiration from the Roman originals abundantly accessible in what had been the provinces of Gallia and Germania.

The spirit of secularism, grandiloquence, and, to call a spade a spade, enormous personal vanity which found fulfillment in these epitaphs *alla Romana* can be traced back, however, far beyond the deliberate imitation of classical prototypes, whose influence must be considered as an effective instrument rather than the cause of the phenomenon. In Italy the resurgence of the commemorative point of view can be observed at the very beginning of the Renaissance movement, that is to say, the first decades of the fourteenth century. And it was, along with (or even in advance of) the knights and generals, whose equestrian statues will be touched upon later, the professors—first the great jurists in the University of Bologna, soon after their colleagues in other disciplines and other seats of learning—who first insisted on being remembered rather than saved and preferred the perpetuation of their academic function, lecturing, *per saecula saeculorum*, to the anticipation of their admission to paradise.

Funny though this sounds—and, in a sense, is—there is a serious and legitimate foundation for professorial conceit. Teaching, viz., the transmission of knowledge "from generation to generation," carries with it an element of perpetuity such as no other form of human activity can claim. We should not forget the beautiful lines of the great Arab poet, Hariri: "What could be nobler than to plant the seeds of wisdom in fresh receptive soil where they will come up and bear fruit forever? The sound of thy speech will longer endure in the young than will the traces of thy writing on tablets: thy words will be alive when death has broken the bones of thy jaw." Nor should we overlook the fact that the professors of Bologna, Pavia, Padua, and Montpellier were, in their modest way, the forerunners and pacemakers of Renaissance humanism. Dante, Petrarch, and Boccaccio, even Ariosto and Tasso, began their careers (not always willingly but never without benefit) as students of law; Marsilio Ficino studied medicine in his youth; and Rabelais practiced it for the better part of his life.

Even in the thirteenth century the sarcophagi of the Bolognese professors (in Italy, we remember, "ensarcophagusment" always survived along with interment) were often raised on colonnettes and surmounted by a pyramidal canopy *(piramide)*, the age-old symbol of enduring fame (fig. 286); but they were adorned only with ornaments and symbols. On the remarkable tomb of Rolandino dei Passageri (d. 1300; fig. 287), however, still seen *in situ* on the little Piazza San Domenico—a tomb remarkable also because it is, like Petrarch's in Arquà, a kind of public monument—the flat reliefs of the sarcophagus display, in addition to Rolandino's effigy *en gisant*, what was to become the very signature of professorial tombs: the school or lecture scene (fig. 282) in which we see the teacher in action as he addresses a group of students eagerly absorbing his words or, at least, taking them down in their notebooks.

Both lecturer and audience are here represented in profile; but while this scheme persisted for a long time—e. g., in Master Roso da Parma's tomb (fig. 289) of the famous anatomist Mundinus (Mondino dei Liuzzi) and his brother Luccio (of 1318)—it was soon supplemented (in fact, as early as 1318, the very year of the Mundinus tomb) by a more dignified, not to say hieratic, arrangement wherein the professor, majestically enthroned *in cathedra* and represented in strict frontality, appears in the center while the students are arrayed on either side (fig. 290).

In these two versions—of which the second came to be preferred in Italy, whereas the first, and only the first, occasionally invaded France in the course of the fourteenth century—the school or lecture scene survived for centuries, modernized, in most cases, only with regard to setting, costume, and perspective (as, for example, in Antonio Rossellino's tomb of an early jurist, Filippo Lazzari, in S. Domenico at Pistoia). In one forever memorable instance, however, it reappeared in purely classical disguise: in one of Andrea Riccio's eight bronze reliefs from the tomb, originally in S. Fermo at Verona (fig. 291), of two famous physicians and teachers of medicine, Marcantonio della Torre (d. 1511), chiefly remembered as the collaborator of Leonardo da Vinci, and his father Girolamo.

This unfortunately dismembered monument, the sculptural portions of which are now preserved in the Louvre, displays the life, death, and, if one may say so, apotheosis of the two scientists (it is difficult to decide which of the reliefs commemorate the father and which the son)[1] as though they and their associates had lived under Augustus or Hadrian. The school scene (fig. 292), with the lecturer as well as the students dressed *all'antica*, is staged amidst Roman ruins and palm trees and superintended, as it were, by the statues of Minerva, Apollo, and Hygeia. When the hero (here probably Marcantonio, who died of a malarial fever at the age of thirty) collapses on his bed, he resembles the dying Adonis on Roman sarcophagi (fig. 293). Before his death a sacrifice is offered to Aesculapius (fig. 294). After the inevitable has happened, his fate is lamented, according to the *conclamatio* ritual, by women pulling their hair and throwing up their arms (fig. 295). Instead of being transported to heaven, his soul—receiving preferential treatment by a kindly Charon because it carries a book! (fig. 297)—descends into a Virgilian nether world where it is ferried across the River Styx and admitted to the Elysian Fields, which resound with music and poetry (fig. 298). The dedication of his tomb (a fairly faithful replica of the S. Fermo monument itself, except that its decoration includes a death's-head, an hourglass, and a couple of books) takes the shape of a classical *lustratio* (fig. 296). And the whole program culminates in a relief which shows nothing less than the triumph of human genius over Death himself (fig. 299). Pegasus and a vase containing a laurel wreath—the former so well-known a symbol of intellectual "uplift" and "immortal fame" that no further explanation seemed necessary, the latter explicitly inscribed VIRTVS—confront a wobbly skeleton whose scythe has fallen to the ground.

So frankly pagan a funerary monument is, however, no less rare than is so frankly Averroistic an epitaph as that of Cesare Cremonini, professor at Padua and a good personal friend as well as a scientific opponent of Galileo, which reads (or is said to have read): "Hic iacet Cremoninus totus" ("Here lies all of Cremonini").

Apart from such exceptional cases (among them the transformation of the church of S. Francesco at Rimini into a supermausoleum where the sarcophagi of the Malatesta family and the "Diva Isotta," protected by the planets rather than saints, take the place of altars so that outraged contemporaries denounced it as sacrilegious), the funerary art of the Renaissance—and even more so that of the Baroque—attempted to follow the precept of Erasmus of Rotterdam: "Nos vetera instauramus, nova non prodimus" ("We reinstate the old without forsaking the new").

In Italy as well as in the North, the modernization of sepulchral art, that is to say, the adoption of a *buona maniera moderna* patterned upon classical models, first tended to affect the character of the monuments only with respect to form but not with respect to program. Sarcophagi, whether freestanding, placed in arched recesses outside (*avelli*) or inside a church, or projecting, high up, from its wall (a custom redundantly reflected in Tintoretto's *Finding of the Relics of St. Mark*; fig. 300), were shaped and decorated *all'antica* without much thought for iconography; in fact, the appeal of classical forms, combined with the fascination of precious, skillfully treated materials, could dwarf the interest in subject matter to such an extent that effigies as well as narrative reliefs were deemed unnecessary, as in the sarcophagus housing the parents of Cosimo de' Medici (fig. 301) or Verrocchio's splendid bronze and porphyry sarcophagus of the same Cosimo's two younger sons, Giovanni and Piero (fig. 302).

Even when the effigy was retained, as in Jacopo della Quercia's famous tomb of Ilaria del Carretto (d. 1406; figs. 303, 304)—where, however, the image, delicate to the point of evanescence, may antedate

[1] For biographical and iconographical details, see F. Saxl, "Pagan Sacrifice in the Italian Renaissance," *Journal of the Warburg Institute*, II, 1939, pp. 346 ff., particularly pp. 355 ff.

the rest of the monument by ten or fifteen years—the decoration of the *tumba* or sarcophagus could be limited to garland-bearing putti, memorial tablets, heraldic devices, or, in a specimen characteristically produced in Rome, mere strigilation (fig. 305). And in the fashioning of tomb slabs the medieval tradition proved so powerful that their partial modernization resulted in a contradiction opposite to, yet no less glaring than, that present in, say, the monuments of Siegfried von Eppstein or Peter von Aspelt in Mainz (fig. 214).

In these Northern examples, we recall, the aliveness and apparently upright position of the effigies were at variance with their horizontal placement and, more particularly, with the presence of a pillow. In the Italian tomb slabs (where, as in the three-dimensional effigies, the deceased is represented as a dead body, hands crossed and eyes closed) this contradiction was reduced to a minimum or entirely absent as long as the architectural environment was either merely adumbrated in a linear design or not indicated at all, as is the case, for example, in Lorenzo Ghiberti's tomb of Leonardo Dati (fig. 306) or Jacopo della Quercia's tombs of Lorenzo Trenta and his wife (fig. 307). But when Donatello in his tomb slabs of Giovanni Crivelli (fig. 308) and Bishop Giovanni Pecci of Siena (fig. 309) administered to Lorenzo Ghiberti what has been called "a sharp rebuke" (both in the name of classical antiquity and modern naturalism), he produced a new paradox.

His ambition was to place the figure within a convincing architectural setting styled *all'antica* and rendered in perspective in such a manner that a beholder standing in front of the monument would receive an impression of three-dimensionality. Thus, while Siegfried von Eppstein, Peter von Aspelt, and innumerable other Northern worthies had been wide awake and active while ostensibly lying down, Donatello's Crivelli sleeps the eternal sleep while ostensibly standing upright in a niche of classical cast, the base line of its conch curved downward in a kind of *prospettiva di sotto in su*; and in the Pecci tomb the situation is further complicated, and aggravated, by the fact that this classical niche, its worm's-eye perspective even more marked, turns out to be, upon closer inspection, the concave inner surface of a bier with handles and feet visible at the bottom but not at the top.

The problem was solved, to the extent that it could be solved, by "Simone Ghini" in his tomb of Pope Martin V (ca. 1435—40; fig. 310) in St. John in the Lateran—the only known example of a papal monument in only two dimensions—where the perspective artifice produces a fairly convincing illusion of three-dimensionality. Here the figure of the dead pontiff seems to lie in a deep trough or vat the upper surface of which is symmetrically defined by classicizing pilasters and arches while the depth of its walls is indicated by advancing lines so sharply descending that they converge considerably beneath the lower margin of the plaque. When the beholder takes his stand at a point determined by these vanishing lines so as to look at the work in sharp foreshortening (fig. 311), the flat effigy seems to transform itself into a statue in the round reposing beneath ground level but protected above by what, under the optical conditions just mentioned, assumes the character of a canopy projecting from the upper surface of the "vat" at a right angle.

Even where the funerary sculpture of the Renaissance yielded to classical influence and other modern tendencies not only in form but also in iconography, it did not normally deny the hopes and beliefs of Christianity.

In certain cases we find what may be called a total absorption of "modern" symbolism into the context of a medieval program. Perhaps the most curious example of this kind is the tomb of a canon named Hubert Milemans (erected about the middle of the sixteenth century) in Ste.-Croix at Liége (fig. 312), where the recumbent effigy is surmounted by a Crucifixion while beneath the sarcophagus the not very original idea that death annihilates everything, including human endeavor, friendship, and charity, and that we must ceaselessly watch since every hour brings us nearer to the end with eaglelike speed, is entirely expressed in the then fashionable language of "Egyptian" hieroglyphs.

Less curious but more important are those monuments which attempt to achieve a dynamic equilibrium—an equilibrium implying and expressing a tension still capable of being resolved—between the medieval tradition and the *rinascimento dell'antichità*. When a Florentine Quattrocento sculptor, probably Giuliano da Sangallo, exploited for his decoration of the funeral chapel of the Sassetti family in S. Trinita (fig. 314) two Roman sarcophagi, one showing a children's bacchanal, the other the same Death of Meleager (fig. 313) whose unrestrained pathos had helped Nicola Pisano and Giotto to express the despair of a mother in the *Massacre of the Innocents* and the sorrow of St. John in the *Lamentation of Christ*, these borrowings from the Antique served to humanize and emotionalize but did not paganize the joyful ministrations of medieval angels and the ceremonially regulated grief of medieval *pleureurs* (fig. 315).

The pagan spirit of these marginal reliefs as well as that of the *bucrania* adorning the darkly lustrous sarcophagi themselves is, moreover, exorcised, as it were, by the paintings of Ghirlandaio which dominate the chapel as a whole: the Sibyls in the vaults; the stories from the life of St. Francis on the walls; and the famous Nativity on the high altar. And a much-debated relief produced in Verrocchio's workshop at about the same time (fig. 316) and largely based upon the same Meleager sarcophagus does not attempt— no matter what its original context may have been and whether or not it commemorates the untimely death of the beautiful Francesca Tornabuoni—to reproject a contemporary tragedy into the classical past; rather it may be said to blend in the description of this tragedy the pathos of a Roman *conclamatio* with the inward sorrow pervading a Death of the Virgin.

Yet the fact remains that the Renaissance formally sanctioned rather than merely tolerated the principle of individual (as opposed to what I have called institutional and "gentilitial") commemoration; and that a maximum of posthumous recognition came to be considered a reward not only for sanctity or at least piety but also for political, military, literary, and artistic achievement, in certain cases even for mere beauty.

Apart from the introduction of quasi-emblematical motifs, such as books as symbols of intellectual culture and erudition or the pyramid as a symbol of the "gloria dei principi" (thus for the first time in Raphael's tomb of Agostino Chigi in S. Maria del Popolo, designed in 1515), the iconographical innovations symptomatic of this novel attitude—some of them touched upon a short while ago—may be roughly summarized as follows.

1   The revival of funerary symbolism, mythological or ritual, from classical antiquity.

2   The admission—or, if we look back to classical antiquity, readmission—of the biographical element which, after the downfall of paganism, had normally been restricted to the recording of events worthy of being included in the *Acta Sanctorum*.

3   The inclusion of the Virtues—either the four moral or cardinal Virtues (Prudence, Temperance, Fortitude, and Justice), the three theological Virtues (Faith, Hope, and Charity) or the whole heptad—as character witnesses.

4   The activation of the effigy ("effigy" here taken to mean the *representacion au vif* in contradistinction to the *representacion de la mort*, on the one hand, and to the portrayal of the deceased within a scene of veneration, on the other).

5   The introduction of what I propose to call, for reasons to become apparent later, the "Arts Bereft."

The Revival of Classical Symbolism

The first of these innovations, the tendency to revive classical symbolism and mythology within the framework of sepulchral art, has already been met with in the Sassetti and Della Torre tombs. Originating, of course, in the Italian Quattrocento, this tendency grew into a pervasive force wherever the Renaissance movement took root, and the number of examples is legion. To mention only two further instances, we may refer, first, to the magnificent eagles supporting the *lit de parade* in Bernardo Rossellino's famous tomb of Leonardo Bruni (d. 1444; fig. 317), which, like countless monuments of its kind, is otherwise a fairly accurate translation of a French High Gothic *enfeu* into the language of the Italian Renaissance, except that the claim of the great statesman and historian to temporal immortality is visually stressed by the big book, presumably his *History of Florence*, which reposes on his chest; and, second, to two reliefs on the tomb of Jacopo Cardinal of Portugal (d. 1459; fig. 318), the *opus majus* of Bernardo's younger brother, Antonio. One of these reliefs shows winged charioteers, a Platonizing motif familiar to us from Roman monuments; the other exhibits, more surprisingly, a fairly literal copy of a Mithras relief (fig. 319) which, however, was here used only as a general symbol of good conquering evil, for the specific significance of the scene was demonstrably unknown until the beginning of the seventeenth century.

In Northern funerary sculpture a mythological subject makes its first timid appearance, curiously enough, in the tomb of two small children, the son and daughter of Charles VIII and Anne de Bretagne (fig. 320). The reliefs on their little *tumba* in Tours Cathedral, completed in 1506 by the workshop of Michel Colombe, show—in addition to such classical motifs as lions' feet, centaurs, sirens, and griffins—three scenes from the life of Hercules (the Carrying of the Columns, the Killing of the Hydra, and the Victory over Cacus) juxtaposed with three corresponding scenes from the Life of Samson. Perhaps it was because the dauphin's brief life itself provided so little material for elaboration that his potential qualities were hopefully compared to the most shining *exempla virtutis* from classical as well as Biblical antiquity.

The Readmission of the Biographical Element and the Inclusion of the Virtues

The second and third innovations—the readmission of the biographical element and the inclusion of the Virtues—can be discussed together because they represent two aspects of one and the same process, a process antedating the *rinascimento dell'antichità* by about one century: the extension to the prominent layman of what had been the privilege of the saint or, as I phrased it, the near-saint.

This monopoly was broken in Italy in the first third of the fourteenth century. The scheme known to us from the tombs of Sts. Giles and Junian and of Pope Clement II (figs. 253, 254) was transformed, if not by Nicola Pisano himself, at least by his followers. The Virtues were no longer represented in reliefs adorning the walls of the sarcophagus or *tumba* but raised to the status of quasi-caryatids. After the fashion of Nicola's holy-water basin at Pistoia and his son Giovanni's pulpits, they mostly appear as full-grown statues, often attached to columns which support a sarcophagus adorned with scenes from the life of the occupant (figs. 321, 322). And it was in this monumentalized form that they were forced to enhance the merits of secular princes and princesses—and, later on, of anybody who could afford it—instead of testifying to the piety of those who, to quote Thiofrid of Echternach once more, had entered their graves "in abundantia virtutum."

The earliest cases on record are the Anjou tombs by Tino di Camaino of Siena (and Pisa), who had been called to Naples by Robert the Wise but died too early (in 1337) to commemorate his royal master himself. What he did produce were the tomb of Robert's mother, Mary of Hungary (d. 1325), in S. Maria di Donnaregina; that of his son, Charles of Calabria (d. 1328), in S. Chiara (fig. 397);[1] and those of Charles's two wives, Catherine and Mary, the latter also laid to rest in S. Chiara, the former in S. Lorenzo. Whether some special significance attaches to the fact that the male members of the family were placed

---

[1] Such was the impression made by this monument that it was promoted to the role of "The Tomb of Hector" in at least two manuscripts of Guido Colonna's *Historia destructionis Troiae;* see H. Buchthal, "Hector's Tomb," *De Artibus Opuscula XL; Essays in Honor of Erwin Panofsky*, New York, 1961, pp. 29 ff.

under the protection of all the Virtues (in Charles of Calabria's case even eight rather than seven), whereas Robert's mother and Charles's two wives had to be satisfied, respectively, with the four cardinal or the three theological ones, I dare not decide. Certain it is, however, that the Anjou tombs established a tradition which grew rather slowly in the Italian Trecento (the tomb of Francesco Pazzi in S. Croce at Florence) and Quattrocento (the most remarkable example being, of course, Donatello's and Michelozzo's tomb of Baldassare Coscia, formerly known as Pope John XXIII [fig. 323], where the three theological Virtues are placed in classicizing niches), but assumed the proportions of an international rage from the sixteenth century.

We can easily conceive that the secularization of the Virtues coincided with the secularization of biographical eulogy. At the same time that the tombs of nonsaints, even nonecclesiastics, began to exhibit the Virtues, they also began to display narratives which, in contrast to the stereotyped school or lecture scene, were meant to perpetuate the memory of specific and individual achievements and events. Suffice it to mention the reliefs on the sarcophagus of Cangrande della Scala (d. 1329), minutely describing his administrative and military triumphs, his gracious behavior toward the vanquished and even the translation of his body from Treviso, where he died, to his beloved Verona (figs. 385, 386).[1]

From ca. 1500, the date conventionally accepted as the beginning of the Renaissance in the North, the Virtues and the eulogistic narrative invaded funerary sculpture on the other side of the Alps. The tomb of Louis XII and Anne de Bretagne (fig. 324), executed between 1515 and 1531 by two Italian brothers, Antonio and Giovanni Giusti, shows the two innovations combined. The vigorously projecting base of an arcaded structure (probably inspired by the tomb of Gian Galeazzo Visconti in the Certosa di Pavia) is decorated with biographical reliefs while the four corners of this base serve as seats for the four cardinal Virtues. These are here Italianate in appearance as well as in some of their attributes (the orb of Justice, the lion's skin, borrowed from Hercules, of Fortitude); but their treatment as statues entirely detached from the body of the monument and their diagonal disposition at the corners of a structure of which they form, quite literally, the *cardines*, represent a solution which must be credited to France. And obvious though this solution appears in retrospect, it was arrived at only after considerable experimentation.

In what would seem to be the earliest instance of a Northern tomb exhibiting the Virtues, the tomb of Charles VIII, executed shortly after his death in 1498, destroyed in the French Revolution but known to us through reliable renderings (fig. 325), the artist attempted to make the innovation more palatable to the French taste by revising the new motif according to the standards of the Isle-de-France: the Virtues are represented in reliefs, circular in shape and set into the walls of the *tumba*—the form and number of these reliefs, no fewer than twelve, manifestly inspired by the famous series of Virtues and Vices in the main portal of Notre-Dame.

In that most enchanting of all places dedicated to the memory of the dead, Margaret of Austria's chapel at Brou near Bourg-en-Bresse (fig. 341), where the intricacies of an autumnal Gothic and the freshness of a vernal Renaissance form as complete and enigmatic a unity as do the intentionally contradictory ideas in her omnipresent, calmly disillusioned motto, FORTVNE INFORTVNE FORT VNE ("Luck, Unluck, One Luck"), the figures of the Virtues (figs. 326, 343)—included in the program from as early as ca. 1505 even though the beginning of its execution was delayed until 1507—nestle in the delicate tracery of one of the *tumbae* exactly as do the statuettes in a Flamboyant Gothic portal.[2] And it was only in the tomb of Francis II of Brittany and Marguerite de Foix (fig. 327), begun by Michel Colombe and Girolamo da Fiesole in 1499, that they attained the status of independent figures placed diagonally at the corners of the monu-

---

[1] An even richer array of biographical scenes—sixteen altogether—may be seen on the tomb of Bishop Guido Tarlati in the Cathedral of Arezzo (1330) by Agostino di Giovanni and Agnolo di Ventura of Siena.

[2] The same arrangement appears, incidentally, in Gil de Siloé's tomb of Juan II of Castile and Isabel of Portugal in the Charterhouse of Miraflores near Burgos.

ment. Their iconography, however, here—as in half a dozen other monuments of the French Renaissance —still reflects a complex and somewhat pedantic system evolved in the fifteenth century (and still employed by Peter Bruegel): Prudence is equipped with a compass in addition to mirror and serpent, Fortitude with a tower, Temperance not only with a bridle but also with a table clock, etc.[1]

After this "Virtues-at-the-corners" type had reached its final form in the tomb of Louis XII and Anne de Bretagne (1515–31)—and, with the Virtues standing rather than seated, in Primaticcio's and Germain Pilon's admirable tomb of Henry II and Catherine de Médicis (fig. 331)—it spread all over the European continent from Toledo (Alonso Berruguete's tomb of Cardinal Tavera) to Innsbruck (the tomb of Maximilian already mentioned) and Munich (Peter Candid's tomb of Louis of Bavaria in the Frauen-kirche). Major resistance was offered in Italy, where the traditional predilection for wall tombs operated in favor of different solutions, as well as in the Netherlands, northern Germany, and Scandinavia, which tended to prefer the incorporation of the Virtues into a kind of table tomb *alla moderna*. This latter type was especially popularized by the Antwerp sculptor, Cornelis Floris (1514–75), and one of his ideal tomb designs (fig. 332) is distinguished by an amusing little innovation derived from emblem books and printer's marks: the figure of Hope carries a crow because the Romans had interpreted the cry of this bird *("cras, cras")* as an invitation to hope for a better "tomorrow."

The Activation of the Effigy: The Kneeling Effigy; the "statue accoudée"; the Equestrian Statue; the Image "in Majesty"

Turning back to the tomb of Charles VIII (fig. 325), we realize that it marks a new departure not only in the inclusion of the Virtues but also in what has been referred to as the activation of the effigy. The spell of recumbency has been broken, and the king instead of reposing on a *lit de parade*, attended by four angels, is shown on his knees before a huge *prie-dieu* on which he has deposited his crown and prayer book. The author of this work, the Modenese sculptor Guido Mazzoni (enticed from Italy by Charles VIII in person), specialized—like his pupil, Antonio Begarelli—in those illusionistic groupings of life-sized, colored terra-cotta figures which Michelangelo admired with the generosity always accorded to the violinist by the pianist ("if these terra cottas were transformed into marble, woe to the statues of the ancients") but which are apt to remind the modern beholder of waxworks *à la* Madame Tussaud. But in applying this illusionism to a funerary effigy executed in gilded bronze and enamel, Guido Mazzoni started a revolution even by the standards of the Italian Renaissance.

A short while ago I referred to the typical Quattrocento wall tomb, as represented by Bernardo Rossellino's monument of Leonardo Bruni (fig. 317), as a "fairly accurate translation of a French Gothic *enfeu* into the language of the Italian Renaissance." I intentionally refrained from stressing the fact that Rossellino's work, like those of his followers, represents the climax of a development which entailed not only a transformation but also some deletions.

Among the earliest attempts to adapt the fully developed *enfeu* to the taste and spirit of the nascent Renaissance were the tomb of Clement IV at Viterbo, by the Roman *marmorarius* Petrus Oderisii (begun between 1268 and 1271, and Arnolfo di Cambio's tomb of Guillaume Cardinal de Braye (d. 1282) in S. Domenico at Orvieto (fig. 333).[2] In the latter the French Gothic archetype is already changed in various ways. The

[1] For this system, see, in addition to E. van Moë, "Les Ethiques, Poétiques et Economiques d'Aristote," *Les Trésors des Bibliothèques de France*, III, fascicule IX, 1930, pp. 3 ff.; R. Tuve, "Notes on the Virtues and Vices," *Journal of the Warburg and Courtauld Institutes*, XXVI, 1963, pp. 264 ff., particularly pp. 277 ff.; for "the clock of Temperance," popularized by Heinrich Suso's *Horologium Sapientiae* of ca. 1339, see H. Michel, "L'Horloge de Sapience et l'histoire de l'horlogerie," *Physis, Rivista di Storia della Scienza*, II, 1961, pp. 291 ff.

[2] If we can trust the engraving in *Propyleum ad Acta Sanctorum*

recumbent effigy is conceived, as was the Italian custom, as an image of a dead body, eyes closed and hands crossed, which reposes on a *lit de parade* placed on top of the sarcophagus proper; this *lit de parade* is protected by a kind of tabernacle the curtains of which are drawn by two angels; and, above all, the deceased is represented twice. He appears not only as a *gisant* lying in state but also, elevated to a higher level, in the guise of a living human being kneeling before the Virgin Mary and presented to her by St. Peter, that is to say, in the guise of a "sponsored donor" after the fashion of the five kneeling figures on the tomb of Cardinal Lagrange (fig. 264), a monument which we can now define as an overgrown hybrid between the "double-decker tomb" and the *enfeu* reshaped by Arnolfo di Cambio.

Of all these innovations only the superimposition of *lit de parade* and sarcophagus has been retained in Bernardo Rossellino's tomb of Leonardo Bruni (fig. 317) and such derivations of it as Desiderio da Settignano's tomb of Carlo Marsuppini (d. 1453) in S. Croce at Florence or Mino da Fiesole's tomb of Margrave Hugo of Tuscany (completed 1481–82) in the Badia. The curtains, though faintly echoed in Donatello's tomb of Baldassare Coscia (fig. 323) and Antonio Rossellino's tomb of the Cardinal of Portugal (fig. 318), have been discarded in favor of garlands, and the "sponsored" donor's figure has disappeared.

This figure had in fact a fairly short life in Italian wall tombs and seems to have survived the fourteenth century only in Rome, where it was very much *en vogue* from the last years of the thirteenth century and where we still find it in the tomb of Pope Pius II in S. Andrea della Valle and in that of Bartolommeo Cardinal Roverella in Santa Cecilia (datable 1483, seven years after the prelate's death). Suffice it to mention an interesting group of Roman tombs in which, according to local tradition, the upper zone of the structure, symbolic of the celestial spheres, is filled with a mosaic rather than a group of statues or a relief: the tomb of Guilelmus Durandus, Bishop of Mende (fig. 334), well known to art historians as the author of the *Rationale divinorum officiorum* (d. 1296), in S. Maria sopra Minerva; that of Gonsalvo Cardinal Rodriguez (d. 1298) in S. M. Maggiore; that of Matteo d'Acquasparta (d. 1302) in S. Maria in Araceli; and, above all, that of Pope Boniface VIII (d. 1303) of which only the effigy and two angels survive in the crypt of St. Peter's but the general disposition of which we know through two drawings by Jacopo Grimaldi (fig. 335).[1]

Elsewhere in the Italian Trecento the idea of resurrection or beatification was expressed, if at all, in a variety of different ways. In Nino Pisano's tomb of Archbishop Simone Saltarelli of Pisa (d. 1342; fig. 336) there survived the by now archaic representation of the ascending soul as a diminutive nude figure carried aloft by angels. The recumbent effigy of Neri Corsini, Bishop of Fiesole (d. 1377; fig. 337), in the second cloister of S. Spirito, rests under the direct protection of a huge fresco (a medium more thoroughly at home in Tuscany than was the mosaic) which shows the Resurrection of Christ. And in one memorable case—so boldly parachronistic that it foreshadows the Baroque rather than the High Renaissance—the body of the deceased itself is assisted to "rise from the dead" as if in anticipation of the Last Judgment: in Giovanni Pisano's unfortunately dismembered monument of Margaret of Brabant (fig. 338), the wife of Emperor Henry VII, who had died at Genoa on December 11, 1311.[2]

Wherever the "sponsored" donor's portrait occurs in Italian wall tombs it does not stand by itself. Invariably presented by a saint, it as invariably supplements a recumbent effigy, and in at least one case—the tomb of Robert of Anjou (fig. 398), which I have briefly mentioned in the preceding chapter and

---

Maii, Antwerp, 1742, p. 378 (kindly brought to my attention by Professor G. B. Ladner), the French *enfeu* type as such was introduced in Italy, a few years before Arnolfo di Cambio's tomb of the Cardinal de Braye, in Piero Oderisi's tomb of Clement IV (d. 1268) in S. Francesco at Orvieto. This tomb, completed in 1272 and now destroyed except for the *gisant*, already showed the latter surmounted by a Madonna and a kneeling figure which here, however, represents not the "sponsored donor" but St. Hedwig who had been canonized by Clement IV in 1257. Still absent are the *lit de parade* and the curtain-drawing angels.

[1] Vatican Library, Cod. Barb. lat. 2733, kindly brought to my attention by Professor G. B. Ladner.
[2] This interpretation would seem to be confirmed by the tomb of a gentleman of the Bardi family (about 1340) in the Bardi di Vernio Chapel, S. Croce, Florence (fig. 339), where the sarcophagus is surmounted by a fresco showing the resurrected occupant awaiting his fate at the Last Judgment. See Eve Borsook, *The Mural Painters of Tuscany from Cimabue to Andrea del Sarto*, London, 1960, pl. 12 and p. 131.

to which we shall shortly revert—it even coexists with the image (rare at the time) of the deceased in majesty. It is, then, not a *representacion au vif* as opposed to a *representacion de la mort*; rather it is, if one may say so, a *representacion de l'âme bienheureuse* as opposed to a *representacion de l'être humain:* a new "humanistic" substitute for the image of the soul in the guise of a little nude figure carried aloft by angels. And where this childlike image is retained (as in the tomb of Archbishop Saltarelli) the "elevated" donor's portrait is, consequently, absent.

In short, the kneeling donor's portrait on Italian wall tombs from those of Clement IV and Cardinal de Braye (fig. 333) to that of Cardinal Roverella (fig. 340) is not an "effigy." When Guido Mazzoni in his tomb of Charles VIII (fig. 325) removed the kneeling figure from the throne room of the Madonna and deprived it of a celestial sponsor, this isolation and monumentalization amounted to a promotion of what had been an adjunct of the effigy to the status of an effigy in its own right: an effigy which shows the deceased not only restored to life but endowed with the capacity for self-determined action. Small wonder that, wherever this emancipated kneeling figure recurs in later monuments, the traditional *representacion au vif* (viz., the effigy recumbent but apparently alive and splendidly arrayed) invariably disappears whereas the *representacion de la mort* (viz., the representation of the enshrouded corpse) may be retained.

The number of such monuments, all directly or indirectly derived from the tomb of Charles VIII, is legion. But we can easily see that so radical an innovation could not be accepted without some resistance, even in a milieu as progressive as that of Margaret of Austria.

The tombs at Brou—erected, we recall, under her close personal supervision and retaining the traditional contrast between the *representacion au vif* and the *representacion de la mort*—do not as yet accept the kneeling effigy even though distinctly modernistic tendencies, among them the admission of the Virtues, are evident in other respects.

These three magnificent monuments (figs. 341–45) are carefully graded according to rank so as to solve what must have been a most intricate problem in funerary etiquette. Margaret of Austria, Governess of the Netherlands and daughter of a German Emperor (Maximilian I), was buried in the chapel of a monastery that stands in territory belonging to her third—and only real—husband, Philibert of Savoy (who in 1504 had left her a widow of only twenty-two), and had been founded—at least vowed—by the latter's mother, Margaret of Bourbon. There had, therefore, to be three tombs. And while Philibert's deserved distinction on the grounds of territorial and matrimonial precedence, that of his wife demanded distinction on the ground of her imperial status. The problem was dealt with in the most ingenious manner. The tomb of Philibert is a "double-decker tomb" placed in the very center of the choir so as to dominate the whole ensemble; it is the only one of the three structures visible to a beholder entering the church from the west. It has, however, no canopy. The tomb of Margaret of Austria is also a "double-decker tomb," and it is also a freestanding monument. It is, however, placed off center, jutting out into space between the choir and southern transept; but this less prominent position is counterbalanced by the fact that it does have a canopy. The tomb of Margaret of Bourbon, finally, faces that of her daughter-in-law; but it is inferior to hers not only because of the less favorable implications of the north as opposed to the south, but also in that it is recessed into a wall that separates the choir from the sacristy, in that it lacks a canopy, and in that it shows the deceased only once, *en gisant* but *au vif*.

While the ensemble of these tombs was devised by an artist named Jan van Roome and executed by a group of minor masters, the five effigies (as well as the enchanting putti) were reserved for Lady Margaret's favorite sculptor, Conrat Meit, who began his work in 1526. These effigies—which, at the special request of the Governess and against the suggestion of her chief adviser, Jean Lemaire de Belges, display the natural beauty of the material (marble and alabaster) without any coloring—rank among the noblest products of funerary sculpture: Conrad Meit's unsurpassed talent for complex and exuberant detail was matched by his discretion in expressing the contrast between the *representacion au vif* and the *representacion de la mort*—terms, incidentally, which I have borrowed from the very contract concluded between him and his patroness. His *transis* are still sharply distinguished from his *gisants* (it is, in my opinion, confusing to extend the latter term to recumbent images represented as mere corpses, regardless of their social status in life); but they are no longer horrid, let alone repulsive. Death, here conceived as the "brother to Sleep" rather than as the "fell sergeant," has deprived the princes of their rank but neither of their beauty nor their human dignity.

In this respect the spirit of the Renaissance asserted itself even within the realm of the macabre. While Northern sixteenth-century art continued to contrast the effigy of the living—now mostly "activated"—with that of the dead, it attempted to avoid, as far as possible, the more lurid aspects of the Late Gothic *transi* (not to be confused with such representations of death in person as Ligier Richier's world-famous statue on the tomb of René de Châlons in Bar-le-Duc); and the presence of vermin, as in the effigy of Jeanne de Bourbon, Countess of Auvergne (now in the Louvre; fig. 347), tends to be rare after 1500.

In the tombs at Brou, then, the *representacions au vif* have retained their traditional, recumbent position. Not so in the nearly contemporary monument of Louis XII and Anne de Bretagne already mentioned (fig. 324). Here the recumbent effigies have been replaced—under the influence, of course, of the tomb of Louis's predecessor, Charles VIII—by kneeling figures intently praying before their *prie-dieu* (fig. 346); and it is these activated effigies—so thoroughly different from the "sponsored donors" in the Italian wall tombs—which are, for the first time in a tomb commemorating a reigning king and queen of France, contrasted with the portrayals of Their Majesties as *transis*. These *transis*, like those at Brou, do not show any marks of decay. In the faces of Louis XII and Anne de Bretagne (fig. 348), particularly in that of the latter, the sculptors even managed to capture a diaphanous, Cimmerian beauty which would have been the envy of the Pre-Raphaelites—or, for that matter, of Rodin when he attempted his *Paolo and Francesca*. We are, however, not spared (which seems to be a *hapax legomenon)* the horrifying aspect of the sutures resulting from the removal of the heart and entrails prior to embalming and burial (fig. 349)—a process to which the history of art owes some extraordinary monuments.[1]

Since in the case of exalted personages some kind of sacredness attached to every part of their bodies, the organs removed before embalming were often bequeathed by their previous owners to certain favorite churches or monasteries (William the Conqueror, for example, whose body reposes in St.-Etienne at Caen, left his heart to the Cathedral of Rouen and his entrails to the church of Châlus). Here they were given separate burial, so to speak, and in medieval times these "tombeaux des entrailles" of the French nobles, particularly monarchs, were distinguished from those marking the resting place of their bodies chiefly by a symbolic bag or purse placed upon the breast of the effigy. At times, they were smaller in size, as is the case with the tiny images produced by Jean de Liège for the "tombeau des entrailles" of Charles IV and Jeanne d'Evreux (now in the Louvre); but more often than not they were as nearly life-sized as the regular effigies; suffice it to compare André Beauneveu's statue on the tomb proper of Charles V (d. 1380), still in St.-Denis (fig. 350), with the same master's statue on the "tombeau des entrailles," transferred to the Louvre from the monastery of Maubuisson (fig. 351).

The Renaissance dispensed with an effigy on the "tombeau des entrailles" but elaborated, instead, the resting place of the heart. The urn enclosing the heart of Francis I, executed by Pierre Bontemps in 1550 (figs. 352, 409–12), is comparatively modest in size and remarkable for its iconography—to which we shall revert—rather than for its not very felicitous form. But other "heart monuments," e. g., that for the heart of Louis, Cardinal of Bourbon and Archbishop of Reims, and that of Charles de Balsac, formerly in Noyon Cathedral, grew into enormous columns which, in at least one case, that of the Connétable Anne de Montmorency, could form the center of a whole chapel;[2] and Germain Pilon's monument for the heart of

[1] Cf. now R. E. Giesey, *The Royal Funeral Ceremony in Renaissance France* (Travaux d'Humanisme et Renaissance, XXXVII), Geneva, 1960.

[2] For the heart monuments of Louis, Cardinal of Bourbon, see Cabinet des Estampes, Rés. Pe 1, Tome 1, fol. 39. For that of Charles de Balsac, Rés. Pe 3, fol. 21; for the general disposition of

Henry II (fig. 353), executed only ten years after that for the heart of Francis I, is one of the most beautiful things in the Louvre.

To revert, after this brief excursion into the province of the *Embalmers' Quarterly*, to the main subject of our discussion: after its first appearance on the tomb of Charles VIII, the kneeling effigy successfully challenged the recumbent one for more than two centuries and far beyond the borders of France. Here the tomb of Louis XII and Anne de Bretagne was imitated as well as criticized in that of his successor, Francis I (d. 1547), and his wife Claude, a daughter of Anne de Bretagne (fig. 354), which owes its architectural framework to Philibert de l'Orme and its rather pedestrian sculptural decoration to Pierre Bontemps (figs. 328–30). Even without this sculptural decoration, where the Resurrection of Christ, hidden within the vault, is all but eclipsed by representations of battle scenes, the king's passage over the Alps and a triumph *all'antica*, the very fact that the whole structure consciously emulates a Roman triumphal arch would proclaim the intention to glorify the exploits of the "grand François" rather than provide for the salvation of his soul; but the gloomy, tunnellike interior of this triumphal arch shelters again the effigies of the king and his queen *en transis*, and on its platform the kneeling images have multiplied into a whole family—an arrangement soon to be duplicated in Pompeo Leoni's tombs of Charles V and Philip II in the Escorial (fig. 355).

And as the work of the Giusti brothers was criticized by Philibert de l'Orme and Pierre Bontemps, their work in turn was criticized by Primaticcio and Germain Pilon in their resplendent monument of Henry II and Catherine de Médicis (fig. 331), already mentioned in connection with the problem of the Virtues. Now we can appreciate it as both the climax and the end of the development that had begun with the tomb of Louis XII and Anne de Bretagne—viz., the combination of kneeling effigies *au vif* with recumbent *transis*—a concept eagerly adopted by both the aristocracy and the high clergy and occasionally resulting in the paradoxical spectacle of a great gentleman praying to God directly behind his own corpse (fig. 356).

Far from inspiring horror (as does an *abbozzo* produced by Girolamo della Robbia and rejected because he took too seriously the command to represent the queen, then forty-five, "as she would look a few days after death"; fig. 357), Pilon's magnificent nudes (fig. 358)—the king reminiscent of an Achilles or Patroclus, the queen, perhaps intentionally, of a *Venus pudica*—inspire a feeling of admiration for strength and beauty, intensified rather than diminished by the idea of mortality. Their spirit is, like that of Greek tragedy, heroic rather than devout. But just for this reason we can understand that the days of the *transi* were numbered, and it was Catherine de Médicis herself who, near the end of her life, explicitly repudiated it.

In 1583, when the grandiose but subsequently abandoned plan for a "Chapelle des Valois"—to be added to the basilica of St.-Denis as a mausoleum for Catherine, her husband, and her children, and dominated by a magnificent Resurrection group from the hand of Germain Pilon (fig. 359)—seemed to be nearing completion, she ordered, for the basilica proper, a second monument displaying only her and Henry II's effigies *en gisant:* a monument opposing high medieval formality to modern sentiment—a monument, in fact, which is no more nor less than an attempt at reconstructing a royal *tumba* of the thirteenth or fourteenth centuries. As if wishing to deny what the earlier tomb had affirmed, Catherine de Médicis had herself and her husband (here bearing a remarkable resemblance to Edward VII of England) represented in even more ritualistic fashion than, say, Philip the Bold or Blanche of Castile: stiffly recumbent in full regalia, crowned with the "imperial" crown, hands joined in prayer, and only the eyes, particularly those of the queen, revealing a spirit very different from that of the Middle Ages (figs. 360, 361).

the figures originally surrounding the monument for the heart of Anne de Montmorency (the column itself now in the Louvre),   Rés. Pe 11, fols. 15, 16.

The kneeling figure minus the *transi* survived for many centuries in its native France, where it could even be incorporated into the context of a wall tomb (fig. 362) or, sometimes in so grotesque a fashion as in the monument of Jean de Salazar and Marie de la Trémouille (formerly in Sens Cathedral; fig. 363), into that of a table tomb, and it remained the leading type for a long time to come; we may refer, apart from the comparatively modest works of Barthélemy Boudin, Gilles Guérin, and Jacques Sarrasin, to Antoine Coyzevox's well-known tombs of Mazarin and Colbert. It also survived in Spain, in the Netherlands, in Germany (where it supplanted, in the tomb of Maximilian, a recumbent image contemplated as late as 1527), and in England. In Italy, however, the kneeling image occurs, before its rehabilitation by Bernini, only sporadically and—apart from the tombs of Paul V and Sixtus V in S. Maria Maggiore—mostly in centers open to French or Spanish influence, such as Naples, Sicily, Turin, and Genoa.

One of the latest and most beautiful *transis*,[1] another masterpiece of Germain Pilon, belongs to the tomb of Valentine Balbiani (figs. 364–366), wife of the ill-famed Chancellor René de Birague.[2] Commissioned shortly after her death in 1572 but probably not begun until about 1580, this exquisite work, showing the dead woman in a state of extreme emaciation which moves and even ennobles rather than repels, is no longer a statue in the round but a flat relief; and by virtue of its very delicacy this flat relief played only a comparatively unobtrusive part within the ensemble, of which, unfortunately, only fragments have come down to us. The image of death is here subordinated to the image of life; and the latter in turn exemplifies a form of activation which we have not encountered thus far: the lady, accompanied by her lap dog, is represented neither recumbent nor kneeling but reclining in a restful meditative attitude, turned toward the beholder so as to give the impression of facing him. The upper part of her body is slightly raised, and while one hand gracefully holds a prayer book, the other supports her head with the age-old gesture of "sweetly sad" sorrow.

Of this reclining pose it has been said: "The mediaeval *gisant* has raised himself and, in recollection of the Antique, rests on his elbow as on Etruscan tombs."[3] Yet there is reason to doubt that the undeniable similarity between these *statues accoudées* (sporadically accepted in France from the times of Pierre Bontemps but so unfamiliar in other Northern countries that John Webster could ridicule them, as late as 1611–12, as a "new fashion" according to which "princes' images on their tombs do not lie, as they were wont, seeming to pray up to heaven, but with their hands under their cheeks as if they had died of the toothache")[4] and the effigies on Etruscan—and Roman—sarcophagi can be sufficiently explained by the direct imitation of classical models.

Such a direct imitation of the Antique might be expected to take place—and actually did take place in the further course of events—in Italy, where the reclining attitude occurs at a considerably earlier date.

---

[1] For a somewhat belated *transi*—which is, however, of Dutch rather than French origin and quite "unschrecklich," as Lessing would say, in that the deceased is shown as he looked directly after death and is decorously arrayed in a kind of dressing gown and nightcap—see Hendrik de Keyser's tomb of William the Silent in the Nieuwe Kerk at Delft (executed from 1614 to 1623; fig. 413).

[2] For an interesting and in part rather attractive group of late-sixteenth-century *transis* in Châlons-sur-Marne, see L. Pressouyre, "Sculptures funéraires du XVIᵉ siècle à Châlons-sur-Marne," *Gazette des Beaux-Arts*, 6th ser., LIX, 1962, pp. 143 ff.

[3] M. E. Sainte-Beuve, "La statue tombale de Marguerite de Mandelot," *Gazette des Beaux-Arts*, 6th ser., XLVIII, 1956, pp. 61 ff.

[4] *Duchess of Malfi*, IV, 2. The development of the "activated" effigy is nicely summarized in the poem prefixed to Dart's *Westminster* (ca. 1723), quoted in K. A. Esdaile and S. Sitwell, *op. cit.*, p. 54:

Upon their backs the ancient Statues lie,
Devoutly fix'd, with Hands uplifted high,
Intreating Pray'rs of all the passers-by.
At length they changed the Posture by degrees,
And plac'd the Marble Vot'ry on its knees,
There Warriors rough devoutly Heav'n adore,
And Statesmen kneel who never knelt before . . .
Next a less pious Posture they provide,
On Cushion lolling, stretch'd with careless Pride;
With wringing Hands the little Cherubs moan,
And Fun'ral Lamps appear to blaze in stone,
And Marble Urns with juster Beauty stand,
And rich Relievo shows the Master's Hand,
On the neat Altar with a Busto grac'd
In Roman Pride, like that which Sheffyld plac'd.

But in Italy itself images of this kind cannot be traced back beyond Andrea Sansovino's twin tombs of Cardinals Girolamo Rosso and Ascanio Sforza in S. Maria del Popolo (fig. 367). These memorable monuments—memorable also because they, the works of a Tuscan, first introduced into the Eternal City a type of wall tomb derived from Roman triumphal arches (fig. 368) but apparently developed in Venice—were not begun until 1505 and 1507 respectively. They thus considerably postdate a most extraordinary group of Spanish tombs, all products of the same workshop, in which the step from the recumbent to the reclining effigy had been taken from ten to twenty-five years before and the style of which evinces the influence of the French *détente* rather than that of classical antiquity: the tombs of Don Iñigo López de Mendoza, first Count of Tendilla (d. 1479), and his wife in San Ginés, Guadalajara (figs. 369, 370), and that of Don Martín Vázquez de Arce (d. 1486) in the cathedral of nearby Sigüenza (fig. 371).

Far from expressing, as Webster charged, the mundanity of persons who, instead of fixing their eyes "upon the stars," seem to turn their faces "upon the world," these tombs are pervaded by a spirit, perhaps specifically Spanish, of somber piety. In all of them religious books play a prominent part, and while the Mendoza couple still maintain an attitude halfway between the *statue accoudée* and the recumbent image, Don Martín Vázquez de Arce (called, in contradistinction to his father, the "Doncel") has raised himself to a position strikingly similar to that here under discussion. And while the Count and Countess of Tendilla and the "Doncel" are not shown "with their hands under their cheeks," this posture of melancholy contemplation is represented by the disconsolate armorbearers crouching at the feet of their effigies.

For both stylistic and iconographical reasons I am, therefore, inclined to believe that these studious Spanish *demi-gisants*, as we may call them, are derived from representations of melancholy poets or philosophers reclining on their beds—representations particularly frequent in French fifteenth-century art and popularized by woodcuts precisely at the time when the statues at San Ginés and Sigüenza were carved. A comparison between the "Doncel" and, for example, the frontispiece of *Les Faits Maistre Alain Chartier* (fig. 372), printed at Paris in 1489, speaks for itself. If this hypothesis—and it is no more than that—should be accepted, these Spanish monuments would confront us with a last pseudomorphosis—a pseudomorphosis, however, which in this case was a prelude to actual influence: Andrea Sansovino, who was in the Iberian peninsula from 1491 to 1493 and then again from 1496 to 1501, may have remembered the tombs at San Ginés and Sigüenza, but, after his arrival in Rome, he revised them *all'antica*.

Once introduced into the main stream of Europe an funerary art, the *demi-gisant*, whatever its antecedents, became no less popular and, because of its greater flexibility, even more fruitful than the kneeling effigy. A married couple or a pair of brothers could be combined in innumerable different ways: in stately, slightly bored companionship, as in Pierre-Etienne Monnot's tomb of John Cecil, fifth Earl of Exeter, and his wife (fig. 373); in animated conversation, as in Francesco Aprile's Bolognetti tomb in the church of Gesù e Maria in Rome (fig. 374); or even, in England, in such a way that the privilege of facing eternity in a state of moderate wakefulness was reserved to the husband while his lady—placed, as was fairly usual in British tombs, on a lower level—had to be satisfied with perpetual recumbency (fig. 375). Much more important, however, is the fact that the reclining but activated effigy could be interpreted, depending on whether the occupant of the tomb was thought of as dead or still alive, either as the portrayal of a person rising from the grave—a concept always fraught with the danger of involuntary humor, as when Jean-Baptiste Pigalle's emaciated Claude Henri d'Harcourt (Paris, Notre-Dame) half emerges from his bier as from a bathtub, but also capable of producing a monument as moving as Jean-Baptiste Tuby's tomb of Julienne Le Bé (fig. 376), the mother of Charles Le Brun—or as the portrayal of a person giving up his ghost to God. Since Giovanni Pisano's "Resurrection" of Margaret of Brabant (fig. 338) was too bold an anticipation to have any immediate following, it is in Sansovino's *demi-gisants* that we may recognize the ancestors, however remote, of Pigalle's triumphal Maréchal de Saxe, as well as of Girardon's dying Richelieu (fig. 377) and even Bernini's Lodovica Albertoni (fig. 444).

The kneeling effigy, then, is essentially French, and the reclining effigy or *demi-gisant* is Italian only insofar as it was adapted to Renaissance standards in Rome rather than in its homeland, Spain. No one, however, can dispute to Italy a third possibility of activating the effigy: that of representing the deceased on horseback.

In the North only one instance of this kind seems to have been preserved: the tomb of Louis de Brézé (the husband of Diane de Poitiers) in Rouen Cathedral (fig. 378); it was constructed, probably over a period of time, during the years following his death in 1531. This stately monument is a modernized *enfeu*, crowned by a winged allegorical female whose attributes include the bridle of Temperance, the sword of Fortitude and Justice, and the serpent of Prudence and who is seated on a throne of thorns symbolic of both Patience and "Virtue in general." The deceased was originally represented three times: as a *transi* recumbent on a "Roman" sarcophagus; in a bust portrait (now lost) emerging from behind this sarcophagus; and in an equestrian statue whose architectural and sculptural enframement must be ascribed to none other than Jean Goujon. Apart from this monument only one other French example has come to my notice: the tomb of Nicolas du Châtelet who fell in the battle of Dreux in 1562, originally in the Church of Vauvillars (Haute-Saône) and now entirely destroyed (fig. 379).[1]

The intrusion of an over-life-sized equestrian statue upon a Christian tomb seems so unusual that the most recent and very expert discussion of the monument of Louis de Brézé, referring to it as "unique," explains the motif as a borrowing from secular architecture such as the castles of Blois (fig. 380) or Assier. That this assumption is not necessary is evident, however, from so well known a monument as Giovanni Antonio Amadeo's tomb of Bartolommeo Colleoni in Bergamo (1470–76; fig. 381); and this tomb—the equestrian statue carved in wood and gilded, the rest of the decoration executed in stone and exhibiting a particularly incongruous mixture of Christian scenes, classical heroes, and Virtues—has a long history.

The equestrian statue was, so much is true, of secular origin, and in the religious art of the Middle Ages a figure on horseback often suggested the vice of Pride. On the other hand, the most famous of the equestrian statues left by classical antiquity, the *Marcus Aurelius* on the Capitol, had come to be reinterpreted as a monument to Constantine, that is to say, to the victory of Christianity over paganism; and in this capacity it was repeated, about thirty times, in Romanesque art. When these pseudo-Constantines had disappeared at the beginning of the thirteenth century, the equestrian statue was resecularized, so to speak: it was revived as a monument of civic liberties or civic pride, first in sculpture, as in Benedetto Antelami's *Oldrado da Tresseno* (1233) in the Palazzo della Ragione at Milan, later in painting, as in Simone Martini's *Guidoriccio de' Fogliani* (1328) in the Palazzo Pubblico at Siena.

At the same time (to be precise, from the turn of the thirteenth century), the equestrian figure invaded the domain of funerary sculpture; but this invasion was, significantly, independent of what was going on in the town halls and in the market squares. In funerary art, the development of the equestrian figure did not begin, as might be expected, with monumental images bestowing upon the deceased the quiet dignity of a Roman emperor and ultimately derived from classical prototypes. It rather began with a small-sized relief which portrays the deceased brandishing his sword and galloping into battle as is the case on countless Gothic seals. It was only after the evolution had run its course for nearly one and a half centuries that the great masters of the Quattrocento could reapproach, not to say rediscover, such monuments as the *Marcus Aurelius*, or the so-called *Regisole* at Pavia.

The relief in question (we can safely dismiss as a charming curiosity a niello plaque of ca. 1260 in St.-Memmie near Châlons-sur-Marne which shows a young knight named Thiébauz Rupez as a mounted

[1]   This tomb had already been removed and dismantled, "ôtée et cassée," when Dom A. Calmet (*Histoire généalogique de la Maison Châtelet*, Nancy, 1741, pp. 203 ff.) saw the fragments collected by "le Sieur Poisson demeurant à Vauvillars" and "incrustées dans le mur de son cabinet avec une copie de l'Epithaphe."

falconer accompanied by his two dogs—as if some drawing by Villard d'Honnecourt had been incongruously fitted into the trapezoidal space of the slab) is found in the second cloister of SS. Annunziata at Florence (fig. 382) and commemorates one Guilelmus (allegedly surnamed Beraldus or Berardus). Lieutenant (Balius) to Amerigo of Narbonne, who saved the day for the Florentines at Campaldino in 1289, he had been killed in this battle, and there can be little doubt that his unusual heroization was meant to honor a nobleman, presumably of French extraction, who, fighting side by side with Dante, had given his life for the cause of Florence. Small wonder that his tombstone represents him as he must have appeared on his seal—the typical seal of a Gothic knight, exemplified by countless instances in France and England (fig. 383).[1]

In Tuscany this monument of ca. 1290—remarkably "Gothic" even in style—remained, significantly, without immediate following. In North Italy, however, beginning with the Scaligeri tombs at Verona, we can observe what amounts to an Ascension of the Horse.

The fairly modest sarcophagus of Alberto I della Scala (d. 1301) already represents the prince on horseback (fig. 384). But this equestrian image is still executed in relief and placed between two saints, St. James the Great and Mary Magdalene; the corners of the lid are guarded by the symbols of the Evangelists, and on the rear wall Alberto is shown kneeling before the Virgin. The tomb of Cangrande della Scala, already mentioned in a different context, offers a very different aspect. It is no longer a simple sarcophagus but an enormous structure attached to the church (fig. 385). The reliefs on the sarcophagus tell the story of Cangrande's life (fig. 386) and eulogize him as the great statesman and military leader that he was (though one of them still displays the Man of Sorrows and the Annunciation). On top of this sarcophagus there is Cangrande's effigy reposing on a *lit de parade*, his eyes closed but his round face still "pleno de alegreça," "full of cheer," as a contemporary poet puts it. The whole structure, however, is surmounted by his equestrian statue, his posture and facial expression proclaiming the triumph of a personality (fig. 387) which even in death glows with superior intelligence, lordly, good-natured insouciance, and no small measure of self-satisfaction.

This towering monument established a special and long-lasting tradition in North Italy. The tomb of Cangrande as well as those of his successors (Mastino II and Cansignorio) were still outside their family church. But even before the century was over, the horse of Bernabò Visconti (d. 1385) forced its way into the church's interior: Visconti's rather unattractive equestrian statue, flanked by two Virtues and surmounting a sarcophagus which exhibits saints and scenes from the Passion, was originally placed directly behind the main altar of S. Giovanni in Conca at Milan. In the first decade of the fifteenth century, in the monument of the *condottiere* Paolo Savelli (d. 1405) in the Frari Church at Venice (fig. 388), the noble animal, already reminiscent of the Antique in its ceremonial gait but placed upon a still Gothic sarcophagus, was incorporated in a wall tomb; and this new type developed, roughly, in three directions.

On its North Italian home ground[2] the equestrian wall tomb, as it may be called, acquired the somewhat hybrid style exemplified by the Colleoni tomb in Bergamo. In the provincial environment of the Abruzzi a kind of regressive transformation produced the charming monument of Lello II Camponeschi at Aquila (d. 1432 and, significantly, the work of a Northerner named Gualtiero d'Alemagna; fig. 389), where the sarcophagus of the young nobleman—its reliefs showing the Coronation of the Virgin between Apostles and Prophets—is surmounted by a composition which may be described as a "goldenes Rössel" in stone, a characteristic reflection of the "International Style" of about 1400. Fusing the equestrian motif with the elements of a regular *enfeu* in a semi-pictorial space not subjected to any archi-

---

[1] Another image of a knight derived from a seal occurs on the sarcophagus of Sire de Palays in the Musée des Augustins, Toulouse (reproduced in *Trésors des Musées de Province*, I, Paris 1957); its significance, however, seems to be purely heraldic.

[2] I owe to my friend Michelangelo Muraro the acquaintance with a somewhat out-of-the-way article where further information about equestrian tomb statues in Venetian territory may be found: F. Pappani, "Delle Statue equestri erette a'suoi Capitani Generali di Terra dalla Repubblica di Venezia," *Bollettino d'Arti, Industrie, Numismatica e Curiosità Veneziane*, III, 1880, pp. 72 ff.

tectural organization, this composition shows the young nobleman's effigy *en gisant* extended on the ground and guarded by his faithful dog as well as two ministering angels; but in the background, emerging on a rocky ledge, he appears once more on horseback, mounted on an enormous, bashful-looking steed that has abandoned all aspirations to classical grandeur. In Florence, finally, where the tombstone of 1289 had failed to produce a continuous tradition, two great Quattrocento painters, vying with each other in an attempt to prove that the brush is no less powerful an instrument than the chisel, commemorated two loyal *condottieri* in murals which, while merely simulating such equestrian wall tombs as actually existed in North Italy, surpass them in plastic volume and rhythmic energy and resolutely deny the Gothic past in favor of a purely "classical" style: Paolo Uccello's *Giovanni Acuto* (John Hawkwood) of 1436 (fig. 390) and Andrea del Castagno's *Niccolò da Tolentino* of 1456 (fig. 391).

So powerful was the tradition established by the Scaligeri tombs and culminating in these two murals that it produced a curious repercussion—or, to put it colloquially, boomeranged—in Donatello's *Gattamelata* (fig. 392) on the southwest corner of the Santo in Padua (1446–47). To all practical intents and purposes this world-renowned monument has nothing to do with funerary art: the body of the great *condottiere* is safely buried inside the church. Yet it was thought fitting to elaborate its enormous pedestal into the likeness of a mortuary chamber (fig. 393) identified as such by the telltale motif of the Door of Hades, which we remember so well from Roman sarcophagi and which Donatello employed, with a subtle variation, not once but twice: the door on the east side (fig. 394), facing the church, is (as in several classical examples) very slightly ajar so as to convey the idea of "entrance";[1] whereas that on the west side, facing the "world," is firmly closed so as to convey the idea of "no exit." Here the development has come full circle. Owing to its long association with tombs, the equestrian statue, originally secular, had acquired so strong a sepulchral flavor that its first reappearance as a public monument had to be justified, as it were, by its apparent conversion into a cenotaph.

The equestrian statue was not the only secular—or, at least, nonsepulchral—image to be interpolated, ex post facto, so to speak, into the schema of a funerary monument. The same thing happened, also in Italy and also in the early decades of the fourteenth century, to what may be called the "image in majesty," viz., the statue of a ruler enthroned. But while the funerary adaptation of the equestrian statue produced a continuous tradition which, however, did not normally outlast the fifteenth century (the tombs of Louis de Brézé and Nicolas de Châtelet are, from an Italian point of view, anachronisms), the funerary adaptation of the image in majesty—directly subjecting the beholder to the power of one who, in a sense, continues to "bear rule over all the earth"—remained exceptional until the very end of the Quattrocento. In fact, only three major instances are known in all Trecento art: the tomb of an emperor, the tomb of a king who was this emperor's most formidable enemy, and the tomb of this king's son.[2]

[1] In an even more "classicistic" spirit this motif was employed in an impressive design for a tomb by Rubens (Amsterdam, Rijksprentenkabinet; see J. S. Held, "Rubens' Designs for Sepulchral Monuments," *Art Quarterly*, XXIII, 1960, pp. 247 ff., fig. 2).

[2] We must exclude, I think, the tomb of Philippe de Courtenay, titular king of Constantinople (d. 1283) in the Lower Church of Assisi. Whether this tomb was produced by Ramo di Paganello immediately after Philippe de Courtenay's death (as proposed by W. R. Valentiner, "The Master of the Tomb of Philippe de Courtenay at Assisi," *Art Quarterly*, XIV, 1951, pp. 3 ff.) or by an anonymous master some twenty or thirty years later (so, among others, G. Gerossa, "Chi è il Sovrano sepolto in San Francesco d'Assisi?", *Dedalo*, VIII, 1927–28, pp. 67 ff.), it is generally admitted that it belongs to the type best represented by Arnolfo di Cambio's tomb of Cardinal de Braye (fig. 333). And it is plainly impossible, both from an aesthetic point of view and from the point of view of funereal etiquette, that a monument of this close-knit group (cf. the tombs of Bishop Durandus, fig. 334, Cardinal Rodriguez, Matteo d'Acquasparta and Pope Boniface VIII, fig. 335) should have been planned in such a way that the image of the Virgin Mary, shifted off axis, shares the space of the upper zone (symbolizing the celestial spheres!) with an effigy which portrays the deceased not sponsored by a saint and reverently kneeling before our Lady but in lone splendor, seated with legs haughtily crossed and, to make things worse, with a lion at his feet. The inevitable conclusion, I believe, is that, when the tomb was set up, the normal "sponsored donor's group" and its counterpart had remained unexecuted or, possibly, had been destroyed or defaced by some accident; and that the present arrangement of the upper zone (though demonstrably antedating 1580) is a makeshift affair which combines the Madonna with an effigy originally destined for an entirely different, secular purpose.

The tomb of the emperor (fig. 395), again a work of that great innovator, Tino di Camaino, is that of Henry VII (d. 1313), which has been reconstructed from a number of fragments preserved in the Camposanto at Pisa. If this reconstruction is correct (and it is not without significance that just the elements here under discussion are still thought by some to belong to a secular monument and not to a tomb), the emperor was represented twice: below, as a conventional *gisant* attended by curtain-drawing angels; above, enthroned and surrounded by four of his councilors, who are shown standing (fig. 396).

In more modest form, the effigy "in majesty" recurs in the center of Tino di Camaino's tomb of Charles of Calabria (d. 1328; fig. 397); and a climax of monumentality—not only as regards the size and position of the effigy but also in that the whole monument is a three-dimensional *edificium* set into space like a rood screen—is reached in the tomb of Charles of Calabria's father, Robert of Anjou (d. 1343; fig. 398), executed by two minor Florentine sculptors named Giovanni and Pace and already mentioned on a previous occasion. Here the king, protected by the Apostles as well as the Virtues (both represented by statuettes ensconced in the framework), recurs no fewer than four times. In the bottom zone he is portrayed in the center of his family; above that, he lies in state on a *lit de parade* (fig. 399); high up, within an arch whose gable shows Christ in an angel-borne mandorla, he appears as a "sponsored donor" presented to the Madonna by St. Francis and St. Clare; and in the large space between the lintel of this arch and the *lit de parade* he sits enthroned, orb and scepter in hand, an impassible idol which "fait le vide autour de lui."

None of these monuments, commemorating the most powerful men of their age, had much immediate following. The tomb of the well-known canonist, Cino dei Sinibaldi (d. 1337), in Pistoia Cathedral (fig. 400) may be defined as a scholastic parody of Tino's tomb of Henry VII: with the by now conventional "school scene" in mind, the artist—or, rather, artists—converted the statue of an emperor enthroned and flanked by four standing councilors into the statue of a professor (Cino, a native of Pistoia, had spent most of his life at Perugia and Bologna) delivering a lecture from his academic chair and flanked by six standing students. The tomb of René of Anjou (fig. 267; more fully discussed above) would seem to be dependent on that of Robert the Wise, but not only postdates the latter by more than a century, but intentionally distorts a monument of imperious power and pride into one of self-dispraise and frustration. And another work of Tino di Camaino's, the incompletely preserved tomb of Bishop Antonio degli Orsi (d. 1321) in Florence Cathedral (fig. 401), belongs in a totally different category. While it includes a portrait of the bishop on his episcopal throne, this portrait shows him dead instead of alive and is thus anything but an "image in majesty": far from being contrasted with a recumbent effigy, the seated figure is here nothing but a somewhat whimsical substitute for the former—which is confirmed by the fact that the otherwise customary *gisant* is conspicuously absent (fig. 402).

It was, as I have said, not until the very end of the fifteenth century that the "image in majesty" initiated a continuous tradition; and even then this tradition—except for such unusual cases as Hendrik de Keyser's tomb of William the Silent (figs. 413–416), which honors a *pater patriae*, or Michelangelo's Medici tombs (figs. 429, 430), where the effigies transcend the limitations of individual likenesses—gave expression to the spiritual power of the popes rather than to the temporal power of kings and emperors.

The decisive step was taken in the last work of Antonio Pollaiuolo, the tomb of Pope Innocent VIII (completed in 1498, the year of the artist's death) in St. Peter's (fig. 403).

In it the Pope is represented in two impressive statues. One, flanked by—or, if you like, set out against—four flat reliefs depicting the cardinal Virtues, shows him *in cathedra*; the other represents him *en gisant* on a sarcophagus now placed beneath the enthroned figure but originally set upon the mighty cornice surmounting it so that the Pope seemed to repose under the direct protection of the three theological Virtues that appear in a semicircular tympanum, the figure of Charity—centrally placed, enframed by a mandorla and seated—playing the part allotted to the Madonna in more conventional wall tombs.

The effigy *in cathedra* portrays the pontiff holding in his left hand not, as has occasionally been said, the "blade removed from the lance of heresy" but, on the contrary, the blade of the spear of Longinus, a precious relic which he had received, less than two months before his death on July 25, 1492, as a personal present from Sultan Bajazet and kept in his private apartments up to the very end. His right arm is raised in lordly benediction.

The Motif of the "Arts Bereft"

What Pollaiuolo has done in this monument is, needless to say, to incorporate into a wall tomb an image patterned upon those papal *Ehrenstatuen* which from the end of the thirteenth century were erected all over Italy in commemoration of visits or special benefactions and showed the Vicar of Christ *in cathedra* (fig. 404), extending his apostolic blessing to the individual community as well as to the faithful in general; in the cathedral of his native Florence, Pollaiuolo could even have seen the earliest extant representative of this species, the statue of Boniface VIII (1296). There would thus be no reason to suspect a direct connection between his tomb of Innocent VIII and that of Henry VII or Robert of Anjou—were it not for the curious fact that the tomb of Robert of Anjou anticipates the second papal monument produced by Pollaiuolo in the use of a motif then even more unusual than the "image in majesty": the Liberal Arts.

Taking the place of the traditional *pleureurs* and lamenting the death of a patron with similarly decorous gestures, all seven of the Liberal Arts appear behind the recumbent effigy of Robert the Wise; and here their presence can be explained—which seems to have been forgotten in more recent literature—by the direct and personal influence of the one man who so often embarrasses historians by doing or saying what should have been done or said only some one hundred or one hundred and fifty years later: Petrarch. Looking upon King Robert as a benefactor to whom he professed to owe the wreath of the poet laureate, he had composed an epitaph *(Epistolae poeticae*, II, 8), apparently intended for the monument itself since it begins with the line: "Hic sacra Magnanimi requiescunt ossa Roberti." And although none of Petrarch's words were inscribed on the monument (instead of his polished "Omnis in hoc virtus secum iacet orba sepulcro," we read the rather inelegant "Cernite Robertum regem virtute refertum"), one of his thoughts was incorporated in its iconography: "Morte sua viduae septem concorditer artes / Et musae flevere novem" ("Bereft by Robert's death, the Seven Arts, / Sharing their grief with the Nine Muses, wept").

That there may be more than coincidence in the similarity between Pollaiuolo's tomb of Innocent VIII and the much earlier monument to Robert of Anjou is indicated by the fact that Pollaiuolo revived this unique motif of the "Arts Bereft" in his first papal monument (completed in 1493), that of Innocent's predecessor, Sixtus IV (figs. 405, 406)—exactly one hundred and fifty years after the death of Robert the Wise.

In this astonishing monument, also of bronze and also preserved in St. Peter's, the *tumba* has grown into what may be described as a *tumulus*, a form much imitated, later on, all over Europe and particularly in Spain. It consists of a huge, oblong pyramid, truncated so that its upper surface has room not only for the recumbent effigy of the Pope (fig. 407), for his coat of arms and the commemorative inscription, but also for the seven Virtues (disposed, in anticipation of their arrangement on the tomb of Innocent VIII, in such a manner that Charity protects the pontiff's head while Hope and Faith hover above his shoulders). The concave slopes of this pyramid, however, show, for the first time since the tomb of Robert of Anjou, the Liberal Arts. The implication is still, needless to say, that they deplore the loss of a man who had both protected and mastered them; they differ from their fourteenth-century ancestresses—apart, of course, from the style—not only in that they do not show any grief, but also in that the orthodox heptad is augmented by Perspective (i. e., Optics) as well as by Philosophy and Theology, who share the place of honor near the head of the effigy. And the spirit of the *rinascimento dell'antichità* is eloquently manifested by the representation of Theology (fig. 408) in the guise of a nude, reclining Diana—a bold equation justified by the fact that sacred doctrine was believed to be illumined yet dazzled by the light of the Trinity (which, therefore, here appears as a triple head encircled by a flaming halo) much as the moon-goddess is by the light of the sun.

Once reintroduced and reformulated by Pollaiuolo, both the idea of portraying the departed enthroned and the idea of including personifications other than the Virtues were eagerly accepted and elaborated in later funerary art. The statue of Innocent VIII *in cathedra* set a pattern followed, with suitable concessions to the style and fashion of the day, by artists such as Bandinelli (or, rather, Nanni di Baccio Bigio), Guglielmo della Porta, Baldassare Longhena, Alessandro Algardi, Pierre Legros, and, as we shall see, Bernini. And the Liberal Arts on the tomb of Sixtus IV not only "multiplied after their kind" but also underwent all sorts of interesting mutations.

The reliefs on the urn formerly containing the heart of Francis I (figs. 409–12), already mentioned, reveal, rather engagingly, that this heart had belonged to the concrete and imaginative rather than to the abstract and intellectual forms of human endeavor: grammar, rhetoric, dialectic, and arithmetic are banished, whereas astronomy, geometry, two kinds of music (instrumental and vocal), poetry, and the "three arts of design," architecture, sculpture, and painting, are admitted. And in the end the personifications seen on tombs could range from Time and Death to Piety, Fame or the Genius of Mankind, from the Spirit of Filial or Conjugal Love to *La France*, *Italia* (e. g., on the tomb of Vittorio Alfieri), or other fatherlands. A particularly fascinating example is Hendrik de Keyser's tomb of William the Silent (figs. 413–16), already mentioned. Here the great liberator—represented, we recall, both *en transi* and enthroned, though both these effigies are on the same level—is protected by obelisks (symbols of the "gloria dei principi"), glorified by Fame and extolled by four personifications borrowed, with minor changes, from Ripa's *Iconologia*: Justice, Fortitude (here also standing for Patience, since she holds a thorn in her right hand), Religion (with book and church model), and Liberty *(Aurea Libertas)* who carries a scepter and a hat because the Roman ritual of *manumissio* (the freeing of a slave) included the ceremonial covering of the future citizen's head with a hat or cap *(pileus)*.

The influence of Pollaiuolo's tombs extended even to the most famous and titanic funerary monuments ever undertaken in the Christian Era: Michelangelo's tomb of Pope Julius II (d. 1513) and his Medici Chapel—each of them surrounded by problems which have given rise to entire libraries and are in part still unsolved.

As commissioned and designed (for St. Peter's) in 1505, the tomb of Julius II—a nephew of Sixtus IV—was a big, freestanding mausoleum of impressive proportions (about 24 feet wide and 36 feet long) whose dark interior, apparently the earliest elliptical room in modern architecture, was to house the Pope's sarcophagus. As far as its architectural structure and sculptural decoration are concerned, we know for certain that the lower story of the front wall—essentially corresponding to that of the rear wall—is faithfully reflected in that drawing (fig. 417) which has been mentioned in connection with a Roman sarcophagus familiar to, and used by, Michelangelo. This front wall showed, on either side of a door, a niche containing a winged Victory with a vanquished foe at her feet and flanked by hermae to which nude "Slaves" are fettered; the only question is whether the much longer side walls were also articulated by two or, as I prefer to think, three of such niche-and-hermae units.

As to the rest, we depend on Michelangelo's two biographers, Giorgio Vasari and Ascanio Condivi, whose descriptions—written about half a century after the fact and combining with information supplied by Michelangelo and the evidence of old drawings (or, possibly, a model) the authors' own impressions of the monument as finally erected—disagree in several respects. Certain it is that the corners of the second story were occupied by four seated statues one of which represented Moses (as for the three others, we are free to accept or to reject Vasari's assertion that they portrayed St. Paul, the Active Life, and the Contemplative Life); that space was left for bronze reliefs narrating "the exploits of so great a pontiff''; and that the whole structure culminated in two figures (according to Condivi, angels; according to Vasari, Cybele and Caelus) who carried what is variously described as an *arca* ("casket") and a *bara* (either "bier" or "litter"), their facial expression conveying the idea that the death of the Pope was lamented on earth and greeted with joy in heaven.

Neither of the biographers, it should be noted, explicitly mentions an effigy. There can be no doubt, however, that such an effigy was contemplated: in 1508 a blocked-out "figure of His Holiness" was shipped to Michelangelo from Carrara, and I am still convinced that it is this *abbozzo* which is identical with the unfinished papal statue found in Michelangelo's workshop after his death in 1564 and subsequently transformed, by the Lorraine sculptor Nicolas Cordier, into a *St. Gregory Enthroned*. This *St. Gregory* can still be seen in S. Gregorio al Cielo in Rome and would thus appear to demonstrate that the effigy on the tomb of 1505 was to represent the pontiff seated rather than recumbent (figs. 418, 419).[1] But even if this argument should be questioned, the fact remains that the word *bara* could and did designate in sixteenth-century usage a "litter" or *sella gestatoria* as well as a bier (no less illustrious an author than Machiavelli speaks of an old gentleman suffering from gout as suddenly making his appearance *portato in bara*, "borne on a litter," and the Italian translation of Seneca's letters renders the passage referring to those fastidious characters who are carried about the market place above the heads of ordinary folk on a high litter as "questi delicati che si fanno portare per la piazza *in queste alte bare*").[2] Furthermore, a recumbent effigy placed more than twenty-five feet above ground level and facing the beholder—if one may say so— with its feet would have been visible only from a considerable distance and even then would have offered a most peculiar aspect.[3]

Even the contract of 1513 (drawn up after the plan of burying the Pope in St. Peter's had proved unfeasible), which transformed the hitherto freestanding monument into a structure attached to a wall (fig. 420) and placed the effigy at a considerably lower level (only about eighteen feet above ground), did not envisage this effigy as "recumbent" (fig. 421) but as an image "held up by two figures on either side of the head while two others are at its feet" ("a capo à essere i' mezzo di due figure ch'el tengono sospeso, ed a piè i' mezzo du'altre").

Not until 1532, when the monument—its contemplated projection from the wall reduced from more than twenty feet to less than ten in a contract of 1516 and practically eliminated ten years later—had irrevocably shrunk to a wall tomb pure and simple, did the image of the Pope, now intended to be seen in profile, appear in the guise of a Sansovinesque *demi-gisant*; it was, in fact, to a pupil of Sansovino, Tommaso di Pietro Boscoli, that its execution was entrusted when the tomb was finally erected, between 1542 and 1545, in S. Pietro in Vincoli, the Pope's titular church while he was a cardinal (fig. 422).

---

[1] See J. Hess, "Michelangelo and Cordier," *Burlington Magazine*, LXXXII, 1943, pp. 55 ff. When C. de Tolnay, *Michelangelo*, IV; *The Tomb of Julius II*, Princeton, 1954, p. 15, states that the figure found in Michelangelo's workshop after his death—and, therefore, Cordier's *St. Gregory*—"must have been" one of the two papal statues (representing Leo X and Clement VII) destined for the Medici Chapel and known to have been quarried and blocked out in 1524, he would seem to presuppose precisely what has to be proved and what is not very probable in view of the technical and legal circumstances: the marble blocks destined for the Medici tombs were naturally left in Michelangelo's *Florentine* workshop when he left Florence forever in 1534 and were later used for different purposes; whereas the *abbozzo* completed by Cordier was found in Michelangelo's *Roman* workshop. It is true, however, that in my original reconstruction, proposed some time before Cordier's *St. Gregory* was discovered, the papal effigy and the figures supporting it are much too large; I have corrected this error in figs. 418 and 419.

[2] Both these quotations are taken from the *Vocabulario degli Accademici della Crusca*, where also a third one can be found and where the word *bara*, in the sense here under discussion, is defined as "una sorte di lettiga." For the benefit of those who wish to locate these passages and this definition in the *Vocabulario* (De Tolnay, *op. cit.*, IV, p. 84, Note 7) I am glad to state that they can be found (apart from the Venice edition dedicated to Prince Eugene, I, 1806, par. 1, p. 312) in the current edition, the famous "*Quinta Impressione*," II, Florence, 1866, par. 2, p. 57.

[3] Ettlinger, *op. cit.*, p. 270, Note 2 (without referring, incidentally, to Cordier's *St. Gregory*), calls attention to the very elevated position of such effigies as that of "Pope John XXIII" (our fig. 323); but cases like these, viz., wall tombs in which the effigy (frequently tilted towards the beholder so as to counteract the optical distortion) is seen *in profile* cannot legitimately be compared with projects for a freestanding or at least emphatically projecting mausoleum the effigy of which was meant to present itself *in front view*.

This gradual transformation of a full-fledged mausoleum, enclosing a mortuary chamber and on its exterior displaying more than forty marble statues (not counting the biographical bronze reliefs), into an ordinary wall tomb that shows, besides the famous *Moses* and the dismal effigy of the Pope, only the statues of Leah and Rachel, a Sibyl, a Prophet, and the Madonna (the last three figures executed by assistants) was partly enforced by circumstances: the necessity of shifting Julius II's burial place from the biggest church in Christendom to one of the smallest; the conflicting claims on Michelangelo's time and energy; and, above all, his own innate aversion to organized "teamwork." But at the same time this *tragedia del sepolcro* bears witness to the spirit of the Counter-Reformation and, perhaps even more, to the aging Michelangelo's renunciation of the "fables of the world."

The composition of 1505, fusing the influence of Roman sarcophagi with that of Pollaiuolo's tomb of Sixtus IV—and, possibly, with that of the "triumphal-arch scheme" known to the master from his short stay in Venice in 1495 and just being imported into Rome by Sansovino—was dominated by the wish to glorify the Pope as a kind of Pantocrator and as a man who had succeeded in harmonizing the threefold antithesis between the Old Testament and the New, between the classical and the Christian ideals of human conduct (achieving, in Ficino's words, a "concordantia Mosis et Platonis"), and, finally, between this life and the next.

However much the ultimate symbolic content of the figures may have come to be tinged by the personal convictions and experiences of Michelangelo, certain it is that the groups and figures of the lower story were meant to celebrate—as in the tomb of Sixtus IV, though in a more secular key—the victory of the Virtues on the one hand and the grief of the Arts deprived of their patron—including, as Vasari informs us, Architecture, Sculpture, and Painting, "each of them designated by its attributes"—on the other (the monkeys attached to the famous *Slaves* in the Louvre [figs. 423–26] may well refer, all Neo-Platonic symbolism notwithstanding, to the old adage *ars simia naturae)*;[1] that the statue in the "mezzanine" represented the peaceful coexistence of the Old Testament with the New and of the contemplative life with the active; and that the whole structure culminated in the pontiff's triumphant *adventus* in heaven— or, as the Neo-Platonists would say, the "return of the soul to whence it came."

The project of 1513 (fig. 420) no longer provides for biographical reliefs but introduces, instead, the specifically Christian motif of the Virgin Mary, which had had no room in the original program; and in its final form (fig. 422), with both the Victories and the Slaves discarded and the Pope meekly reclining under the protection of Fancelli's *Madonna*, the monument might be called a throwback to the medieval *enfeu* and the Early Renaissance wall tomb—were it not for the dominating presence of the *Moses* (originally, we recall, intended for the right-hand corner of the second story), for the survival of the contrast between the active and the contemplative life (though now represented by the Biblical figures of Leah and Rachel), and, needless to say, for the extraordinary architecture of the upper story which, as De Tolnay has shown, expresses more than anything "the master's final turn of mind."[2]

Unlike the tomb of Julius II, the Medici Chapel—intended for the tombs of Lorenzo the Magnificent (d. 1492) and his brother Giuliano (killed by the Pazzi in 1478) as well as those of the younger Lorenzo, Duke of Urbino (d. 1519), and the younger Giuliano, Duke of Nemours (d. 1516)—is an unfinished but not a distorted document of Michelangelo's true intentions. These intentions crystallized into a final program as early as the beginning of 1521, less than two years after the death of Lorenzo the Younger had given rise to the whole project; but even within this brief space of time a change can be observed from a freestanding monument to wall tombs and from an almost purely secular conception to one which fused the beliefs of orthodox Christianity with Neo-Platonic ideas.

---

[1] See H. W. Janson, *Apes and Ape Lore in the Middle Ages and the Renaissance*, London, 1952, pp. 295 ff.   [2] De Tolnay, *op. cit.*, IV, p. 75.

At the beginning Michelangelo planned to unite the four tombs in a structure either conceived as a so-called Janus arch *(arcus quadrifrons)* or as a kind of enormously magnified *cippus*, its decoration consisting only of four reliefs (possibly representing the Four Seasons) and eight statues of mourners. This project, hardly compatible with the limitations of the space, was soon abandoned in favor of two double wall tombs—one for the Magnifici, the other for the Duchi—which would have occupied the side walls of the chapel while the entrance wall, facing the altar, would have displayed a Madonna flanked by the family saints of the Medici, Cosmas and Damian. The final solution, blending the Christian and the secular element into an inextricable unity, was found by allotting the side walls to the tombs of the Duchi alone whereas a double tomb on the entrance wall ("la sepoltura in testa," fig. 427) was to accommodate the sarcophagi of both Magnifici as well as the statues of the Madonna and the family saints.

Of this combination of double tomb and *Sacra Conversazione* only the statues of the Madonna and the saints were executed (fig. 428); the single tombs of the Duchi, however, their seated effigies surmounting their sarcophagi on which recline the famous *Times of Day*, were nearly completed (figs. 429, 430). I say "nearly" because even here a number of important elements are missing: first, the frescoes— probably representing such prefigurations of salvation as the Resurrection and the Brazen Serpent—which should have filled the big lunettes above the tombs; second, the rich decoration on top of the epistyle— including, in addition to the backs of the now truncated empty thrones (to which we shall revert), a central trophy, festoons, and small nude figures in a crouching position; third, four allegorical statues envisaged for the niches on either side of the effigies (we know that those intended to flank the statue of Giuliano, and thus to correspond to the figures of Day and Night, would have been, as in the Julius tomb of 1505, personifications of heaven and earth, whereas the subject of the figures next to the statue of Lorenzo is not determined); and, finally, four statues of reclining river-gods which would have been accommodated, rather uncomfortably, in the corners beneath the sarcophagi.

The iconographical significance, not to mention the symbolic content, of so complex a program can hardly be reduced to a simple formula; nor can I attempt to evaluate the countless *explications de texte* which have been devoted to the Medici Chapel by generations of scholars.[1] Nearly all of these exegeses contain some elements of truth, and none of them, I think, has been refuted by a recent proposal to discard all philosophical and cosmological concepts in favor of a politico-dynastic interpretation aggravated by psychoanalysis.[2]

That a funeral chapel dedicated to the most prominent members of a most prominent family contains an element of individual and dynastic glorification goes without saying. But this does not necessarily mean that its entire content can be reduced to a "grandiose allegory of princely and papal power." It is true that one of the projects for the *sepoltura in testa* (fig. 427) includes a figure of Fame, "holding the epitaphs in place and neither moving forward nor backward because they [the Magnifici] are dead and their activity has come to an end"; but it should not be overlooked that this project never materialized and that no reference to Fame is found in the final redaction. It is also true that, while "Roman armor is scarcely the normal attire for departed souls, it is most appropriate to Captains of the Roman Church" (a title, by the way, which belongs only to Giuliano, Duke of Nemours, but not to Lorenzo, Duke of Urbino); but it is equally true that Roman armor—as well as Roman trophies—is no less appropriate to the heroized or deified dead as opposed to the living.

The basic impression conveyed by the ducal tombs—an impression that would have been even stronger had the river-gods and the frescoes in the lunettes been executed—is that of gradual ascent from the lowest spheres of existence to the highest; and this impression is confirmed, from an iconographical point

[1] See particularly De Tolnay, *op. cit.*, III, *passim*; for earlier interpretations, cf. H. Thode, *Michelangelo, kritische Untersuchungen*, I, Berlin, 1908, pp. 500 ff.

[2] F. Hartt, "The Meaning of Michelangelo's Medici Chapel," *Essays in Honor of Georg Swarzenski*, Chicago, 1951, pp. 145 ff.

of view, by the presence of the empty thrones, an obvious reference to the Roman ceremony known as *sellisternium*, wherein an empty throne was held in readiness for gods and, after the death of Caesar, for deified emperors. Nor is it an accident that the effigies of the dukes emerge, as it were, from the stream of time by virtue of surmounting the four *Times of Day*, which, according to Condivi, signify "il tempo che consuma tutto," and with reference to which Michelangelo himself had said: "Day and Night speak and say 'We have with our swift course brought about the death of Duke Giuliano, and it is only right that he has taken his revenge'" (that is to say, by depriving Day and Night of light and with his closed eyes sealing theirs).

These two images—and this is borne out by the fact that Giuliano's was intended to be flanked by statues personifying heaven and earth—thus do indicate a state halfway between terrestrial and celestial life (the ideas of heroization or deification merging, so to speak, with that of Christian salvation); and it can hardly be questioned that Michelangelo, in order to stress the universal and transcendent significance of this ascent, not only intentionally refrained from aiming at individual likeness but in the characterization of his heroes anticipated the Miltonian contrast between two universal types of human existence as such: the contrast between *L'Allegro* and *Il Penseroso*—the contrast between the bright-faced, open-minded, and openhanded (witness the coins in his left hand) Giuliano and the somber, self-centered, and parsimonious (witness the closed cashbox on which he rests his left elbow)[1] Lorenzo, already referred to as "il pensoso Duca" by Vasari. In these two figures Michelangelo restated, beyond all personal glorification, the eternal antithesis between the active and the contemplative, the Jovian and the Saturnine, ways of life—both roads to immortality—which was one of the leitmotifs of Neo-Platonic thought and constituted, we recall, about the only constant in the strange eventful history of the Julius tomb.

In sum: the "allegory of princely and papal power" has outgrown all the limitations of empirical experience and historicity; and this is confirmed rather than refuted by the contemplated river-gods whose supposed significance is presented as the strongest argument in favor of a dynastic interpretation. Their cosmological or philosophical implications as symbols of space—and, more specifically, of a world still lower and darker than that governed by time—have been contested on the strength of a poem by Gandolfo Porrino (composed sometime before 1546) which is believed to identify two of the figures as the Tiber and the Arno, the fluvial symbols of Rome and Florence. The other pair of figures, it has been assumed, were intended to personify two of the smaller rivers of Tuscany, so that the whole tetrad would have defined the extent of the Medici's territorial power. In reality, however, Porrino's poem has nothing whatever to do with the river-gods in the Medici Chapel (referred to simply as *i fiumi* in all other sources); and the best thing the iconographer can do is to forget it.[2] To imagine Michelangelo

---

[1] As Professor Edgar Wind informs me, some zoologists incline to identify the animal whose head appears on this cashbox not with a lynx (a creature no less compatible with my interpretation since it signifies avarice as well as watchfulness); but while it is true that the whiskers suggest a feline rather than a bat, the sleepy eyes, small pointed nose, and long blunt ears are definite characteristics of the latter. See now O. Cederlöf, "Fladdermusen," *Symbolister*, I (*Tidskrift för Konstvetenskap*, XXX), Malmö, 1957, pp. 89 ff., particularly pp. 111 ff.

[2] For Porrino's poem, already quoted in Benedetto Varchi's *Due lezioni* (delivered in 1546) and referred to, e. g., in Thode, *op. cit.*, p. 505, see Hartt, *op. cit.*, p. 153. Porrino blames Michelangelo for having neglected his artistic duties in favor of spiritual conversation and concludes with the following couplet:

E i magnanini re del Tebro e d'Arno

I gran sepolcri aspettaranno indarno.

Under the assumption that the *sepolcri* is the subject of the sentence, these two lines have been construed to mean that "the grand tombs

will await in vain the magnanimous kings of the Tiber and the Arno" and thus to criticize the nondelivery of the river-gods for the Medici Chapel. This interpretation is, however untenable. In the first place, it would be hard to understand why Porrino should have been so indignant about the absence of two comparatively unimportant river-gods when so many essential things, particularly the *sepoltura in testa* in its entirety, were missing; in the second place, the personification of a geographical feature such as a river or mountain cannot possibly be called the "king"—least of all, the "magnanimous king"—of the very feature which it personifies; Madame de Pompadour or the City of Paris might be called the "Queen of the Seine," but a personification of the River Seine itself could not be so called. We have, therefore, to assume that the *magnanimi re*, and not the *sepolcri*, is the subject of the sentence, which thus has to be translated as follows: "And the magnanimous rulers of the Tiber and the Arno will await their grand tombs in vain." And this means, very simply, that both Julius II (the "king of the Tiber") and the Magnifici ("the kings of the Arno") were still trying hard to decide whether the alleged Tiber and the alleged Arno should be matched by "the Sieve, the Ombrone, the Arbia, the Orcia, the Greve, the Chiana or the Albegna" (all unspectacular at best and practically nonexistent in the dry season) is, in fact, almost as mirth-provoking as to conceive of the attribute of St. Damian, the medicine cup, as a receptacle for the "flow of milk" from the breasts of the *Maria lactans.*

After this fleeting glance at Michelangelo let us conclude with an even more fleeting one at Gian Lorenzo Bernini (1598–1680); and the omission of the intervening tomb makers—confronted with the hopeless choice between either trying to rival Michelangelo, as did Guglielmo della Porta in his tomb of Paul III, or by-passing him, as did Flaminio Ponzio and Domenico Fontana in their tombs of Paul V and Sixtus V, respectively—is no great loss.

We know from Bernini's own son, Domenico, that his father was proud of having "somehow accomplished a fusion of painting and sculpture" ("sapputo accoppiare in un certo modo la Pittura e la Scoltura"). But in addition to abolishing the borderline between two different media, Bernini defied a number of other even more essential barriers: the barriers between empirical time and metaphysical time (or eternity); the barriers between pleasure and pain; and, ultimately, the barriers between life and death. I say "defied" and not "denied" because his style—in contrast to the *trompe-l'œil* effects occasionally attempted and achieved wherever art had learned to handle the tools of perspective—did not treat all these dualisms as nonexistent: it clearly acknowledged and then resolved them.

In his long life Bernini handled, and reshaped, all possible types of funerary sculpture, from modest *memorie* (epitaphs with bust portraits, the genre that had most successfully survived the somewhat barren interval between the declining years of Michelangelo and the emergence of Bernini himself), which were erected in honor of distinguished but not overwhelmingly important persons in the smaller Roman churches, to the grandiose tombs of two popes in St. Peter's.

Even within the limitations of the *memoria* a comparison between three works—one early, one middle period, one late—will show the extraordinary range of Bernini's development.

The epitaphs of Mons. Giovanni Battista Santoni of ca. 1615–16 in S. Prassede or Mons. Pedro de Foix Montoya of 1621 in S. Maria di Monserrato (fig. 431) do not conspicuously depart from the late-sixteenth-century tradition of funerary portraiture as represented, for example, by the anonymous tomb of Francesco Toleto (d. 1596) in S. Maria Maggiore (figs. 432, 433).

In the epitaph of a pious nun, Suor Maria Raggi, erected in 1643 in S. Maria sopra Minerva (fig. 434), we witness, however, the paradoxical reconciliation of multiple opposites, achieved by a violent intrusion of the miraculous upon reality. The basic idea is the transportation of the deceased to heaven—a motif that can be traced back, we recall, to the tomb slabs of the twelfth century, the *enfeus* of the thirteenth, and the wall tombs of the fourteenth. But here it is no longer the soul, symbolized by a child, that is borne aloft by angels; it is a material object, viz., a portrait medallion, and the whole group is set out against what represents—yet was never supposed to be mistaken for—a glorious wind-swept cloth of honor which is suspended from a cross.

In a *memoria* of ca. 1670 (in S. Lorenzo in Lucina; fig. 435), finally, Dr. Gabriele Fonseca, a great physician, seems to cross the borderline between life on earth and life in heaven by way of an inward rather than an outward miracle— a visionary experience in the flesh rather than an apotheosis in effigy. His hands, the left placed on his heart, clutch his doctor's gown as in a spasm of pain; but his eyes seem to see the radiance of the spheres to which he is about to ascend: he belongs to this world as well as the next.

without a burial place when the poem was written. We remember, in fact, that Julius II was not laid to rest in S. Pietro in Vincoli until 1545; and the remains of the Magnifici were not transferred to the Medici Chapel until 1559 (and even then, they were deposited in an indifferent piece of masonry rather than a proper sarcophagus).

In the *memoria* of Alessandro Valtrini (fig. 436)—quite similar to that of Suor Maria Raggi and only slightly earlier—the portrait medallion is carried by Death rather than angels: in Bernini's world the very power that puts an end to life bestows immortality, not only in a spiritual but even in a temporal sense. And this leads us to the first of his big papal tombs, that of Urban VIII, begun as early as 1628 but not completed until 1647 (fig. 437).

It is obvious (almost too obvious to be mentioned) that the composition of this monument—the Pope, his hand raised in blessing, towering above a voluted sarcophagus flanked by two Virtues—was inspired by Guglielmo della Porta's monument of Paul III (d. 1549; fig. 438) which faces it. But no less obvious are the differences. Quite apart from the grandeur, even violence, of the Pope's gesture and the strong and contrasting emotions displayed by the two Virtues, an entirely new relationship has been established both among the figures and between the figures and the beholder. The Virtues—no longer reclining on the sarcophagus after the model of Michelangelo's *Times of Day* but standing beside it—are living human beings rather than statues; they transcend, though not too emphatically, the lateral boundaries of the niche in which the tomb is placed; and there has been added the figure of Death (fig. 439), who—perched, as it were, between the volutes of the sarcophagus—belongs to a mythical species halfway between the concrete and human (the Pope) and the abstract and allegorical (the Virtues). From an iconographical point of view it is noteworthy, first, that one of the moral Virtues (Prudence) has been replaced by one of the theological ones (Charity), so that the Pope is characterized as the Vicar of Christ, whose attributes are justice and mercy, rather than as a ruler of men, whose attributes are justice and prudence;[1] and, second, that Death himself, entrusted with the task of immortalizing the name of the pontiff in a huge book (referred to as *Liber Mortis* in a somewhat analogous monument) which, in its size and format, gives the impression of a memorial tablet to be affixed to the pedestal of the effigy, has become a guarantor of immortality.

Yet the tomb of Urban VIII is almost conventional as compared to that of Alexander VII (figs. 440, 441), which may be called Bernini's last work (executed between 1671 and 1678). Here the borderline between aesthetic and natural space has been further blurred by the omission of the sarcophagus and the introduction of a door which—half concealed by a curtain of jasper pulled up by Death—directly connects, or seems to connect, the space in which we find ourselves with the vault that shelters the remains of the pontiff; and, moreover, by the fact that the two personifications in front so vigorously overlap the lateral boundaries of the niche that they seem to belong, quite literally, to two worlds.

I have referred to "two personifications in front" because their number has now been augmented to four, arranged *en carreau* as in the tombs in St.-Denis which we discussed some time ago. And of these royal tombs—and their numerous relatives—the monument of Alexander VII is reminiscent in an even more important respect: the Pope is no longer represented enthroned and blessing but on his knees and praying—though not in profile, as in the earlier examples, but in front view, as if he were "praying for the whole of Christianity" (to borrow a beautiful phrase from Rudolf Wittkower, to whom I owe nearly all I can say about Bernini).[2]

Whether or not this curious reversion to the non-Roman and non-Tuscan tradition of the sixteenth century was inspired by Bernini's recollection of his Neapolitan boyhood or—perhaps more probably—by the suggestion of a Spanish cardinal, Domenico Pimentel, whose tomb he had designed (though not personally executed; fig. 442) some twenty years before, I do not dare decide. In one crucial respect, however, Bernini departed from all previous iconography. It has justly been observed (by Wittkower) that the part played by Death in the tomb of Alexander VII is very different from that which he plays in the

---

[1] It should be noted, however, that the tomb of Paul III had originally been devised as a freestanding structure displaying, in addition to Justice and Prudence, Charity and Temperance. After the tomb was removed to its present location (in 1599), the latter two figures (now called, in my opinion incorrectly, "Peace" and "Abundance") were transported to the Palazzo Farnese, where they can still be admired.

[2] R. Wittkower, *Gian Lorenzo Bernini*, London, 1955, p. 26.

tomb of Urban VIII. Raising an hourglass, Death seems here to be cast in the more conventional role of a destroyer, and not, as in the earlier tomb, in that of a vindicator. In reality, however, he participates even more effectively—though, so to speak, by indirection—in a task of glorification and vindication the overt part of which has devolved upon the shoulders of one of the four personifications. This personification, which should have shocked the modern iconographers even more severely than it did shock the seventeenth-century moralists, is Truth (fig. 441), originally naked—so much so that Innocent XI caused her to be covered by a metal garment painted white—but still displaying her age-old attribute, the sun.

Here, then, a group of three Virtues (Charity and, in the background, Prudence and Justice) has been completed by a figure which does not properly "belong."[1] Truth—in contrast to Veracity, which is a "part of Justice"— is not, and was hardly ever considered to be, a Virtue; that is to say, she does not personify a maxim of commendable conduct. Rather she personifies—like Health, Wealth, Peace, or Prosperity—the object and aim of a virtue: she is, to quote Thomas Aquinas' famous definition, not "virtus sed objectum vel finis virtutis" (*Summa theologiae*, II, 2, qu. 109, art. 1, concl. 1). She represents, in short, not something which is, or should be, practiced by men but something which should, and ultimately will, prevail among men—if and when it is revealed by Time according to the old adage "Veritas filia temporis." Bernini himself had started, but never completed, a group entitled *Truth Revealed by Time* (fig. 443) when he felt that he had been wronged by public opinion and the then ruling pope, Innocent X. And I believe that this bold intrusion of Truth into a group of Virtues—an intrusion which must have been even more evident, from a purely visual point of view, when she still stood out from the three others in her pristine nudity—has a very personal reference to the later years of Alexander VII, a man frustrated, to the point of unparalleled humiliations, in his heroic attempts to assert the power of the Holy See against that of Louis XIV and unsuccessful in his efforts to unite all Christian nations against the Turks.

It is, I believe, in connection with the unusual presence of Truth that the behavior of Death in Alexander's monument must be explained. Raised with such emphasis, and placed on exactly the same level as the sun of Truth, his hourglass, familiar symbol of time and transience, here signifies not only the power that ends life but also the power that reveals truth. While proclaiming the triumph of Time over Life, Death achieves, however unwillingly, the triumph of Truth over Time; and that he hides his face in the folds of the curtain may indicate not so much (as Bernini's contemporary biographer would have it) that he is ashamed of having deprived the world of so admirable a pope as that he—but not his hourglass—is forced into "obscurity," much as the moon is forced into obscurity by the sun in the firmament, by a power transcending that of even a Virtue: the sun of Truth.

While working on the tomb of Alexander VII Bernini created a funerary monument quite different from it in overt content yet closely akin to it in spirit: the tomb of the Blessed Lodovica Albertoni in S. Francesco a Ripa (fig. 444). What is implied in the Fonseca bust is here explicitly stated. The Blessed Lodovica is represented *in extremis*, her eyes growing dim. Instead of "activating" the dead, Bernini perpetuated the moment of dying: the agony of death merges, in one ineffable experience, with the bliss of eternal life. To borrow from Rudolf Wittkower once more: "The statue is placed at the far end of the Altieri Chapel in an isolated recess behind the altar ... [but] the visitor standing in the nave of the church is looking through darkness into light: above the altar he finds lit, as by magic, the mirage of the dying Blessed ... the altar itself is transformed into a sepulcrum...."[2]

[1] The memorial chapel of the De Silva family in S. Isidoro, decorated under Bernini's supervision and consecrated in 1663 (Wittkower, *op. cit.*, pp. 227f., figs. 82, 83), does not constitute a valid exception. Here the figure of Truth does not intrude upon a group of Virtues but, in one of the two epitaphs, forms the counterpart of Mercy while, in the other, Justice is juxtaposed with Peace, the cycle thus literally illustrating Psalm 84 : 10, which is explicitly referred to in the inscriptions: "Mercy and truth are met together; righteousness and peace have kissed each other." In this case, too, the figures of Truth (originally nude) and Mercy (originally pressing milk from her breasts) were subsequently covered with metal drapery.

[2] Wittkower, *op. cit.*, p. 237.

To end this hasty survey of funerary sculpture with Bernini is not entirely arbitrary. After him—and in part owing to his own achievement, which all but severed subjective experience from pretersubjective ritual—the days of funerary sculpture, and of religious art in general, were numbered. "Modern tombs," says Henry James, "are a skeptical affair ... the ancient sculptors have left us nothing to say in regard to the great, final contrast."

Occasionally we sense a touch of originality, even greatness, in the works of Antonio Canova or of that admirable Swedish *tumbarius*, Johan Tobias Sergel, whose less-known funerary monuments[1] are as remarkably imaginative as his deservedly famous cenotaph of Descartes, where the age-old idea "the universe is ruled by Death" (most beautifully expressed in a design by Stefano della Bella; fig. 445) is converted into a triumphant "The universe is illumined by genius (fig. 446)."[2]

On the whole, however, all those who came after Bernini were caught in a dilemma—or, rather, trilemma—between pomposity, sentimentality, and deliberate archaism. He who attempts to write the history of eighteenth-, nineteenth-, and twentieth-century art must look for his material outside the churches and outside the cemeteries.

---

[1] See R. Josephson, *Sergels Fantasi*, Stockholm, 1956, particularly I, pp. 280 ff., pp. 301 ff.; II, pp. 354 ff.

[2] Stefano della Bella's drawing, showing Death as the "prime mover" of the earth, was originally destined for the tomb of a Medici, possibly Francesco, son of Grand Duke Cosimo II, who died in 1634; but the fact that the Medici arms have been crossed out with irascible pen strokes would seem to indicate that the project had been rejected. It may be added that the third and fourth lines of the mutilated inscription on the right can safely be completed into "In ogni te[mpo]/ In ogni lo[co]"—"Always and everywhere."

I

From Egypt to the "Tomb of the Nereids"

FIGURES 1–49

1

1, 2 Harp from Ur (detail). University Museum, Philadelphia

2

4

3 *Billy Goat* from Ur. University Museum,
Philadelphia

4   MASTER BERTRAM. *Sacrifice of Isaac* Kunsthalle,
Hamburg

5   Soul-Bird (Bā). The Metropolitan Museum of
Art, New York (Rogers Fund, 1944)

6   Mural showing "Soul-Birds" and "Image-Soul."
Tomb of Irinufer, Thebes

7

8

7 Painted Mummy Cartonnage, showing the
Deceased Brought Before Osiris by Horus. Staatliche Museen, Berlin

8 The Deceased Transported to His Grave on a
Boat-Shaped Hearse. Tomb of Sebek-nakht, El-Kab

9 *Rahotep and Nofret.* Museum, Cairo

10 False Door and Portrait Statue of Ateti, from Saqqara. Museum, Cairo

11 *Offerings to the Dead*, from Tomb of Rii. Staatliche Museen, Berlin

12 *A Hunting Party on the Nile*, from Tomb of Mereruka. Saqqara

11

12

13

13   *The Fields of Iaru*, from Tomb No. 1 (Sennod-
jem). Thebes. Photograph by The Egyptian Expedition, The Metropolitan Museum of Art, New York

14 *Ushabti* Figurines. University Museum,
Princeton

14

15

16

15 *Chertihotep*. Staatliche Museen, Berlin

16 *Amenhotep IV and His Family*. Staatliche
Museen, Berlin

17

18

19

17 Mortuary Temple of Ramses II, Second Court. Thebes

18 *Lamentation Over a High Priest*. Staatliche Museen, Berlin

19 Gold Plate from Pharsalus. Museum, Volos

20

21a   21b

20 *Lekythos* (detail). Staatliche Museen, Berlin

21a, b *Lekythos* (details). National Museum,
Athens

22 Erechtheum, Porch of the Maidens. Acropolis,
Athens

22

23   Stele from Philadelphia, Lydia

24   Spartan Relief from Chrysapha. Staatliche
Museen, Berlin

25

26

25, 26   Reliefs from Tomb of the Harpies, Xanthos.
British Museum, London

27

28

29

27 Relief from Tomb of the Harpies, Xanthos.
British Museum, London

28 *Lekythos* (detail). National Museum, Athens   29 The Kerameikos Cemetery. Athens

30

31

30   Stele of Agakles. National Museum, Athens   31   Stele of Polyeuktos. National Museum, Athens

32 Stele of Chairedemos and Lyceas. National
Museum, Piraeus

33 Stele of Timarista and Krito. National Museum, Rhodes

34

35

36

35 Fragment of a Stele. Staatliche Museen, Berlin

36 *Lekythos* of Timotheos, Phelleus, and Phanokrite (detail). Schliemann's House, Athens

34 Stele of Dexileos. Kerameikos Museum, Athens

ΔΗΜΟΚΛΕΙΔΗΣ : ΔΗΜΗΤΡΙΟ

37 ALXENOR OF NAXOS. Stele from Orchomenos.
National Museum, Athens

38 Stele of Democleides the Sailor. National
Museum, Athens

39

39 *Lekythos* of Myrrhine (detail), formerly Athens.
Collection Stephanos Skuluris

40 Stele of a Youth, from the River Ilissus.
National Museum, Athens

4.1

4.2

4.1   Stele of Panaitios. National Museum, Athens

4.2   *Lekythos* of Leonike. The Metropolitan Museum of Art, New York

43   Stele of Hegeso. National Museum, Athens

44

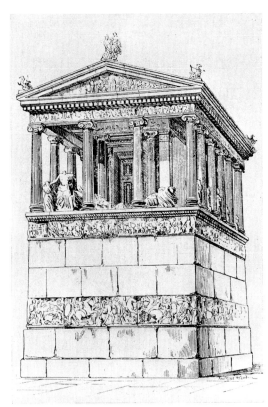

44 *Battle Scene*, from Tomb of the Nereids, Xanthos. British Museum, London

45 Tomb of the Nereids, Xanthos, reconstruction (after Collignon).

45

46

47

46 *Conquest of a City*, from Tomb of the Nereids, Xanthos. British Museum, London

47 *Satrap Receiving Surrender*, from Tomb of the Nereids, Xanthos. British Museum, London

48

49

48　Pedimental Figure, from Tomb of the Nereids,
Xanthos. British Museum, London

49　*Nereid* from Tomb of the Nereids, Xanthos.
British Museum, London

II

From the Mausoleum

to the End of Paganism

FIGURES 50-135

50 *Battle of Greeks and Amazons,* from the
Mausoleum, Halicarnassus, 359–351 B. C. British
Museum, London

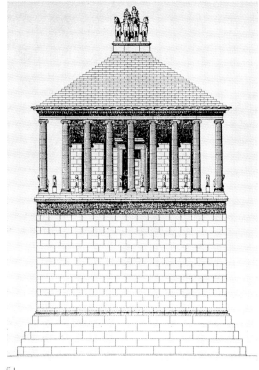

51 Mausoleum, Halicarnassus, reconstruction
(after Krischen)

51

52

53

54

56

52 *Mausolus*, from the Mausoleum, Halicarnassus.
British Museum, London

53 *Chariot Race* (fragment), from the Mausoleum,
Halicarnassus. British Museum, London

54 Sarcophagus from Galgoi, Cyprus. The Metropolitan Museum of Art, New York

55 *Perseus and Medusa* (detail of sarcophagus
shown in Figure 54)

56 Sarcophagus of Tabuit, King of Sidon. Museum, Istanbul

57 a

57 c

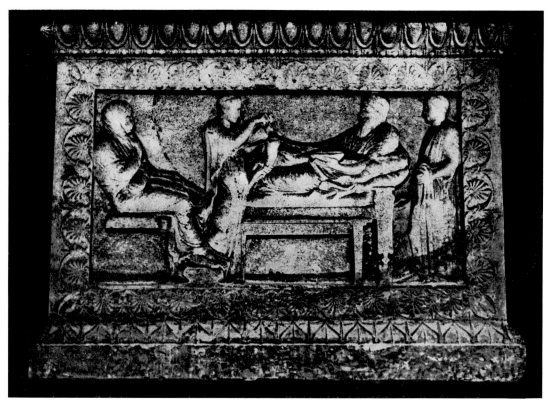

57 b

57 d

58a

58b

58c

58a, b, c "Lycian" Sarcophagus. Museum, Istanbul

59

60

61

60 Sarcophagus from Sidamara. Museum, Istanbul

61 Sarcophagus of the Mourning Women. Museum, Istanbul

62 *Battle Scene* (left half), from the Alexander Sarcophagus. Museum, Istanbul

63 *Battle Scene* (right half), from the Alexander Sarcophagus. Museum, Istanbul

64 *Lion Hunt* (left half), from the Alexander Sarcophagus. Museum, Istanbul

65 *Lion Hunt* (right half), from the Alexander Sarcophagus. Museum, Istanbul

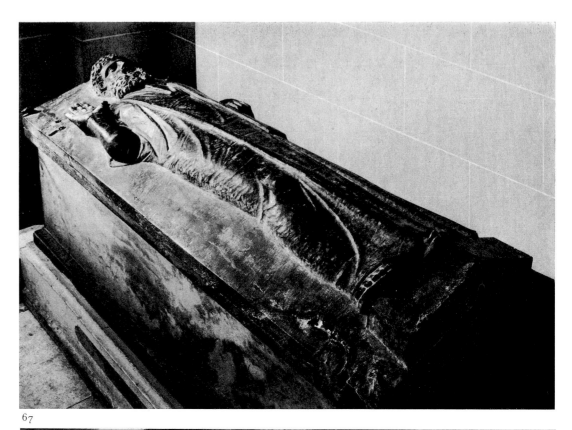

66

67

68

67 Sarcophagus of a Punic Priest. Louvre, Paris

66 Sarcophagus of a Punic Priestess. Musée de
Lavigerie, Carthage

68 Tomb of St. Erminold, 1283. Abbey Church,
Prüfening

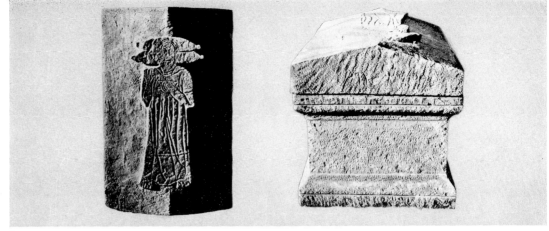

69

70

69 Sarcophagus of Baalsillec. Musée de Lavigerie, Carthage

70 Inghirami Tomb, from Volterra. Archaeological Museum, Florence

71 Etruscan Urn (detail). Museum, Chiusi

72 *The Death of Man*, from the Rohan *Book of Hours* (MS. Lat. 9471, fol. 135). Bibliothèque Nationale, Paris

73

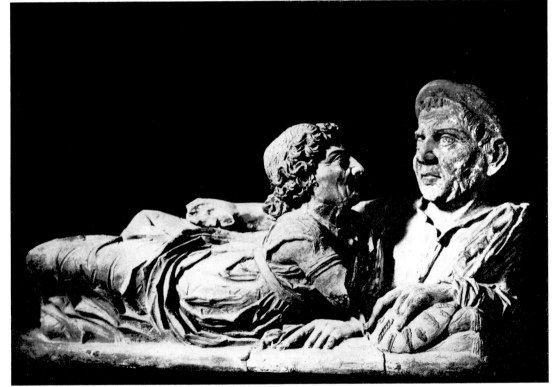

74

75

76

77

78

79

76　Etruscan Stele. Museo Civico, Bologna

78　Etruscan Sarcophagus, from Vulci. Museum
of Fine Arts, Boston

77　Etruscan Sarcophagus. Museum, Tarquinia

79　Etruscan Urn. Museum, Chiusi

80   Etruscan Urn. Museum, Chiusi

81   Etruscan Urn. Archaeological Museum,
Florence

82   Cover of an Etruscan Sarcophagus. Ny Carlsberg Museum, Copenhagen

83

84

83   Etruscan Urn. Museum, Chiusi

84   Sarcophagus of Larthia Seianti. Archaeological
Museum, Florence

85

86

87

85   Etruscan Sarcophagus, from Cerveteri. Villa Giulia Museum, Rome

86   Etruscan Sarcophagus, from Cerveteri. Louvre, Paris

87   Etruscan Urn. Museo Guarnacci, Volterra

88

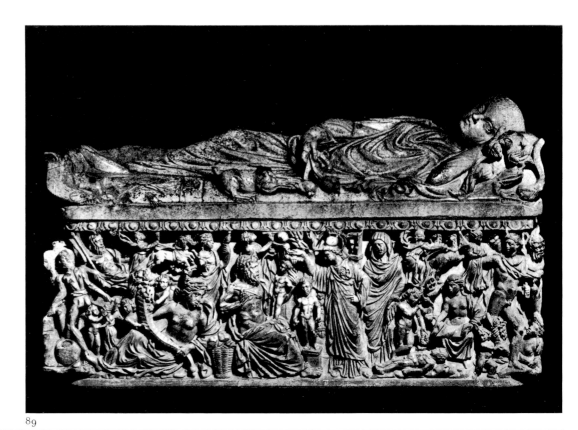

89

90

88 Stele of Saturninus. British Museum, London

89 Prometheus Sarcophagus. Capitoline Museum,
Rome

90 Lid of a Sarcophagus. Terme Museum, Rome

91

92

93

94

91 Stele of Vetienius Urbicus, Bugler, from Cologne. National Museum, St.-Germain-en-Laye

92 Tombstone of L. Vibius and Family. Vatican Museum, Rome

93 Tombstone. Vatican Museum, Rome

94 Sepulchral Altar of Cornelia Tyche and Julia Secunda. Louvre, Paris

95

96

95   Tomb of M. Vergilius Eurysaces. Porta Maggiore, Rome

96   Detail of Figure 95

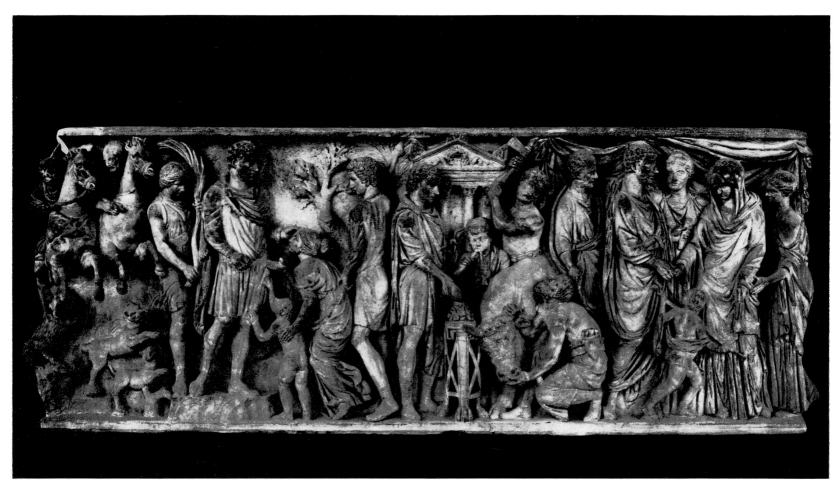

97 a

97 b

97 c

97 a, b, c   Biographical Sarcophagus. Uffizi,
Florence

98a

98b

98a, b Sarcophagus, from Simpelveld. Archaeological Museum, Leiden

99

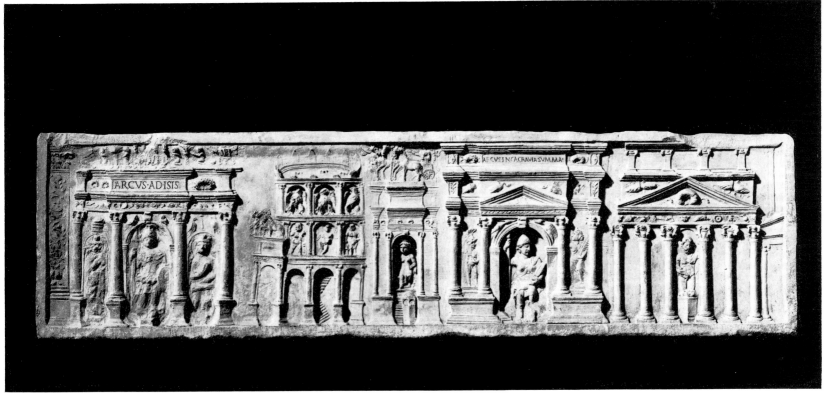

100

99, 100   Reliefs from Tomb of the Haterii. Lateran
Museum, Rome

101

102

101 Relief from Tomb of the Haterii. Lateran
Museum, Rome

102 Sarcophagus. Vatican Museum, Rome

103 Persephone Sarcophagus. Uffizi, Florence

104 Stele of a Decurio (detail). Ptuj (Pettau),
Yugoslavia

105

105 Dionysiac Sarcophagus (front). Walters Art
Gallery, Baltimore

106 Dionysiac Sarcophagus (back). Walters Art
Gallery, Baltimore

107 Dionysiac Sarcophagus. The Metropolitan
Museum of Art, New York

108a

108b

108c

108a, b, c *The Story of Ariadne*, from a Garland Sarcophagus. The Metropolitan Museum of Art, New York

109

110

109 Urn. Vatican Museum, Rome

110 Sarcophagus of Caecilia Metella. Palazzo Farnese, Rome

111 Sarcophagus. Terme Museum, Rome

111

115

116

117

118

119

117   Sarcophagus. Vatican Museum, Rome

118   Sarcophagus (detail). The Metropolitan Museum of Art, New York

119   *Columnar Meleager Sarcophagus* (drawing executed for Cassiano del Pozzo)

120a

120b

120a, b Columnar Hercules Sarcophagus.
Borghese Gallery, Rome

121a

121b

121 a, b, c, d   Sarcophagus, from St. Irene.
Museum, Istanbul

121 c

121 d

122 *Noli me tangere*, from Bronze Doors of
St. Bernward, 1015. Cathedral, Hildesheim

123 Sarcophagus. Isola Sacra, Porto di Roma

124

MVNIFICENTIA. PII SEXTI. P.M.

125

124   Sarcophagus. Vatican Museum, Rome

125   Sarcophagus. Palazzo Giustiniani, Rome

126

127

126 Sarcophagus (detail). Louvre, Paris

127 Sarcophagus, from Palazzo Barberini. Dumbarton Oaks, Washington, D. C.

128

129

128 Fragment of a Sarcophagus. British Museum,
London

129 Sarcophagus of M. Sempronius Neicocrates.
British Museum, London

130 Sarcophagus. Palazzo Torlonia, Rome

130

MVNIFICENTIA PII SEXTI P M

131

132

131 Sarcophagus. Vatican Museum, Rome

132 Columnar Hercules Sarcophagus. British
Museum, London

134

133

135

133　　*Cippus* of Abascantus. Museum, Urbino　　　　134　　Sarcophagus. Vatican Museum, Rome　　　　135　　Sarcophagus. Vatican Museum, Rome

III

The Early Christian Period and

the Middle Ages North of the Alps

FIGURES 136-271

136

137

136   Sarcophagus of St. Helena. Vatican Museum,
Rome

137   Tomb Slab of Valentia. Musée Alaoui, Tunis

138

139

138   Sarcophagus. Chartreuse, Valbonne (Isère)

139   Sarcophagus. Palazzo dei Conservatori, Rome

140

140   Sarcophagus (detail). Lateran Museum, Rome

141   Sarcophagus, from Via della Lungara. Terme Museum, Rome

142   Sarcophagus. Domitilla Catacomb, Rome

141

142

143   Fragment of a Sarcophagus from Istanbul.
Staatliche Museen, Berlin

144   Sarcophagus. S. Francesco, Ravenna

145   Sarcophagus. Lateran Museum, Rome

143

144

145

146

147

148

149

150

151

152

153

152   Sarcophagus. Museum, Arles

153   Sarcophagus of Titus Julius Gorgonius. Cathedral, Ancona

154   Sarcophagus. Notre-Dame, Manosque (Basses-Alpes)

154

155

156

157

155 Sarcophagus. Lateran Museum, Rome

156 Sarcophagus of Adelphia and Valerius. Museum, Syracuse

157 Sarcophagus of Junius Bassus. Vatican Grottoes, Rome

158 Sarcophagus (front). S. Ambrogio, Milan

159

160a

160b

159   Sarcophagus (back). S. Ambrogio, Milan

160a, b   Sarcophagus (sides). S. Ambrogio, Milan

161

162

161 Sarcophagus, from Via Salaria. Lateran Museum, Rome

162 Sarcophagus. S. Maria Antiqua, Rome

163 Sarcophagus. Church, Le Mas-d'Aire (Landes)

163

164 a

164 b

164 a, b   Two Fragments of a Sarcophagus. Staatliche Museen, Berlin

165

166

165 Sarcophagus of Constantina. Vatican Gallery, 166 Sarcophagus, from Sarigüzel. Museum, Istanbul
Rome

167

168

167   Sarcophagus. Lateran Museum, Rome

168   Prometheus Sarcophagus. Louvre, Paris

169

170

171

172

169   Stele, from Terenouthis. Kelsey Museum of Archaeology, University of Michigan, Ann Arbor

170   Stele, from Terenouthis. Kelsey Museum of Archaeology, University of Michigan, Ann Arbor

171   Stele, from Terenouthis. Kelsey Museum of Archaeology, University of Michigan, Ann Arbor

172   Stele of the Children of Antipatros. Kerameikos Museum, Athens

173 *The Vigils of the Dead*, from a Book of Hours (MS. Lat. 10538, fol. 137v). Bibliothèque Nationale, Paris

174 *The Mass of the Dead*, from the Milan Book of Hours (fol. 116). Museo Civico, Turin

173

174

175

176

177

175 Tomb Slab of Cresconia. Formerly Cemetery, Thabraca

176 Female Portrait, from the Fayyûm. University, Strasbourg

177 Tomb of Crescentia, from Thabraca. Musée Alaoui, Tunis

178

179

Planc. XXVIII. du To. 1.

180

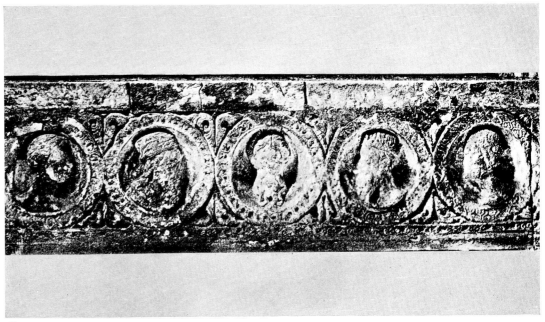

181

182

183

184

185

186

187

188

189

190

191

192

183 "Reiterstein," from Hornhausen. Museum, Halle

184 Front and Back of a Tombstone. Isle of Man

185 Front and Back of a Stele from Niederdollendorf. Rheinisches Landesmuseum, Bonn

186 Tombstone, from Gondorf, Rheinisches Landesmuseum, Bonn

187 Tomb Slab, from Leutesdorf. Rheinisches Landesmuseum, Bonn

188 Tomb Slab, from Andernach. Rheinisches Landesmuseum, Bonn

189 Tomb Slab of Optimus. Museo Paleocristiano, Tarragona

190 Enamel Plaque of Geoffroi Plantagenet, from St.-Julien. Museum, Le Mans

191 Tomb Slab of William, Count of Flanders (died 1109), from St.-Bertin. Museum, St.-Omer. Photo courtesy Dr. Henri Stern

192 Tomb Slab of Abbot Gilbert (died 1152), from St. Maria Laach. Rheinisches Landesmuseum, Bonn

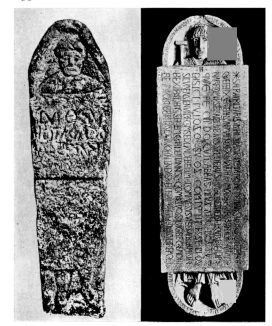

193 Drawing after Tomb Slab of St. Arnulf. Stadtmuseum, Cologne

194 Tomb Slab of Bishop Frumald of Arras (died 1184). Museum, Arras. Photo courtesy Dr. Henri Stern

195 Tomb Slab of the Dominican General Muñoz de Zamora (died 1300). S. Sabina, Rome

196 Tomb Slab of St. Isarn (right), and its Gallo-Roman Model. Archaeological Museum, Marseilles

197 Tomb Slab of Rudolf of Swabia (died 1080). Cathedral, Merseburg

198 *St. Pantaleon*, from MS. Harley 2889, fol. 66 v. British Museum, London

199 Tomb Slab of Duke Widukind. Church, Enger (Westphalia)

200

201

202

200   Tomb Slab of Archbishop Frederick of Wettin
(died 1152). Cathedral, Magdeburg

201   Tomb Slab of Archbishop Wichmann
(died 1192). Cathedral, Magdeburg

202   Tomb Slab of Bishop Evrard de Fouilloi
(died 1220). Cathedral, Amiens

203

204

205

203   Effigy of Pope Clement II. Cathedral, Bamberg

204   Effigy of Count Henry III of Sayn. Germanisches Nationalmuseum, Nuremberg

205   Tomb Slab of Hugues Libergier (died 1263). Cathedral, Reims

206   *Tomb of Daphnis*, woodcut from *Publii Virgilii Maronis Opera*. Strasbourg, 1502

206

207

208

209

210

207 Capital Representing the Tomb of St. Séverin. St.-Séverin, Bordeaux

208 Wölflin of Rufach. Double Tomb of Philip and Ulrich, Counts of Werd (died 1332 and 1334, respectively). St.-Guillaume, Strasbourg

209 *Spinario* (detail of Figure 200)

210 *Spinario*. Capitoline Museum, Rome

211 Tomb of Bishop Gunther. Cathedral, Bamberg

211

212 Brass of Sir Edward Cerne (died 1393) and
Lady Elyne Cerne. Church, Draycott Cerne, Wilts.

213 Tomb Slab of Archbishop Siegfried III of
Eppstein (died 1249). Cathedral, Mainz

214 Tomb Slab of Archbishop Peter von Aspelt
(died 1320). Cathedral, Mainz

215 Tomb of Archbishop John of Nassau (died
1419). Cathedral, Mainz

216

217

218

216   Tomb of Archbishop Konrad von Daun (died 1434). Cathedral, Mainz

217   Tomb of Adalbert of Saxony (died 1484). Cathedral, Mainz

218   TILMAN RIEMENSCHNEIDER. Tomb of Bishop Rudolf von Scherenberg (died 1495). Cathedral, Würzburg

219

220

221

219　Tomb of a Knight. Church, Dorchester, Oxon.

220　Tomb of Sir Roger Kirdeston (died 1337). St. Mary's, Reepham, Norfolk

221　Tomb of King Henry II of England (died 1189) and Eleanor of Aquitaine (died 1204). Abbey Church, Fontevrault

222

223

224

225

222   Tomb of Duke Henry the Lion and Duchess Mathilda. Cathedral, Brunswick

223   Tomb of Bernhard von Breydenbach (died 1497). Cathedral, Mainz

224   Tomb of Bishop Wolfhart von Roth (died 1302), Head of Effigy seen from directly above. Cathedral, Augsburg

225   Effigy of Bishop Wolfhart von Roth, seen from foot of tomb

226

227

228

226   Reliefs on Foot Rests, Tomb of Louis II of
Bourbon (died 1410) and Anne d'Auvergne (died
1416). Church, Souvigny

227   Tomb Slab of Ulrich Kastenmayer (died 1432).
St. James, Straubing

228   Epitaph. St. Peter, Erfurt

229

229 Epitaph of Jean Fiévez. Royal Museum, Brussels

230

231

232

230 Epitaph of Jean du Bos (died 1438) and
Cathérine Bernard. Cathedral, Tournai

231 NICOLAUS GERHAERT VON LEYDEN. Epitaph of
Conrad von Busang(?), 1464. Cathedral, Strasbourg

232 JAN VAN EYCK. *Madonna with Canon Van der
Paele.* Museum, Bruges

233 Epitaph. Cathedral, Tournai

234 Epitaph of Jacques Isack (died 1401). Cathedral, Tournai

235 Sarcophagus of Doña Sancha (back). Convent of Santa Cruz, Jaca

236 Sarcophagus of Doña Sancha (front)

233

234

235

236

237

238

239

237 Tomb Slab of St. Reinheldis. Church, Riesenbeck (Westphalia)

238 Tomb Slab of Sulpicius Cultor. St.-Martin, Plaimpied (Cher)

239 *Apotheosis of Romulus*. British Museum, London

240

241

242

240 *"Death and Transfiguration" of Abbot Lambert of St.-Bertin in St.-Omer* (died 1125), from MS. 46, fol. 1 v. Municipal Library, Boulogne

241 Tomb Slab of Presbyter Bruno (died 1194). Cathedral, Hildesheim

242 *Entombment*, Tomb of Bernard de Mèze. Abbey Church, St.-Guilhem-le-Désert

243 Tomb of St. Hilary. St.-Hilaire, Poitiers

243

244 Drawing after the Tomb of Abbot Arnoult(?),
formerly at St.-Père, Chartres. Collection Roger de
Gaignières

245 *Porte Romane.* Cathedral, Reims

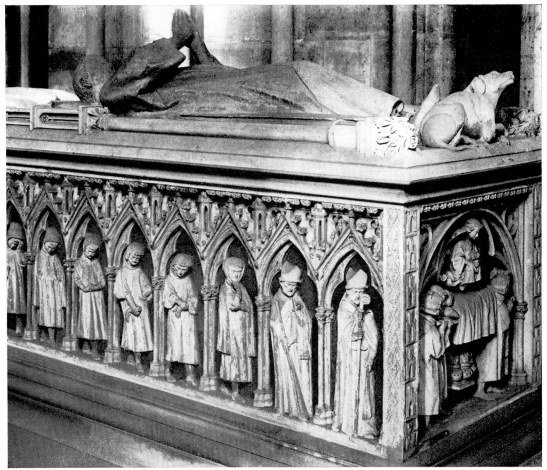

246

247

246 Tomb of Louis de France (died 1260). Abbey
Church, St.-Denis

247 Tomb of the Landgraves Otto and John of
Hesse. St. Elizabeth, Marburg

248

249

250a

250b

251

248 CLAUS SLUTER. Tomb of Philip the Bold
(detail). Chartreuse de Champmol, Dijon

249 CLAUS SLUTER. *Pleureur*. Cluny Museum,
Paris

250 a, b "*Gravenbeeldjes*," from the Tomb of Isabella of Bourbon, formerly at St.-Michel, Antwerp.
Rijksmuseum, Amsterdam

251 Tomb of Maximilian I. Hofkirche, Innsbruck

252

253 a

253 b

254 a

254 b

252　Tomb of Archbishop Philip von Heinsberg.
Cathedral, Cologne

253 a, b　Reliefs from the Tomb of Pope Clement
II. Cathedral, Bamberg

254 a, b　Reliefs from the Tomb of Pope Clement
II. Cathedral, Bamberg

255

256

257

258

259

263   Effigy of Jean Cardinal de Lagrange *en transi* (died 1402). Calvet Museum, Avignon

264   Drawing after the Tomb of Jean Cardinal de Lagrange in its original state in Avignon Cathedral

264

265

266a

266b

267

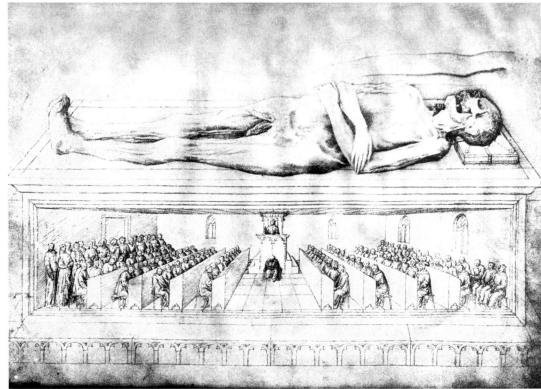

268

269 MASACCIO. *The Holy Trinity with the Virgin, St. John, and Two Donors.* S. Maria Novella, Florence

270 Tomb Slab of Antonio Amati. S. Trinita, Florence

267 Drawing after the Tomb of René of Anjou, formerly in Angers Cathedral. Collection Roger de Gaignières

268 JACOPO BELLINI. Drawing of the Imaginary Tomb of a Professor. Louvre, Paris

271 Drawing of the Tomb of Jean de Beauvau (died 1479), formerly in Angers Cathedral. Collection Roger de Gaignières

269

270

271

IV

The Renaissance,

Its Antecedents and Its Sequel

FIGURES 272-446

272

272 ANTONIO DELLA PORTA and PACE GAGGINI. Tomb of Raoul de Lannoy and His Wife. Church, Folleville (Somme)

273 GIROLAMO VISCARDI. Tomb of the Dukes of Orléans, 1502. Abbey Church, St.-Denis

273

274

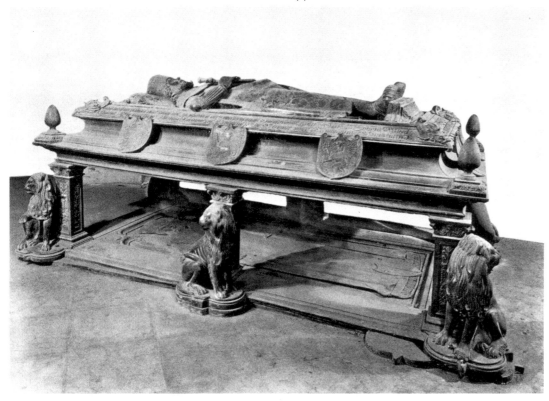

275

276

274 PETER VISCHER. Henneberg Tomb. Church, Römhild

275 HANS VISCHER. Tomb of the Electors Joachim and Johann Cicero. Staatliche Museen, Berlin

276 PETER VISCHER THE YOUNGER. Tomb Slab of Gottlieb Wigerinck. Marienkirche, Lübeck

277

278

279

277　Tilman Riemenschneider. Tomb of Bishop
Lorenz von Bibra. Cathedral, Würzburg

278　Hans Backofen. Tomb of Uriel von Gemmingen. Cathedral, Mainz

279　Detail of Figure 278

280 ADOLF DAUCHER and/or SEBASTIAN LOSCHER.
Fugger Tombs. St. Anne, Augsburg

281

282

283

284

281 HANS BURGKMAIR. *Sterbebild of Conrad Celtes.* Woodcut

282 Detail of Figure 287

283 Epitaph of Johannes Cuspinianus. St. Stephen, Vienna

284 Epitaph of Bishop Donato Medici, 1475. Cathedral, Pistoia

285 Epitaph of Andrea Bregno. S. Maria sopra Minerva, Rome

286 Tomb of Rolandino dei Romanzi. Museo Civico, Bologna

285

286

287

287 Tomb of Rolandino dei Passageri. Piazza S. Domenico, Bologna

288 Epitaph of Stefano and Maddalena Satri. S. Omobono, Rome

288

289

290

289   MASTER ROSO DA PARMA. Tomb of the Brothers Liuzzi, 1318. SS. Vitale e Agricola, Bologna

290   Tomb of Michele da Bertalia, 1328. Museo
Civico, Bologna

292

291

293

291 ANDREA RICCIO. Tomb of Girolamo and Marcantonio della Torre. S. Fermo, Verona. (the originals
of the bronze reliefs on the sarcophagus are in
the Louvre, Paris)

292 *Girolamo Teaching in Verona.* Detail of
Figure 291

293 *Girolamo Taken Ill.* Detail of Figure 291

294

295

294　*A Sacrifice for the Cure of Girolamo*. Detail
of Figure 291

295　*The Death of Girolamo*. Detail of Figure 291

296

297

296   *The Funeral.* Detail of Figure 291

297   *The Passage of the Soul.* Detail of Figure 291

298

299

298   *Girolamo in Elysium.* Detail of Figure 291

299   *Terrestrial Fame.* Detail of Figure 291

300

300 TINTORETTO. *The Finding of the Relics of St. Mark*. Brera Gallery, Milan

301

302

301 ANDREA DI LAZZARO CAVALCANTI. Sarcophagus of Giovanni and Piccarda de' Medici. Old
Sacristy, S. Lorenzo, Florence

302 ANDREA DEL VERROCCHIO. Sarcophagus of Giovanni and Piero de' Medici. Old Sacristy, S. Lorenzo, Florence

303

304

303 JACOPO DELLA QUERCIA. Tomb of Ilaria del Carretto. Cathedral, Lucca

304 Detail of Figure 303. Photo courtesy Prof. Charles Seymour, Jr.

305

306

307

308

305   Sarcophagus of Lorenzo di Luca Valle. St. John
Lateran, Rome

306   LORENZO GHIBERTI. Tomb of Leonardo Dati.
S. Maria Novella, Florence

307   JACOPO DELLA QUERCIA. Tomb of the Wife of
Lorenzo Trenta. S. Frediano, Florence

308   DONATELLO. Tomb of Giovanni Crivelli.
S. Maria in Aracœli, Rome

309 DONATELLO. Tomb of Bishop Giovanni Pecci. Cathedral, Siena

310 FOLLOWER OF DONATELLO. Tomb of Pope Martin V. St. John Lateran, Rome

311 Tomb of Pope Martin V, seen from foot of tomb

312 a, b Tomb of Canon Hubert Milemans (died 1558). Ste.-Croix, Liége

313 Meleager Sarcophagus. Museum, Ostia

314 GIULIANO DA SANGALLO(?). Tomb of Francesco Sassetti. S. Trinita, Florence

315 Detail of Figure 314

312 a

312 b

313

314

315

316

317

316 WORKSHOP OF VERROCCHIO. *The Death of Francesca Tornabuoni*. National Museum, Florence

317 BERNARDO ROSSELLINO. Tomb of Leonardo Bruni. S. Croce, Florence

318 ANTONIO ROSSELLINO. Tomb of Jacopo Cardinal of Portugal. S. Miniato, Florence

319

320

319   Detail of Figure 318. Photo courtesy Prof. Clarence Kennedy

320   MICHEL COLOMBE. Tomb of the Children of Charles VIII and Anne de Bretagne. Cathedral, Tours

321   GIOVANNI BALDUCCI. Tomb of St. Peter Martyr. S. Eustorgio, Milan

322   Detail of Figure 321

323   DONATELLO and MICHELOZZO. Tomb of Baldassare Coscia. Baptistery, Florence

324   ANTONIO and GIOVANNI GIUSTI. Tomb of Louis XII and Anne de Bretagne. Abbey Church, St.-Denis

321

322

323

324

325

326

327

325 Drawing after the Tomb of Charles VIII, formerly in St.-Denis. Collection Roger de Gaignières

326 *Virtue*, from the Tomb of Philibert of Savoy. Chapel, Brou (detail of Figure 343)

327 Michel Colombe and Girolamo da Fiesole. Tomb of Francis II of Brittany and Marguerite de Foix. Cathedral, Nantes

329

328 Vault of the Tomb of Francis I. Abbey Church,
St.-Denis

329, 330 Reliefs from the base, Tomb of Francis I

328

330

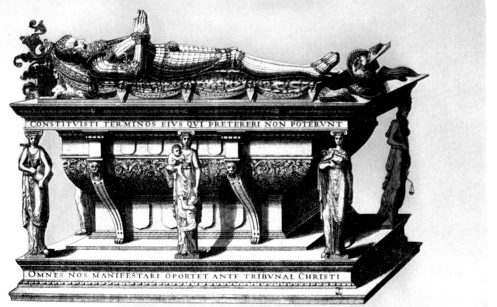

OMNES NOS MANIFESTARI OPORTET ANTE TRIBVNAL CHRISTI

331 FRANCESCO PRIMATICCIO and GERMAIN PILON.
Tomb of Henry II and Catherine de Médicis. Abbey
Church, St.-Denis

332 CORNELIS FLORIS. Tomb of a Knight or
Prince. Engraving

333 ARNOLFO DI CAMBIO. Tomb of Guillaume
Cardinal de Braye (died 1282). S. Domenico, Orvieto

334

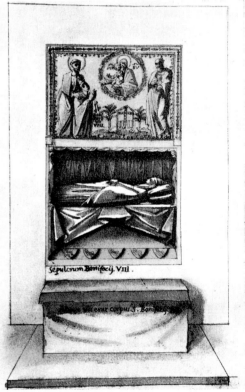

335

334 GIOVANNI COSMATI. Tomb of Guilelmus Durandus, Bishop of Mende (died 1296). S. Maria sopra Minerva, Rome

335 JACOPO GRIMALDI. Drawing after the Tomb of Pope Boniface VIII (died 1303), formerly in St. Peter's. From MS. Barb. Lat. 2733. Vatican Library, Rome. Photo courtesy Prof. G. B. Ladner

336

337

336 Nino Pisano. Tomb of Archbishop Simone
Saltarelli (died 1342). S. Caterina, Pisa

337 Tomb of Bishop Neri Corsini (died 1377). S.
Spirito, Florence

338a

338b

338a, b GIOVANNI PISANO. Fragments from the
Tomb of Margaret of Brabant (died 1311). Palazzo
Bianco, Genoa

339

339   Tomb of a Gentleman of the Bardi Family.
S. Croce, Florence

340   GIOVANNI DALMATA   and   ANDREA BREGNO.
Tomb of Bartolommeo Cardinal Roverella, 1483.
S. Clemente, Rome

340

341

342

343

341   Interior of the Chapel, Brou

342   Tomb of Margaret of Austria. Chapel, Brou

343   Tomb of Philibert of Savoy. Chapel, Brou

344

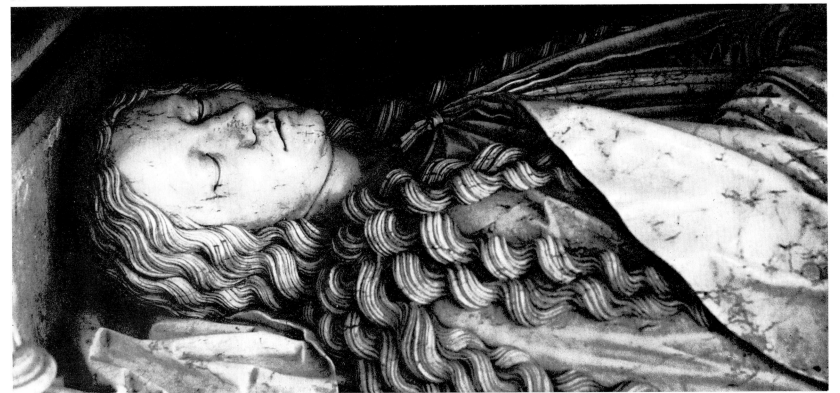

345

344 CONRAD MEIT. Effigy of Margaret of Austria
au vif (detail of Figure 342)

345 CONRAD MEIT, Effigy of Margaret of Austria
en transi (detail of Figure 342)

347

348

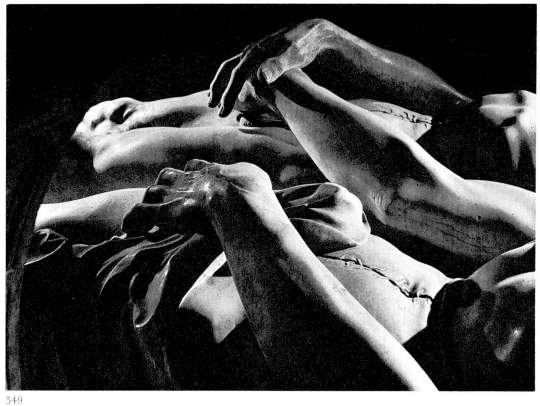

349

346 Kneeling Effigies of Louis XII and Anne de
Bretagne (detail of Figure 324)

347 Effigy of Jeanne de Bourbon, Countess of
Auvergne, *en transi*. Louvre, Paris

348, 349 Effigies of Louis XII and Anne de
Bretagne *en transis* (details of Figure 324)

350 ANDRÉ BEAUNEVEU. Head of the Effigy, Tomb
of Charles V. Abbey Church, St.-Denis

351 ANDRÉ BEAUNEVEU. Effigy of Charles V,
from "tombeau des entrailles." Louvre, Paris

352   PIERRE BONTEMPS. Monument for the Heart
of Francis I. Abbey Church, St.-Denis

353   GERMAIN PILON. Monument for the Heart
of Henry II. Louvre, Paris

354

Philibert de l'Orme and Pierre Bontemps.
Tomb of Francis I. Abbey Church, St.-Denis

355 a

355 b

355 a, b   POMPEO LEONI. Tombs of Charles V and
Philip II and Their Families. Chapel, Escorial

356

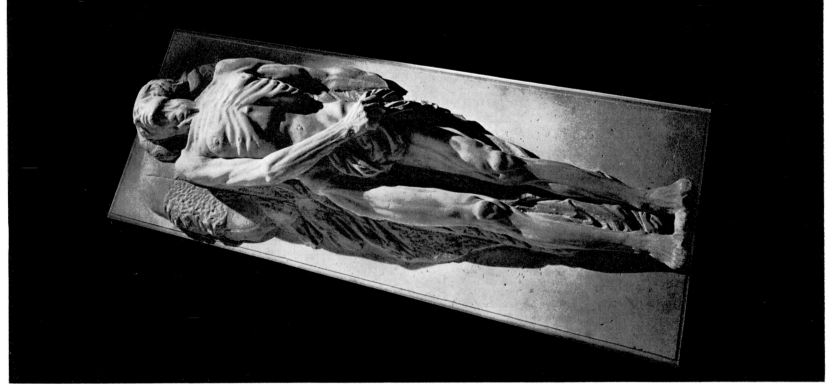

357

356 JACQUES DUBROEUCQ. Tomb of Bishop Eustache de Croy (died 1538). Notre-Dame, St.-Omer

357 GIROLAMO DELLA ROBBIA. Catherine de Médicis *en transi*. Louvre, Paris

358

359

360a

360b

361

362

360a, b WORKSHOP OF GERMAIN PILON. Effigies from Second Monument of Henry II and Catherine de Médicis. Abbey Church, St.-Denis

361 Detail of Figure 360b

362 ROULAND DE ROUX. Tomb of the Cardinals d'Amboise. Cathedral, Rouen

363

364

365

363   Drawing after the Tomb of Jean de Salazar
and Marie de la Trémouille, formerly in Sens
Cathedral. Collection Roger de Gaignières

364   GERMAIN PILON. Tomb of Valentine Balbiani.
Louvre, Paris

365   *Valentine Balbiani en transi*
(detail of Figure 364)

366   Drawing after the Tomb of Valentine Balbiani, formerly in Ste.-Cathérine du Val des Escoliers, Paris. Collection Roger de Gaignières

367   ANDREA SANSOVINO. Tomb of Ascanio Cardinal Sforza, 1505. S. Maria del Popolo, Rome

368   Tullio Lombardo and Assistants. Tomb of Doge Andrea Vendramin. SS. Giovanni e Paolo, Venice

369

370

371

372

369 Tomb of the Countess of Tendilla. S. Ginés, Guadalajara

370 Tomb of the Count of Tendilla. S. Ginés, Guadalajara

371 Tomb of Don Martin Vazquez de Arce. Cathedral, Sigüenza

372 Frontispiece, *Les Faits, dits et ballades*, by Alain Chartier (Paris, 1489)

373

373 PIERRE-ÉTIENNE MONNOT. Tomb of John Cecil and His Wife (died 1700 and 1703, respectively). St. Martins, Stamford, Lincolnshire

374 FRANCESCO APRILE. Tomb of Pietro and Francesco Bolognetti. Gesù e Maria, Rome

374

375

376

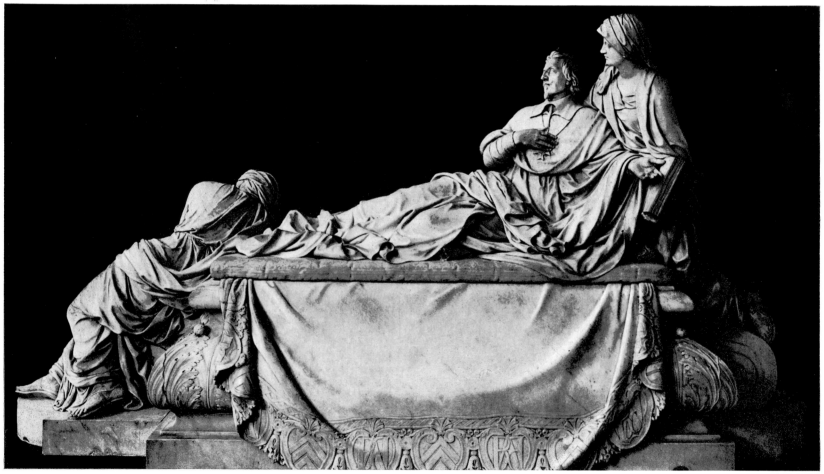

377

375   JOHN SCHOEMAN and THOMAS BURMAN. Tomb
of Sir Thomas and Lady Charlecote, Charlecote
Park, Warwickshire

376   JEAN-BAPTISTE TUBY, Tomb of Julienne Le Bé.
St.-Nicolas-du-Chardonnet, Paris

377   FRANÇOIS GIRARDON. Tomb of Cardinal Richelieu. Sorbonne Chapel, Paris

378 JEAN GOUJON. Tomb of Louis de Brézé. Cathedral, Rouen

379 Engraving after the Tomb of Nicolas du Châtelet (died 1562), formerly at Vauvillars

380 GUIDO MAZZONI. Equestrian Statue of Louis XII. Castle, Blois

381 GIOVANNI ANTONIO AMADEO. Tomb of Bartolommeo Colleoni. Colleoni Chapel, Bergamo

378

379

380

381

382

383

384

382   Tomb of Guilelmus (died 1289). SS. Annunziata, Florence

383   Seal of Robert Fitzwalter. British Museum, London

384   Tomb of Alberto I della Scala. S. Maria Antica, Verona

385

386a

386b

385 Tomb of Cangrande della Scala. S. Maria
Antica, Verona

386a, b Details of Figure 385

387

388

387   Detail of Figure 385   388   Tomb of Paolo Savelli. Frari Church, Venice

389 Tomb of Lello II Camponeschi. S. Giuseppe, Aquila

390 PAOLO UCCELLO. *John Hawkwood*. Cathedral, Florence

391

391 ANDREA DEL CASTAGNO. *Niccolò da Tolentino.*
Cathedral, Florence

392 DONATELLO. Monument of Gattamelata.
Piazza del Santo, Padua

393

394

395

393 Gattamelata Monument, from the West

394 Base of Gattamelata Monument, from the East

395 TINO DI CAMAINO. Tomb of Henry VII, reconstruction (after Valentiner)

396 Tino di Camaino. Statues from the Tomb of
Henry VII. Camposanto, Pisa

397

397   Tɪɴᴏ ᴅɪ Cᴀᴍᴀɪɴᴏ. Tomb of Charles of Calabria. S. Chiara, Naples

398

399

400

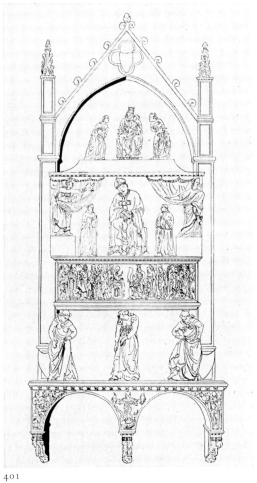

401

402

400 Tomb of Cino dei Sinibaldi (died 1337).
Cathedral, Pistoia

401 TINO DI CAMAINO. Tomb of Bishop Antonio
degli Orsi, 1321, reconstruction (after Valentiner)

402 TINO DI CAMAINO. Statue of the Deceased,
from tomb shown in Figure 401. Cathedral,
Florence

405 ANTONIO DEL POLLAIUOLO. Tomb of Pope
Innocent VIII. St. Peter's, Rome

404

405

404 JACOPINO DA TRADATE. Statue of Pope Martin
V. Cathedral, Milan

405 ANTONIO DEL POLLAIUOLO. Tomb of Pope
Sixtus IV. St. Peter's, Rome

406 Tomb of Pope Sixtus IV, seen from above

407

408

409

407   Detail of Figure 406

408   *Theology* (detail of Figure 405)

409   PIERRE BONTEMPS. *Architecture* (detail of
Figure 352). Photo courtesy Prof. Paul S. Wingert

410

411

410   PIERRE BONTEMPS. *Sculpture* (detail of Figure 352). Photo courtesy Prof. Paul S. Wingert

411   PIERRE BONTEMPS. *Painting* (detail of Figure 352). Photo courtesy Prof. Paul S. Wingert

412

413

414

415

412 PIERRE BONTEMPS. *Geometry* (detail of Figure 352). Photo courtesy Prof. Paul S. Wingert

414 Tomb of William the Silent, side view

413 HENDRIK DE KEYSER. Tomb of William the Silent. New Church, Delft

415 Effigy of William the Silent (detail of Figure 414)

416

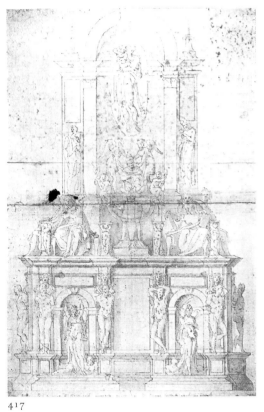

417 MICHELANGELO. Drawing (copy) for Tomb
of Pope Julius II. Staatliche Museen, Berlin

418 MICHELANGELO. Tomb of Julius II, Project of
1505. Tentative Reconstruction of Front Elevation

419 Side Elevation of Figure 418

420   MICHELANGELO. Tomb of Julius II, Project
of 1513. Tentative Reconstruction of Front Elevation

421   Side Elevation of Figure 420

422   MICHELANGELO AND OTHERS. Tomb of Julius
II. S. Pietro in Vincoli, Rome

423

424

425 Detail of Figure 423

426 Detail of Figure 424

427 MICHELANGELO. Drawing for "La Sepoltura in Testa" of the Medici Chapel (Frey 9b). British Museum, London

423 MICHELANGELO. "*The Dying Slave.*" Louvre, Paris

424 MICHELANGELO. "*The Rebellious Slave.*" Louvre, Paris

428 MICHELANGELO. The Medici Chapel, Interior. S. Lorenzo, Florence

425

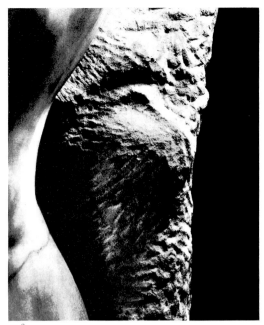

426

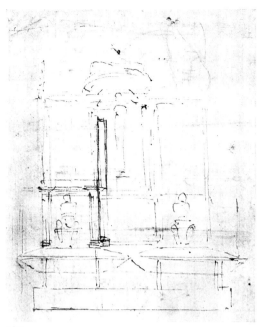

427

428

429

Michelangelo. Tomb of Giuliano de' Medici. Medici Chapel, Florence

430

430   MICHELANGELO. Tomb of Lorenzo de' Medici.
Medici Chapel, Florence

431

432

433

434

431 GIAN LORENZO BERNINI. Epitaph of Monsignor Pedro de Foix Montoya. S. Maria di Monserrato, Rome

432 Tomb of Francesco Cardinal Toleto. S. Maria Maggiore, Rome

433 Detail of Figure 432

434 GIAN LORENZO BERNINI. Epitaph of Suor Maria Raggi. S. Maria sopra Minerva, Rome

435

436

437

435 GIAN LORENZO BERNINI. Epitaph of Dr. Gabriele Fonseca. S. Lorenzo in Lucina, Rome

436 GIAN LORENZO BERNINI. *Memoria* of Alessandro Valtrini. S. Lorenzo in Damaso, Rome

437 GIAN LORENZO BERNINI. Tomb of Pope Urban VIII. St. Peter's, Rome

439

438 Guglielmo della Porta. Tomb of Pope
Paul III. St. Peter's, Rome

439 Detail of Figure 437

441

440   Gian Lorenzo Bernini. Tomb of Pope Alexander VII. St. Peter's, Rome

441   Detail of Figure 440

442

442 GIAN LORENZO BERNINI AND ASSISTANTS. Tomb
of Domenico Cardinal Pimentel. S. Maria sopra
Minerva, Rome

443 GIAN LORENZO BERNINI. *Truth Revealed by
Time*. Borghese Gallery, Rome

SIMVLACRVM·VERITATIS·TEMPORE·DETEGENDAE·
QVOD·LAVRENTIVS·BERNINIVS·EQVES·
OLIM·CALVMNIA·ADPETITVS·
IN·SOLATIVM·DOLORIS·INSCVLPSIT·
ET·TRANSMITTI·POSTERIS·SVIS·IN·PERPETVVM·IVSSIT·
QVO·PRAESENTE·ADMONERENTVR·
INIVRIAS·FERENDAS·POENAS·NON·EXPETENDAS·
ROSPER·ABNEPOS·ILLVSTRI·LOCO·P·D·AN·MDCCCXI·

444 GIAN LORENZO BERNINI. Tomb of the Blessed
Lodovica Albertoni. S. Francesco a Ripa, Rome

444

445

445 STEFANO DELLA BELLA. Design for an Epitaph of Francesco de' Medici Formerly Collection
Jacob Isaacs, Esq., London

446 JOHAN TOBIAS SERGEL. Cenotaph of Descartes,
Adolf Fredrik Church, Stockholm. Photo Höder.
courtesy Dr. Ragnar Josephson

446

Selected Bibliography

A general bibliography for all the subjects discussed in these lectures would have to be so large as to require a separate volume. The following list, arranged according to figure numbers and covering only the works of art illustrated, provides one or two key titles for each monument, usually the most recent scholarly discussion with references to the earlier literature.

Figure

1, 2   H. Frankfort, *The Art and Architecture of the Ancient Orient* (Pelican History of Art), Baltimore, 1954, pp. 30, 35

3   Frankfort, *ibidem*, pp. 23, 31

4   H. Th. Musper, *Gotische Malerei nördlich der Alpen*, Cologne, 1961, pp. 187 f.

5   Unpublished; cf. H. Bonnet, *Reallexikon der ägyptischen Religionsgeschichte*, Berlin, 1952, pp. 74–77, s. v. "Bā"

6   A. Lhote and Hassia, *Les chefs-d'œuvre de la peinture égyptienne*, Paris, 1954, pl. 165

7   H. Schäfer, *Von ägyptischer Kunst*, Leipzig, 1930, pl. 42, 1

8   J. J. Tylor and S. Clarke, *The Tomb of Sebeknekht*, London, 1896, pl. 2

9   W. S. Smith, *The Art and Architecture of Ancient Egypt* (Pelican History of Art), Baltimore, 1958, pp. 41–47

10   K. Lange and M. Hirmer, *Egypt*, London, 1956, p. 306

11   Schäfer, *op. cit.*, pl. 31

12   Lange and Hirmer, *op. cit.*, p. 306

13   W. Wresinski, *Atlas zur altägyptischen Kulturgeschichte*, Leipzig, 1935, I, pl. 19 and comment; Lhote and Hassia, *op. cit.*, pls. 69, 70

14   Unpublished; cf. Bonnet, *op. cit.*, pp. 849–853, s. v. "Uschabti"

15   H. Fechheimer, *Die Plastik der Ägypter*, Berlin, 1923, pp. 34 f., pls. 46, 47; H. Schaefer and W. Andrae, *Die Kunst des alten Orients* (Propyläen-Kunstgeschichte, II), Berlin, 1925, p. 632, pl. 287

16   G. Steindorff, *Die Kunst der Ägypter*, Leipzig, 1928, pl. 177; K. Lange, *König Echnaton und die Amarna-Zeit*, Munich, 1951

17   Smith, *Art and Architecture of Ancient Egypt*, pp. 217 ff.

18   A. Erman, "Aus dem Grabe eines Hohenpriesters von Memphis," *Zeitschrift für ägyptische Sprache*, XXXIII, 1895, pp. 18 ff.; Schäfer, *op. cit.*, pl. 39

19   *Archaiologike Ephemeris*, 1950–51, p. 99

20   W. Riezler, *Weissgrundige attische Lekythoi...*, Munich, 1914, pl. 52

21   Riezler, *ibidem*, pls. 44, 44 a; E. Pfuhl, *Malerei und Zeichnung der Griechen*, Munich, 1923, pl. 542

22   A. W. Lawrence, *Greek Architecture* (Pelican History of Art), Baltimore, 1957, pp. 164 ff.

23   F. Cumont, *Recherches sur le symbolisme funéraire des Romains*, Paris, 1942, p. 33; idem, *Lux perpetua*, Paris, 1949, pp. 153, 279

24   G. M. A. Richter, *Sculpture and Sculptors of the Greeks*, New Haven, 1950, p. 166

25–27   G. Lippold, *Die griechische Plastik* (Handbuch der Archäologie, III, i), Munich, 1950, p. 67

28   Riezler, *op. cit.*, pl. 91; Pfuhl, *op. cit.*, pl. 552.

29   German Archaeological Institute, Athens, *Kerameikos. Ergebnisse der Ausgrabungen*, Berlin, 1939—

30   A. Conze, *Die attischen Grabreliefs*, Berlin, 1893–1922, No. 927

31   Conze, *ibidem*, No. 956

32   R. Lullies and M. Hirmer, *Greek Sculpture*, New York, 1957, p. 61

33   Lullies and Hirmer, *ibidem*, p. 62

34   Lullies and Hirmer, *ibidem*, p. 64

35   Conze, *op. cit.*, No. 1160

36   Conze, *ibidem*, No. 752

37   Lippold, *op. cit.*, p. 114

38   Conze, *op. cit.*, No. 623

39   Conze, *ibidem*, No. 1146; H. Diepolder, *Die attischen Grabreliefs des 5. und 4. Jahrhunderts v. Chr.*, Berlin, 1931, p. 20

40   Lullies and Hirmer, *op. cit.*, p. 71

41   Conze, *op. cit.*, No. 1062

42   G. M. A. Richter, *Catalogue of Greek Sculptures...*, Cambridge, Mass., 1954, No. 88

43   Lullies and Hirmer, *op. cit.*, p. 62

44–49   M. Collignon, *Histoire de la sculpture grecque*, Paris, 1897, II, pp. 217–229; Lippold, *op. cit.*, p. 208; W. B. Dinsmoor, *The Architecture of Ancient Greece*, London, 1950, pp. 256 f.

50–53   Lullies and Hirmer, *op. cit.*, pp. 67 ff.

54, 55   *Antike Denkmäler*, III, 1926, pp. 3 f.; K. Schauenburg, *Perseus in der Kunst des Altertums*, Bonn, 1960, pp. 38, 45

56   O. Hamdy Bey and T. Reinach, *Une nécropole royale à Sidon*, Paris, 1892, pl. 44

57   Hamdy Bey and Reinach, *ibidem*, pls. 21, 22

58   Hamdy Bey and Reinach, *ibidem*, pls. 14, 15; Lippold, *op. cit.*, p. 210

59   R. Delbrueck, "Der römische Sarkophag in Melfi," *Jahrbuch des deutschen archäologischen Instituts*, XXVIII, 1913, pp. 277–308; C. R. Morey, *The Sarcophagus of Claudia Antonia Sabina and the Asiatic Sarcophagi* (Sardis, V, i), Princeton, 1924, figs. 39–41

60   Morey, *ibidem*, figs. 55–57; Cumont, *Recherches*, pp. 90 f.

61   Hamdy Bey and Reinach, *op. cit.*, pls. iv–xi; Collignon, *op. cit.*, pp. 401 ff.; M. Bieber, *The Sculpture of the Hellenistic Age*, New York, 1955 (rev. ed., 1961), p. 22

62–65   Hamdy Bey and Reinach, *op. cit.*, pls. 25–30; Bieber, *op. cit.*, pp. 72 f.

66   H. de Villefosse, "Les sarcophages peints trouvés à Carthage," *Monuments Piot*, XII, 1905, pl. 8; G. and C. Charles-Picard, *La vie quotidienne à Carthage au temps d'Hannibal*, Paris, 1958, p. 75. See also Fig. 69

67   M. Collignon, *Les statues funéraires dans l'art grec*, Paris, 1911, pp. 364 f.; Paris, Musée national du Louvre, *Catalogue sommaire des marbres antiques*, Paris, 1922, No. 3221

68   G. Schmidt, "Beiträge zum Erminoldmeister," *Zeitschrift für Kunstwissenschaft*, XI, 1957, pp. 141–173

69   Carthage, *Musée Lavigerie de Saint-Louis...* (*Musées et collections archéologiques de l'Algérie...*, ed. A. L. Delattre), I, Paris, 1900, pl. 9

70   G. Q. Giglioli, *L'Arte etrusca*, Milan, 1935, pl. 395

71   Giglioli, *ibidem*, pl. 396, 2

72   E. Panofsky, *Early Netherlandish Painting*, Cambridge, Mass., 1953, p. 74; J. Porcher, *The Rohan Book of Hours*, London, 1959, pl. 8

73   Musper, *op. cit.*, p. 20

74   Giglioli, *op. cit.*, pl. 414, 2; M. Pallottino, *Art of the Etruscans*, London, 1955, fig. 113

75   Giglioli, *ibidem*, pl. 69, 2

76   Giglioli, *ibidem*, pl. 237, 4

77   R. Herbig, *Die jüngeretruskischen Steinsarkophage*, Berlin, 1952, No. 96

78   Herbig, *ibidem*, No. 6

79   Giglioli, *op. cit.*, pl. 135, 2

80   D. Levi, *Il museo civico di Chiusi*, Rome, 1935, p. 44

81   Giglioli, *op. cit.*, pl. 336, 2

82   Herbig, *op. cit.*, No. 50

83   Levi, *op. cit.*, p. 78; Giglioli, *op. cit.*, pl. 411

84   Herbig, *op. cit.*, No. 20

85   Giglioli, *op. cit.*, pls. 117–120

86   Giglioli, *ibidem*, pls. 116, 2

87   Giglioli, *ibidem*, pl. 400, 2

88   Cumont, *Recherches*, pp. 433 ff.

89   C. Robert, *Die antiken Sarkophagreliefs*, Berlin, 1890–1939, III, 3, No. 355

90   Cumont, *Recherches*, pp. 392 f.

91   J. Klinkenberg, "Die römischen Grabsteine Kölns," *Bonner Jahrbücher*, CVIII/CIX, 1902, No. 4. See also Fig. 281

92   P. L. Williams, "Two Roman Reliefs in Renaissance Disguise," *Journal of the Warburg and Courtauld Institutes*, IV, 1940–41, pp. 47–66

93   Williams, *ibidem*

94   W. Altmann, *Die römischen Grabaltäre der Kaiserzeit*, Berlin, 1905, No. 279; Williams, *ibidem*

95, 96   E. Nash, *Pictorial Dictionary of Ancient Rome*, London, 1962, II, pp. 329 ff.

97   G. Rodenwaldt, *Über den Stilwandel in der antoninischen Kunst* (Abhandlung der preussischen Akademie der Wissenschaften), Berlin, 1935, pp. 4 f.

98   Cumont, *Lux perpetua*, p. 25

99–101   W. Helbig, *Führer durch die öffentlichen Sammlungen klassischer Altertümer in Rom*, Leipzig, 1912–13, II, Nos. 1192–99; G. M. A. Hanfmann, *The Seasons Sarcophagus in Dumbarton Oaks*, Cambridge, Mass., 1951, No. 323

102   K. Lehmann-Hartleben, "Die antiken Hafenanlagen des Mittelmeers," *Clio* (Beiheft), XIV, 1923, pp. 321 ff.; E. Strong, *Art in Ancient Rome*, New York, 1929, p. 129

103   Robert, *op. cit.*, II, No. 372

104   A. Conze, *Römische Bildwerke einheimischen Fundorts in Oesterreich*, II, Vienna, 1875, pp. 3 ff.; S. Reinach, *Répertoire de reliefs grecs et romains*, Paris, 1909–1912, II, p. 130, 2

105, 106   K. Lehmann and E. C. Olsen, *Dionysiac Sarcophagi in Baltimore*, New York, 1942, passim.

107   C. Alexander, "A Roman Sarcophagus from Badminton House," *The Metropolitan Museum of Art Bulletin*, 1955–56, pp. 39–47

108   Robert, *op. cit.*, II, No. 425

109   Altmann, *op. cit.*, pp. 267 ff.; Cumont, *Recherches*, pp. 412 f.

110   W. Altmann, *Architektur und Ornamentik der antiken Sarkophage*, Berlin, 1902, p. 50; P. Gusman, *L'Art décoratif de Rome...*, Paris, 1912–14, I, pl. 40

111   H. I. Marrou, *Mousikos Anér: étude sur les scènes de la vie intellectuelle sur les monuments funéraires romains*, Grenoble, 1938, p. 33; Cumont, *Recherches*, pp. 338 f.

112   R. Papini, *Campo Santo* (*Catalogo delle cose d'arte e di antichità d'Italia: Pisa*, II), Rome, 1932, No. 45

113   Papini, *op. cit.*, No. 48

114   W. Amelung, *Die Skulpturen des vatikanischen Museums*, Berlin, 1903–1956, I, p. 175, pl. 24

115   Unpublished

116   Papini, *op. cit.*, No. 41; Hanfmann, *op. cit.*, No. 316

117   Amelung, *op. cit.*, II, No. 97 a

118   E. Petersen, "Varia, V; der Sarkophag eines Arztes," *Römische Mitteilungen des deutschen archäologischen Instituts*, XV, 1900, pp. 171 ff.

119   Robert, *op. cit.*, III, 2, No. 309; Cumont, *Recherches*, pp. 332 ff.

120 a, b   Robert, *ibidem*, III, 1, No. 127; Morey, *op. cit.*, pp. 48 f., figs. 85, 86

121   Robert, *op. cit.*, III, 2, No. 144

122   R. Wesenberg, *Bernwardinische Plastik*, Berlin, 1955, pp. 65–116, 172–81

123   G. Calza, *Le necropoli del Porto di Roma nell'Isola Sacra*, Rome, 1940, p. 200

124   Marrou, *op. cit.*, pp. 50, 124; Cumont, *Recherches*, pp. 339 f.

125   A. Rumpf, *Die Meerwesen auf den antiken Sarkophagreliefs* (Robert, *op. cit.*, V), Berlin, 1939, No. 71

126   Cumont, *Recherches*, p. 98, n. 1

127   Cumont, *ibidem*, pp. 487 f.; Hanfmann, *op. cit.*

128   Morey, *op. cit.*, p. 37

129   A. H. Smith, *A Catalogue of Sculpture in the Department of Greek and Roman Antiquities*, British Museum, London, 1892–1904, III, p. 324

130   Robert, *op. cit.*, III, 2, No. 205

131   Amelung, *op. cit.*, II, No. 102k

132   Robert, *op. cit.*, III, 1, No. 131

133   Cumont, *Recherches*, pp. 457–84

134   Marrou, *op. cit.*, p. 107; Cumont, *Recherches*, pp. 307 f.

135   Amelung, *op. cit.*, II, No. 60. See also Figs. 417–21

136 E. Sjöqvist and A. Westholm, "Zur Zeitbestimmung der Helena- und Constantiasarkophage," *Opuscula archaeologica*, I, 1935, pp. 1 ff.; W. F. Volbach and M. Hirmer, *Early Christian Art*, New York, 1961, p. 317, pls. 22, 23

137 P. Gauckler, "Mosaïques tombales d'une chapelle de martyrs à Thabraca," *Monuments Piot*, XIII, 1906, pp. 188–97

138 D. Fossard, "La chronologie des sarcophages d'Aquitaine," *Actes du Vᵉ congrès international d'archéologie chrétienne*, Vatican City, 1957, pp. 321–33.

139 F. Gerke, *Die christlichen Sarkophage vorkonstantinischer Zeit*, Berlin, 1940, pp. 407 f.; Rome, *Cataloghi dei musei comunali di Roma, Musei Capitolini, I monumenti cristiani*, 1952, No. 15

140 J. Wilpert, *I sarcofagi cristiani antichi*, Rome, 1929, I, p. 17; II (1932), p. 351; Pauly-Wissowa, *Real-Encyclopädie der klassischen Altertumswissenschaft*, XXXV, Stuttgart, 1939, cols. 1313–16

141 G. Bovini, *I sarcofagi paleocristiani*, Vatican City, 1949, pp. 99 ff., 267; M. Simon, "Symbolisme et tradition d'atelier dans la première sculpture chrétienne," *Actes du Vᵉ congrès*, pp. 307–19

142 Gerke, *op. cit.*, pp. 55, 59, 320

143 Volbach and Hirmer, *op. cit.*, p. 325, pl. 73

144 Volbach and Hirmer, *ibidem*, p. 345, pl. 174

145 M. Lawrence, "Columnar Sarcophagi in the Latin West," *The Art Bulletin*, XIV, 1932, pp. 139 f., No. 26

146 F. Benoit, "Sarcophages paléochrétiens d'Arles et de Marseilles," *Fouilles et monuments archéologiques en France métropolitaine (Gallia, suppl. V)*, Paris, 1954, p. 37, no. 9

147 H. U. v. Schönebeck, *Der Mailänder Sarkophag und seine Nachfolge*, Vatican City, 1935, pp. 13, 41

148 M. Lawrence, *op. cit.*, pp. 126 f., 169, No. 43

149 Benoit, *op. cit.*, p. 45, No. 39

150 F. Gerke, *Der Trierer Agricius-Sarkophag*, Trier, 1949

151 Bovini, *op. cit.*, pp. 179 ff., 306

152 Benoit, *op. cit.*, p. 35

153 Bovini, *op. cit.*, pp. 240 ff., 340 f.

154 M. Lawrence, *op. cit.*, p. 173, No. 94

155 Bovini, *op. cit.*, pp. 224 f., 333 f.

156 S. L. Agnello, *Il sarcofago di Adelfia* (Amici delle catacombe, xv), Vatican City, 1956; Volbach and Hirmer, *op. cit.*, p. 319, pls. 37–39

157 Volbach and Hirmer, *ibidem*, p. 320, pls. 41–43

158–160 A. Katzenellenbogen, "The Sarcophagus in S. Ambrogio and St. Ambrose," *The Art Bulletin*, XXIX, 1947, pp. 249–59; Volbach and Hirmer, *ibidem*, pp. 320 f., pls. 46, 47

161 Bovini, *op. cit.*, pp. 86–91, 263 f.

162 Volbach and Hirmer, *op. cit.*, pp. 309 f., pls. 4, 5

163 E. Le Blant, *Les sarcophages chrétiens de la Gaule*, Paris, 1886, pp. 98 f., No. 120

164 O. Wulff, *Beschreibung der Bildwerke der christlichen Epochen*, I (Staatliche Museen, Berlin), 1909, p. 3, Nos. 3, 4

165 Volbach and Hirmer, *op. cit.*, p. 317, pl. 24

166 Volbach and Hirmer, *ibidem*, pp. 325 ff., pl. 75

167 A. Heimann, "Trinitas Creatrix Mundi," *Journal of the Warburg Institute*, II, 1938, pp. 42 ff.

168 O. Raggio, "The Myth of Prometheus...," *Journal of the Warburg and Courtauld Institutes*, XXI, 1958, p. 47

169 F. A. Hooper, *Funerary Stelae from Kom Abou Billou* (The University of Michigan, Kelsey Museum of Archaeology, *Studies*, I), Ann Arbor, 1961

170 See Fig. 169

171 See Fig. 169

172 Conze, *op. cit.*, No. 451

173 Panofsky, *Early Netherlandish Painting*, p. 59

174 Panofsky, *ibidem*, pp. 232 ff.

175 P. Gauckler, *Inventaire des mosaïques de la Gaule et de l'Afrique*, II, Paris, 1910, p. 323, No. 1015

176 A. Springer, *Handbuch der Kunstgeschichte*, I, 9th ed., Leipzig, 1911, pl. xvi

177 Gauckler, *Inventaire*, p. 311, No. 964

178 A. K. Porter, "The Tomb of Hincmar and Carolingian Sculpture in France," *The Burlington Magazine*, L, 1927, pp. 75 ff.; R. Hamann-McLean, "Merowingisch oder frühromanisch?," *Jahrbuch des Römisch-*

Germanischen Zentralmuseums, Mainz, IV, 1957, pp. 161–99

179   A. Durau Sanpere and J. Ainaud de Lasarte, *Escultura Gotica* (Ars Hispaniae, VIII), Madrid, 1956, p. 75

180   See Fig. 178

181   J. Adhémar, *Influences antiques dans l'art du moyenage français*, London, 1937, pp. 249 f.; E. Panofsky, *Renaissance and Renascences in Western Art*, Stockholm, 1960, p. 90

182   A. K. Porter, *Romanesque Sculpture of the Pilgrimage Roads*, Boston, 1923, pp. 303 f.

183   W. Holmqvist, *Kunstprobleme der Merowingerzeit*, Stockholm, 1939, pp. 122 f.

184   R. Reitzenstein, "Die nordischen, persischen und christlichen Vorstellungen vom Weltuntergang," *Vorträge der Bibliothek Warburg, 1923–24*, Leipzig, 1926, pp. 158, 163 f.

185   K. Böhmer, "Der fränkische Grabstein von Niederdollendorf am Rhein," *Germania*, XXVIII, 1944–50, pp. 63 ff.

186   F. Rademacher, "Frühkarolingische Grabsteine im Landesmuseum zu Bonn," *Bonner Jahrbücher*, 1938–39, pp. 265, 281

187   *Das Erste Jahrtausend*, Düsseldorf, 1962, II, p. 45, No. 177

188   Rademacher, *op. cit.*, p. 267, No. 4

189   G. Serra Villaro, "I sepolcri nella necropoli di Tarragona," *Rivista di archeologia cristiana*, XIV, 1937, pp. 243 ff., 265; P. B. Huguet, *Arte paleocristiano* (Ars Hispaniae, I), Madrid, 1947, p. 221

190   A. Blanchet, *Inventaire des mosaïques de la Gaule*, Paris, 1909, I, 2, p. 105, No. 1144; M.-M. Gauthier, *Émaux limousins champlevés...*, Paris, 1950, pp. 28 f., 153

191   H. Stern, *Recueil général des mosaïques de la Gaule* (*Gallia*, suppl. X), 1957, pp. 96 ff., No. 9

192   P. Kutter, "Die ältesten figuralen Grabmäler im Rheinland," *Wallraf-Richartz Jahrbuch*, I, 1924, p. 66; S. H. Steinberg and C. Steinberg v. Pape, *Bildnisse geistlicher und weltlicher Fürsten und Herren*, Leipzig, 1931, pp. 94, 140

193   P. Clemen, *Die romanische Monumentalmalerei in den Rheinlanden*, Düsseldorf, 1916, pp. 267 ff.

194   Stern, *op. cit.*, p. 96, No. 8*

195   A. Muñoz, *Il restauro della basilica di Santa Sabina*, Rome, 1938, p. 35

196   Adhémar, *op. cit.*, p. 236

197   H. Swarzenski, *Monuments of Romanesque Art*, London, 1954, p. 55, No. 99, Fig. 227

198   H. Swarzenski, *ibidem*, p. 55, No. 99, Fig. 228

199   Panofsky, *Die deutsche Plastik*, pp. 14 f., 83 f.; G. Angermann, "Das Wittekindrelief...," *58. Jahresbericht des historischen Vereins für die Grafschaft Ravensberg*, 1955, pp. 173–215

200   Panofsky, *ibidem*, pp. 14 ff., 30, 92, 94

201   Panofsky, *ibidem*, pp. 16 f., 30, 93

202   A. Michel, *Histoire de l'art...*, Paris, 1905–1929, II, 2, p. 191; A. Gardner, *Medieval Sculpture in France*, New York, 1931, p. 350

203   S. Müller-Christensen, *Das Grabmal des Papstes Clemens II im Dom zu Bamberg. Mit einer Studie zur Lebensgeschichte des Papstes von Alexander Freiherr von Reitzenstein*, Munich, 1960

204   Panofsky, *Die deutsche Plastik*, p. 126

205   E. Panofsky, *Gothic Architecture and Scholasticism*, New York, 1957, pp. 25 f.

206   A. M. Hind, *An Introduction to a History of Woodcut*, New York, 1935, pp. 280, 284, 342 f.

207   R. Hamann and K. Wilhelm-Kästner, *Die Elisabethkirche zu Marburg...*, Marburg, 1929, II, pp. 119 f.

208   V. Beyer, *La sculpture Strasbourgeoise au XIVe siècle*, Strasbourg-Paris, 1955, pp. 21–26

209, 210   Adhémar, *op. cit.*, pp. 190 f.; W. S. Heckscher, "Dornauszieher," *Real-Lexikon zur deutschen Kunstgeschichte*, IV, Stuttgart, 1958, pp. 292 ff.

211   H. Beenken, *Bildwerke des Bamberger Domes aus dem XIII. Jahrhundert*, Bonn, 1925, p. 23; Wolfgang Lotz, "Historismus in der Sepulkralplastik um 1600," *Anzeiger des Germanischen Nationalmuseums, 1940–54*, Berlin, 1954, pp. 65 f.

212   F. H. Crossley, *English Church Monuments A.D. 1150–1550*, London, 1921, p. 251; M. Stephenson, *A List of Monumental Brasses in the British Isles*, London, 1926, p. 531

213   Panofsky, *Die deutsche Plastik*, pp. 138 f.

214   R. Kautzsch and E. Neeb, *Der Dom zu Mainz* (Die Kunstdenkmäler der Stadt Mainz, II), Darmstadt,

1919, pp. 237f.; P. Metz, *Der Dom zu Mainz*, Augsburg, 1927, p. 101

215 Kautzsch and Neeb, *ibidem*, p. 246

216 Kautzsch and Neeb, *ibidem*, pp. 248f.; W. Pinder, *Die deutsche Plastik des XV. Jahrhunderts*, Munich, 1924, pl. 12

217 Pinder, *ibidem*, pl. 97

218 J. Bier, *Tilman Riemenschneider, Ein Gedenkbuch*, 6th ed., Vienna, 1948, pp. 30–36; K. Gerstenberg, *Tilman Riemenschneider*, 5th ed., Munich, 1962, fig. 44

219 L. Stone, *Sculpture in Britain: the Middle Ages* (Pelican History of Art), Baltimore, 1955, p. 150; P. Brieger, *English Art, 1216–1307*, Oxford, 1957, p. 205

220 Stone, *op. cit.*, pp. 167f.

221 L'Abbé Edouard (pseudonym), *Fontevrault et ses monuments*, Paris, 1873, II, pp. 118f., 138f.; *Congrès archéologique de France*, LXXVII, 1910, pp. 54f. See also fig. 335

222 Panofsky, *Die deutsche Plastik*, pp. 60, 109f. See also fig. 335

223 Kautzsch and Neeb, *op. cit.*, pp. 256ff.; Metz, *op. cit.*, p. 62

224, 225 J. Baum, *Gotische Bildwerke Schwabens*, Augsburg, 1921, pp. 95f., 162

226 F. Deshoullières, *Souvigny et Bourbon-l'Archambault* (Petites monographies des grands édifices de France), Paris, n.d., pp. 50ff.; A. Humbert, *La sculpture sous les ducs de Bourgogne, 1361–1483*, Paris, 1913, p. 151

227 P. Halm, "Die spätgotische Grabplastik Straubings," *Kunst und Kunsthandwerk*, XVII, 1914, pp. 307f.; F. Mader, ed., *Die Kunstdenkmäler von Niederbayern, VI: Stadt Straubing*, Munich, 1921, p. 80

228 E. Panofsky, "Imago Pietatis," *Festschrift Max J. Friedländer*, Leipzig, 1927, p. 277

229 P. Rolland, *La sculpture tournaisienne*, Paris, 1944, pp. 27ff.

230 Rolland, *loc. cit.*

231 O. Wertheimer, *Nicolaus Gerhaert...*, Berlin, 1929, pp. 42ff.; W. Vöge, "Nicolaus von Leyen's Strassburger Epitaph und die holländische Steinplastik," *Oberrheinische Kunst*, IV, 1929–30, pp. 35ff.

232 Panofsky, *Early Netherlandish Painting*, pp. 183ff.

233 Rolland, *loc. cit.*

234 Rolland, *loc. cit.*

235, 236 A. K. Porter, "The Tomb of Doña Sancha..," *The Burlington Magazine*, XLV, 1924, pp. 165–79; J. Gudiol and J. Nuño, *Arquitectura y escultura romanicas* (Ars Hispaniae, V), Madrid, 1948, p. 147

237 Panofsky, *Die deutsche Plastik*, pp. 85ff.

238 Hamann and Wilhelm-Kästner, *op. cit.*, p. 122; F. Deshouillières, *Les églises de France; Cher*, Paris, 1932, pp. 197f.

239 A. Rumpf, "Römische historische Reliefs," *Bonner Jahrbücher*, 1955–56, pp. 127–35

240 H. Swarzenski, *op. cit.*, p. 61, No. 127, fig. 289

241 H. Beenken, *Romanische Skulptur in Deutschland*, Leipzig, 1924, pp. 246f.

242 Hamann and Wilhelm-Kästner, *op. cit.*, p. 120

243 Hamann and Wilhelm-Kästner, *ibidem*, pp. 125f.

244 W. Sauerländer, "Art antique et sculpture autour de 1200; Saint-Denis, Lisieux, Chartres," *Art de France*, I, 1961, pp. 47ff.

245 W. Sauerländer, "Beiträge zur Geschichte der 'frühgotischen' Skulptur," *Zeitschrift für Kunstgeschichte*, XIX, 1956, pp. 1ff.

246 Hamann and Wilhelm-Kästner, *op. cit.*, p. 133; M. Dumolin and G. Outardel, *Les églises de France, V; Paris et la Seine*, Paris, 1936, p. 391

247 Hamann and Wilhelm-Kästner, *op. cit.*, pp. 146f., 184f.

248 H. David, *Claus Sluter*, Paris, 1951, pp. 19–26, 107–127, 170

249 F. de Montemy, "Les pleurants bourguignons du musée de Cluny," *Les musées de France, Bulletin*, 1913, pp. 38ff., No. 3

250 C. M. A. A. Lindeman, "De dateering, herkomst en identificatie der 'Gravenbeeldjes' van Jacques de Gérines," *Oud Holland*, 1941, pp. 49–57, 97–105, 161–68, 193–219; J. Leewenberg, "De tien bronzen 'Plorannen' in het Rijksmuseum te Amsterdam," *Gentsche Bijdragen tot de Kunstgeschiedenis*, XIII, 1951, pp. 13ff.

251 V. Oberhammer, *Die Bronzestandbilder des Maximiliansgrabmales in der Hofkirche zu Innsbruck*, Innsbruck, 1935

252   P. Clemen, *Der Dom zu Köln* (Die Kunstdenkmäler der Rheinprovinz, VI, iii: Die Kunstdenkmäler der Stadt Köln, I, iii), Düsseldorf, 1938, pp. 260 f.

253, 254   See Fig. 203

255   W. Pinder, *Die deutsche Plastik vom ausgehenden Mittelalter bis zum Ende der Renaissance*, Wildpark-Potsdam, 1924, p. 183

256   G. Troescher, *Die burgundische Plastik des ausgehenden Mittelalters*, Frankfurt, 1940, pp. 99 f.

257, 258   Eugène Bloch, "Le tombeau de François I de La Sarra-Montferrand à La Sarraz," *Congrès archéologique de France*, CX, *Suisse Romande*, Paris-Orléans, 1953, pp. 369–74

259   Halm, *op. cit.*, pp. 333 f.; Mader, *op. cit.*, p. 80

260   M. Gerlach, *Alte Grabkunst*, 3rd ed., Vienna, 1920, pl. 11, 6

261   J. Evans, *English Art, 1307–1461*, Oxford, 1949, p. 158

262   A. Gardner, *Alabaster Tombs of the Pre-Reformation Period in England*, Cambridge, 1940, p. 59

263–265   E. Müntz, "A travers le Comtat Venaissin: le mausolée du Cardinal de Langrange à Avignon," *L'Ami des monuments et des arts*, IV, 1890, pp. 91 ff.; E. Mâle, *L'Art religieux de la fin du moyen-âge en France*, Paris, 1922, p. 432; P. Pradel, "Le visage inconnu de Louis d'Orléans frère de Charles VI," *Revue des arts*, 1952, pp. 93–98

266   Th. W. Ross, "Five Fifteenth-Century 'Emblem' Verses from British Museum Addit. MS. 37049," *Speculum*, XXXII, 1957, pp. 274 ff.

267   J. Guibert, *Les dessins archéologiques de Roger de Gaignières*, ser. 1 (tombeaux), Paris, n.d., No. 30; L. de Farcy, *Monographie de la cathédrale d'Angers*, Angers, 1905, II, pp. 287–313; O. Pächt, "René d'Anjou et les Van Eyck," *Cahiers de l'Association Internationale des Etudes Françaises*, 8, Paris, June 1956, pp. 41–65

268   V. Goloubew, *Les dessins de Jacopo Bellini au Louvre et au British Museum*, Brussels, 1908, II, pl. vii

269   U. Schlegel, "Observations on Masaccio's Trinity Fresco in Santa Maria Novella," *The Art Bulletin*, XLV, 1963, pp. 19–33

270   W. and E. Paatz, *Die Kirchen von Florenz*, V, Frankfurt, 1953, p. 289

271   Guibert, *op. cit.*, No. 34; De Farcy, *op. cit.*, p. 163

272   A. Blunt, *Art and Architecture in France, 1500–1700* (Pelican History of Art), Baltimore, 1954, pp. 6 f.

273   Blunt, *ibidem*, p. 14

274   S. Meller, *Peter Vischer der Ältere und seine Werkstatt*, Leipzig, 1925, pp. 140 f.

275   Meller, *ibidem* p. 196

276   Meller, *ibidem*, p. 208

277   K. Gerstenberg, *op. cit.*, fig. 50

278, 279   A. Feulner, *Die deutsche Plastik des XVI. Jahrhunderts*, Munich, 1926, p. 55, pl. 29

280   N. Lieb, *Die Fugger und die Kunst im Zeitalter der Gotik und der frühen Renaissance*, Munich, 1952, pp. 224 f.

281   E. Panofsky, "Conrad Celtes and Kunz von der Rosen: Two Problems in Portrait Identification," *The Art Bulletin*, XXIV, 1942, pp. 39 ff.

282   See Fig. 287

283   H. Tietze, *Geschichte und Beschreibung des St. Stephansdomes in Wien* (Oesterreichische Kunsttopographie, xiii), Vienna, 1931, p. 490, fig. 521

284   H. Gottschalk, *Antonio Rossellino*, Liegnitz, 1930, p. 87

285   H. Egger, "Beiträge zur Andrea Bregno Forschung," *Festschrift Julius Schlosser*, Zurich-Leipzig-Vienna, 1927, pp. 127 f.

286   C. Ricci, *Monumenti sepolcrali di lettori dello studio bolognese*, Bologna, 1886, pl. iii

287   Ricci, *ibidem*, pl. v

288   A. Grisebach, *Römische Portraitbüsten der Gegenreformation*, Leipzig, 1936, p. 42; see also review by Ulrich Middeldorf, *The Art Bulletin*, XX, 1938, p. 115

289   Ricci, *op. cit.*, pl. viii

290   Ricci, *ibidem*, pl. ix

291–299   J. Pope-Hennessy, *Italian Renaissance Sculpture*, London, 1958, pp. 345 f.

300   H. Tietze, *Tintoretto*, London, 1948, p. 355

301   M. Lisner, "Zur frühen Bildhauerarchitektur Donatellos," *Münchner Jahrbuch der bildenden Kunst*, 3rd ser., IX/X, 1958–59, pp. 83 ff.

302 Pope-Hennessy, *Italian Renaissance Sculpture*, pp. 310f.

303, 304 J. Pope-Hennessy, *Italian Gothic Sculpture*, pp. 212f.; O. Morisani, *Tutta la scultura di Jacopo della Quercia*, Milan, 1962, pp. 58ff., pls. 12–27

305 G. S. Davies, *Renascence: The Sculptural Tombs of the Fifteenth Century in Rome*, London, 1910, pp. 230f.

306 R. Krautheimer and T. Krautheimer-Hess, *Lorenzo Ghiberti*, Princeton, 1956, pp. 12f., 138, 143, 147f., 152f.

307 I. B. Supino, *Jacopo della Quercia*, Bologna, 1926, p. 36; Morisani, *op. cit.*, p. 64, pl. 55

308 H. W. Janson, *The Sculpture of Donatello*, Princeton, 1957, II, pp. 101f.

309 Janson, *ibidem*, II, pp. 75–77

310, 311 Janson, *ibidem*, II, pp. 232–35

312 E. Iversen, *The Myth of Egypt and its Hieroglyphs in European Tradition*, Copenhagen, 1961, p. 159

313 R. Calza and E. Nash, *Ostia*, Florence, 1959, pp. 105f., fig. 144

314, 315 W. and E. Paatz, *op. cit.*, V, pp. 295f., 362

316 H. Egger, *Francesca Tornabuoni und ihre Grabstätte in S. Maria Sopra Minerva*, Vienna, 1934

317 Pope-Hennessy, *Italian Renaissance Sculpture*, pp. 297f.

318 F. Hartt, G. Corti, and C. Kennedy, *The Chapel of the Cardinal of Portugal*, Philadelphia, 1964

319 F. Saxl, *Mithras, typengeschichtliche Untersuchungen*, Berlin, 1931, pp. 108f.

320 Blunt, *op. cit.*, p. 17

321, 322 Pope-Hennessy, *Italian Gothic Sculpture*, pp. 199f.

323 Janson, *The Sculpture of Donatello*, II, pp. 59–65

324 Blunt, *op. cit.*, pp. 15f.

325 P. Vitry, *Michel Colombe et la sculpture française de son temps*, Paris, 1901, p. 169

326 See Figs. 341–345

327 Blunt, *op. cit.*, p. 16

328–330 Blunt, *ibidem*, pp. 54, 59f., 77

331 Blunt, *ibidem*, pp. 60f., 98–102

332 R. Hedicke, *Cornelis Floris und die Florisdekoration*, Berlin, 1913, I, pp. 24f.

333 Pope-Hennessy, *Italian Gothic Sculpture*, pp. 184f.

334 E. Hutton, *The Cosmati*, London, 1950, pp. 22, 48

335 G. B. Ladner, "The Gestures of Prayer in Papal Iconography of the Thirteenth and Fourteenth Centuries," *Didascaliae: Studies in Honor of Anselm M. Albareda*, New York, 1961, pp. 245ff.

336 Pope-Hennessy, *Italian Gothic Sculpture*, pp. 194f.

337 W. and E. Paatz, *op. cit.*, V, p. 151

338 H. von Einem, "Das Grabmal der Königin Margarethe in Genua," *Festschrift Hans R. Hahnloser*, Basel-Stuttgart, 1961, pp. 125–150; C. Marcenaro, "Per la tomba di Margherita di Brabante," *Paragone*, January 1961, pp. 3–17

339 E. Borsook, *The Mural Painters of Tuscany*, London, 1960, p. 131, pl. 12

340 L. D. Ettlinger, "Pollaiuolo's Tomb of Sixtus IV," *Journal of the Warburg and Courtauld Institutes*, XVI, 1953, p. 269; Pope-Hennessy, *Italian Renaissance Sculpture*, pp. 334f.

341–345 G. Troescher, *Conrat Meit von Worms*, Freiburg i. Br., 1927, pp. 25–39; D. Roggen and E. Dhanens, "De Ontwerpen van de praalgraven te Brou," *Gentsche Bijdragen tot de Kunstgeschiedenis*, IX, 1943, pp. 127ff.

346 See Fig. 324

347 Paris, Musée national du Louvre, *Catalogue des sculptures du moyen-âge, de la renaissance et des temps modernes*, I, Paris, 1922, p. 37, No. 318

348, 349 See Fig. 324

350 M. Aubert, *La sculpture française au moyen-âge*, Paris, 1946, pp. 335–57; J.-F. Noel and P. Jahan, *Les Gisants*, Paris, 1949, pl. XIII

351 Aubert, *loc. cit.*; Noel and Jahan, *op. cit.*, pls. XIV, XV

352 Blunt, *op. cit.*, p. 77

353 Blunt, *ibidem*, p. 98

354 Blunt, *ibidem*, pp. 54, 59f., 77

355 E. Plon, *Leone Leoni et Pompeo Leoni*, Paris, 1887, pp. 230f.; G. Swarzenski, "A Statue by Pompeo Leoni...," *Bulletin of the Museum of Fine Arts*, Boston, XLIII, 1945, pp. 42f.

356 R. Hedicke, *Jacques Dubroecq von Mons...*, Strasbourg, 1904, p. 97

357 M. Cruttwell, "Girolamo della Robbia et ses œuvres," *Gazette des Beaux-Arts*, XXX, 1904, pp. 27 f.; Noel and Jahan, *op. cit.*, pl. xxiii

358 See Fig. 331

359 Blunt, *op. cit.*, pp. 100 f.

360, 361 Blunt, *ibidem*, p. 107, n.44

362 Blunt, *ibidem*, p. 17

363 H. Bouchot, *Inventaire des dessins exécutés pour Roger de Gaignières...*, Paris, 1891, Nos. 3475, 4109, 4110

364–366 J. Babelon, *Germain Pilon*, Paris, 1927, p. 67; Blunt, *op. cit.*, p. 101

367 J. Pope-Hennessy, *Italian High Renaissance and Baroque Sculpture*, London, 1963, Cat. pp. 47 f.

368 Pope-Hennessy, *Italian Renaissance Sculpture*, pp. 354 f.

369, 370 R. de Orueta, *La escultura funeraria en España, provincias de Ciudad Real, Cuenca, Guadalajara*, Madrid, 1919, pp. 110 f.

371 Orueta, *ibidem*, pp. 128 f.

372 A. Martin, *Le livre illustré en France au XVᵉ siècle*, Paris, 1931, p. 143

373 O. Cook, "Sepulchral Effigies," *The Saturday Book*, XVI, 1956, pp. 217 ff., pl. 5

374 R. Wittkower, *Art and Architecture in Italy, 1600–1750* (Pelican History of Art), Baltimore, 1958, pp. 208 f.

375 Cook, *op. cit.*, pl. 5

376 Michel, *op. cit.*, VI, 2, pp. 732 f.

377 Blunt, *op. cit.*, p. 247

378 Blunt, *ibidem*, pp. 73 f.

379 A. Calmet, *Histoire généalogique de la maison du Châtelet*, Nancy, 1741, p. 203

380 Pope-Hennessy, *Italian Renaissance Sculpture*, pp. 342 f.

381 Pope-Hennessy, *ibidem*, pp. 337 ff.

382 W. and E. Paatz, *op. cit.*, p. 116

383 A. B. Tonnochy, *Catalogue of British Seal Dies in the British Museum*, London, 1952, No. 332

384 F. de Maffei, *Le arche Scaligere di Verona*, Verona, 1955, pp. 9–35

385–387 De Maffei, *ibidem*, pp. 37–57

388 Janson, *Sculpture of Donatello*, p. 158

389 Thieme-Becker, *Allgemeines Lexikon der bildenden Künstler*, XV, Leipzig, 1922, pp. 164 f., s.v. "Gualtiero di Alemagna"; A. Venturi, *Storia dell'arte italiana*, VI, Milan, 1908, pp. 63 ff.

390 W. and E. Paatz, *op. cit.*, III, p. 370; Borsook, *op. cit.*, pp. 149 f., pl. 55

391 W. and E. Paatz, *ibidem*, III, pp. 370, 498; M. Salmi, *Andrea del Castagno*, Novara, 1961, pp. 50 f., pls. 70–74

392–394 Janson, *Sculpture of Donatello*, II, pp. 162–187

395, 396 W. Valentiner, *Tino di Camaino*, Paris, 1935, pl. 6; P. Toesca, *Il Trecento*, Turin, 1951, pp. 258 ff.

397 Toesca, *ibidem*, pp. 266 f.; H. Buchthal, "Hector's Tomb," *De artibus opuscula XL; Essays in Honor of Erwin Panofsky*, New York, 1961, pp. 29–36

398, 399 Pope-Hennessy, *Italian Gothic Sculpture*, pp. 188 f.

400 Valentiner, *op. cit.*, p. 11; Toesca, *op. cit.*, pp. 297 ff.

401 Valentiner, *ibidem*, pl. 27

402 Pope-Hennessy, *Italian Gothic Sculpture*, pp. 186 f.

403 Pope-Hennessy, *Italian Renaissance Sculpture*, p. 318

404 W. Hager, *Die Ehrenstatuen der Päpste*, Leipzig, 1929, pp. 32 f.; C. Baroni, *Scultura gotica lombarda*, Milan, 1944, pp. 159 f.

405–408 Ettlinger, *op. cit.*, pp. 239 ff.

409–412 P. S. Wingert, "The Funerary Urn of Francis I," *The Art Bulletin*, XXI, 1939, pp. 383–96

413–416 E. Neurdenburg, *De Zeventiende Eeuwsche Beeldhouwkunst in de Noordelijke Nederlanden*, Amsterdam, 1948, pp. 42 ff.; K. Fremantle, *The Baroque Town Hall of Amsterdam*, Utrecht, 1959, pp. 120 ff.

417–421 E. Panofsky, "The First Two Projects of Michelangelo's Tomb of Julius II," *The Art Bulletin*, XIX, 1939, pp. 187 ff.; *idem*, *Studies in Iconology*, New York, 1939, pp. 187 ff.; H. von Einem, *Michelangelo*, Stuttgart, 1959, pp. 40 ff., 71 ff., 135 ff.

422–424   C. de Tolnay, *Michelangelo: IV. The Tomb of Julius II*, Princeton, 1954, *passim*; Pope-Hennessy, *Italian High Renaissance and Baroque Sculpture*, Cat. pp. 13–25

425, 426   H. W. Janson, *Apes and Ape Lore in the Middle Ages and the Renaissance*, London, 1952, pp. 295 ff.

427–430   C. de Tolnay, *Michelangelo; III. The Medici Chapel*, Princeton, 1948, *passim*; F. Hartt, "The Meaning of Michelangelo's Medici Chapel," *Essays in Honor of Georg Swarzenski*, Chicago, 1951, pp. 145–55; J. Wilde, "Michelangelo's Designs for the Medici Tombs," *Journal of the Warburg and Courtauld Institutes*, XVIII, 1955, pp. 54 ff.; von Einem, *op. cit.*, pp. 82 ff.; Pope-Hennessy, *Italian High Renaissance and Baroque Sculpture*, Cat. pp. 29–39

431   R. Wittkower, *Gian Lorenzo Bernini*, London, 1955, pp. 14, 181 f.

432, 433   Grisebach, *op. cit.*, pp. 122 f.

434   Wittkower, *Bernini*, pp. 26, 28, 204 f.

435   Wittkower, *ibidem*, pp. 16, 30 f., 236

436   Wittkower, *ibidem*, pp. 26, 38, 203 f.

437   Wittkower, *ibidem*, pp. 20, 24 ff., 39, 193 f.; Pope-Hennessy, *Italian High Renaissance and Baroque Sculpture*, Cat. pp. 127 f.

438   Pope-Hennessy, *ibidem*, Cat. pp. 97 f.

439   See Fig. 437

440, 441   Wittkower, *Bernini*, pp. 21, 26 f., 39, 238 ff.; Pope-Hennessy, *ibidem*, Cat. pp. 128 f.

442   Wittkower, *Bernini*, pp. 27, 217

443   Wittkower, *ibidem*, pp. 38, 209 f.; Pope-Hennessy, *Italian High Renaissance and Baroque Sculpture*, Cat. pp. 131 f.

444   Wittkower, *ibidem*, pp. 13, 19, 26, 39, 236 ff.; Pope-Hennessy, *ibidem*, Cat. p. 136

445   London, The Courtauld Institute, *Catalogue*, Exhibition of Architectural and Decorative Drawings, London, 1941, No. 42

446   R. Josephson, *Sergels Fantasi*, Stockholm, 1956, I, p. 283

Index

by Robert Grinstead

Numbers in *italic type* refer to plates, page numbers followed by the letter n refer to footnotes.

315

317

Photographic Credits

Numbers refer to figure numbers

PHOTOGRAPHS SPECIALLY MADE FOR THE AUTHOR 224, 225, 332, 379, 388, 414, 415, 418, 419, 420, 421

FIGURES REPRODUCED FROM BOOKS 8, 23, 31, 36, 39, 45, 51, 56, 57 a, b, c, d, 58 a, b, c, 61, 66, 69, 125, 135, 138, 142, 163, 172, 175, 177, 180, 181, 184, 196, 202, 206, 228, 231, 260, 264, 265, 268, 281, 395, 401, 445

FIGURES REPRODUCED FROM POSTCARDS 89, 111, 240, 263

PHOTOGRAPHS FURNISHED BY MUSEUMS OR COLLECTIONS WHICH OWN THE WORK IN QUESTION *Amsterdam*, Rijksmuseum, 250 a, b; *Ann Arbor*, Kelsey Museum of Archaeology, University of Michigan, 169, 170, 171; *Baltimore*, The Walters Art Gallery, 105, 106; *Berlin*, Staatliche Museen, 7, 11, 15, 16, 18, 20, 24, 35, 164 a, b, 275, 417; *Bonn*, Rheinisches Landesmuseum, 185, 187, 188; *Boston*, Museum of Fine Arts, 78; *Copenhagen*, Ny Carlsberg Glyptotek, 82; *Dijon*, Musée, 256; *Leiden*, Rijksmuseum van Oudheden, 98 a, b; *London*, British Museum, 25, 26, 27, 44, 46, 47, 48, 49, 53, 88, 128, 129, 132, 198, 239, 383, 427; *Milan*, Pinacoteca di Brera, 300; *New York*, Metropolitan Museum of Art, 5, 42, 54, 55, 107, 108 a, b, c, 118; *Paris*, Bibliothèque Nationale, 72, 173, 244, 267, 271, 325, 363, 366; *Philadelphia*, University Museum, University of Pennsylvania, 1, 2, 3; *Princeton*, Art Museum, Princeton University, 14; *Rome*, Museo di Laterano, 140, 167; Musei del Vaticano, 92, 93, 102, 109, 114, 124, 134; *Split*, Arheološki Muzej, 151; *St.-Germain-en-Laye*, Musée des Antiquités Nationales, 91; *Strasbourg*, Musée de l'Université, 176; *Volos*, Archaeological Museum, 19; *Washington, D. C.*, Dumbarton Oaks Research Library and Collection, 127

OTHER SOURCES *ACL* (Archives centrales inconographiques), Brussels, 174, 229, 230, 231, 232, 233, 234, 312 a, b; Fratelli, *Alinari*, Florence, 37, 38, 70, 71, 74, 75, 76, 79, 80, 81, 83, 84, 87, 96, 99, 101, 103, 110, 144, 150, 153, 156, 162, 270, 284, 285, 286, 287, 291, 292, 293, 294, 295, 296, 297, 298, 299, 303, 306, 307, 314, 315, 316, 317, 318, 323, 333, 334, 337, 340, 367, 368, 381, 382, 384, 385, 387, 389, 396, 397, 400, 402, 422, 431, 432; Foto *Anderson* (C. Lo Bianco & Co), Rome, 77, 90, 100, 136, 145, 147, 155, 161, 165, 195, 210, 288, 305, 308, 310, 374, 386 a, b, 398, 399, 403, 405, 406, 407, 408, 428, 429, 430, 435, 438, 439, 440, 441, 442, 443, 444; *Archives Photographiques des Musées Nationaux*, Paris, 86, 94, 152, 154, 168, 182, 190, 205, 221, 226, 238, 245, 248, 249, 272, 273, 320, 326, 327, 328, 329, 330, 341, 342, 343, 344, 345, 347, 351, 352, 353, 354, 356, 358, 360 a, b, 362, 376, 378, 423; G. *Brogi di Lauriti*, Florence, 304, 309, 336, 392; René *Camilleri*,

Algiers, 148; Wilhelm *Castelli*, Lubeck, 276; M. *Chuzeville*, Paris, 67; *Country Life*, London, 375; *Courtauld Institute of Art*, London, 266 a, b; F. H. *Crossley* (National Buildings Record), London 212, 262; *De Jongh*, Lausanne, 257, 258; *Deutscher Kunstverlag*, Munich, 253 a, b, 254 a, b; *Deutscher Verein für Kunstwissenschaft*, Berlin, 200; *Deutsches Archäologisches Institut*, Athens, 29; *Deutsches Archäologisches Institut*, Istanbul, 60, 121 a, b, c, d; *Deutsches Archäologisches Institut*, Rome, 59, 112, 113, 115, 116, 117, 119, 131, 137, 139; *Fotomero*, Urbino, 133; *Fototeca Unione*, Rome, 95; Alison *Frantz*, Athens, 21 a, b, 22, 28; *Fürstliche und Gräfliche Fuggersche Stiftungs-Administration*, Augsburg, 280; *Gabinetto Fotografico Nazionale*, Rome, 85, 120 a, b, 130, 313, 434, 436; *Photographie Giraudon*, Paris, 126, 359, 364, 365, 425, 426; *Biblioteca Hertziana*, Rome, 433; Prof. Max *Hirmer*, Munich, 9, 10, 12, 17, 32, 33, 34, 40, 43, 50, 52, 62, 63, 64, 65, 157, 166; *Historischer Verein*, Traunstein, 255; Pierre *Jahan*, Paris, 346, 348, 349, 350, 357, 361; Ralph *Kleinhempel*, Hamburg 4; *Landesdenkmalamt*, Straubing, 68; *Landesdenkmalamt Westfalen*, Munster, 237; *Lévy & Neurdain*, Paris, 324, 331; Ingeborg *Limmer*, Bamberg, 211; Fotoarchiv *Marburg*, Marburg, 30, 41, 143, 146, 149, 178, 183, 186, 192, 197, 199, 201, 203, 204, 207, 208, 209, 213, 214, 218, 222, 223, 227, 242, 243, 246, 247, 259, 277, 377, 424; *Mas*, Barcelona, 179, 189, 235, 236, 369, 370, 371; Cornelius *Meffert*, Hamburg, 274; *Metropolitan Museum of Art* (Photo Collection), New York, 13; *Museo Civico* (Photo Collection), Padua, 394; *Museum of Fine Arts* (Photo Collection), Boston, 355 a, b; *National Buildings Record*, London, 220, 261, 373; *Österreichische Nationalbibliothek, Bildarchiv*, Vienna, 251, 283; Foto *Paoletti*, Milan, 404; The *Pierpont Morgan Library*, New York, 372; *Pontificia Commissione Archeologia Sacra*, Rome, 158, 159, 160 a, b; Foto *Poppi*, Bologna, 282; Dr. A. *Raichle*, Ulm, 437; *Rheinisches Bildarchiv*, Cologne, 73, 193, 252; Ludwig *Richter*, Mainz, 215, 216, 217, 278, 279; Jean *Roubier*, Paris, 380; *Rijksdienst voor de Monumentenzorg*, The Hague, 413, 416; *Soprintendenza ai Monumenti di Venezia*, Venice, 393; *Soprintendenza alle Antichità*, Rome, 123, 141; *Soprintendenza alle Gallerie*, Florence, 97 a, b, c, 269, 301, 302, 339, 390, 391; *Thomas-Photos*, Oxford, 219; A. *Villani & Figli*, Bologna, 289, 290, 338 a, b; *Warburg Institute*, London University, London, 311; Photo *Wehmeyer*, Hildesheim, 122, 241

UNKNOWN SOURCES 321, 322

WITHDRAWN